JEWISH FAMILY SERVICE OF LOS ANGELES
is an agency of Jewish Federation Council of Greater Los Angeles
and beneficiary of United Jewish Fund

Around Our Table

CALIFORNIA COOKS KOSHER

AROUND OUR TABLE
California Cooks Kosher

Jewish Family Service of Los Angeles has no reason to doubt that the recipes, ingredients and instructions will work successfully. Although the ingredients and instructions have been tested, the cook should not hesitate to question ingredients and instructions before preparation. Recipes in this book have been collected from various sources, and neither Jewish Family Service of Los Angeles nor any contributor, publisher, printer, distributor or sellor of this book is responsible for errors or omissions.

TABLE OF CONTENTS

*"Creative cooks are made
by a spirit of adventure
together with creative recipes,
like the ones I've seen in
Around Our Table,
California Cooks Kosher."*

Nancy Silverton
Owner and chef,
Campanile, Los Angeles, California

Dinah Shore
Culinary artist

*We remember her
and her enthusiastic support
of our cookbook.*

INTRODUCTION

Let us introduce ourselves.
We, the contributors to this cookbook, are the professionals, the volunteers and the seniors of Jewish Family Senior Services, a multi-service program of Jewish Family Service of Los Angeles, an agency of Jewish Federation Council of Greater Los Angeles.

There are at present four Senior Service Centers throughout the Los Angeles area. Each one is alive with animated seniors enjoying the supportive services that the centers provide to help solve the problems; emotional, physical and social of everyday life. Guided by the ethical and moral values of Judaism, these services are available to seniors of all creeds, races and financial ability.

It is for the continuation of this life-enriching work that the profits from the sale of this book are intended.

KASHRUT

A Short Outline of Kashrut
—Unique to the Traditional Jewish Table

These are foods that may be eaten and others that are forbidden.

Permitted:

All fruits, vegetables, grains, cereals, eggs from proper sources, nuts, etc. and foods derived from them.

All dairy foods from proper sources.

All fish with fins and scales.

All meat from animals that have split hooves and chew their cud, such as beef, lamb, veal.

Domesticated fowl.

Forbidden:

Pork and all pork products, shell fish such as crabs, lobsters, oysters, etc.

Meat and fowl must be slaughtered by one trained to do so (shochet) and must be salted and soaked in water in a prescribed manner.

Meat (fleishig) and dairy (milchig) products must not be mixed or eaten together. Fruits, vegetables, grains, nuts, fish, eggs are neutral or pareve and may be eaten alone or with either meat or dairy foods.

Meat and dairy dishes and all utensils used to prepare or eat them with must be kept separate.

Bread and wine have special significance and special laws govern their preparation.

Special foods are traditionally served at Jewish Holiday meals and on Shabbat. A number of such recipes are included. Special laws govern foods that can be served at Passover.

For further reference, see the many books on the subject.

An invitation—come sit with us
Around our Table. We would like to share with
you this exciting collection of family and guest-
proofed California Kosher recipes. Some are new,
as in Fish Blintzes, and some are updated old, as
in Hasidic Black Bean Soup. Some are simple and
some more complicated, but all have a different
twist. Eclectic as it is, please find this book a
welcome addition to your cuisine arts.

Gathering around our table is important to us.
Although observance varies and living styles
change, the table, which represents the vanished
altar of the Temple in Jerusalem, is still the place
that provides nourishment for the body and the
soul. Every "Simcha" or happy occasion, every
"Shabbat" or Sabbath observance, every religious
holiday calls for special dishes to heighten the
day. Our sages tell us, and we believe them, that
"There is no joy without food and drink".

All the recipes selected for our cookbook are in
keeping with the principles of Kashrut (kosher
preparation) and can be enjoyed by everyone. For
those interested, we include a short summary of
these laws. We suggest that when buying
commercially prepared food you check the label
for kosher ingredients.

Good Appetite
L'tay Avon!
The Editors

CONTRIBUTORS

ARLENE ALTMAN • JOANNE ALTSCHULER • HILDA ASHLEY • SYLVIA ASHMAN • JAN BALLIN • IDA F. BERG • JULIA BIDERMAN • SAMUEL BLOCK • ANITA BRENNER • LOIS BRENNER • JOEL BRESSEL • MICHELLE BRESSEL • EVY CADES • SUNNY CAINE • FANNIE CHAVIN • ELAINE COMESS • RHODA CONRAD • IDA COOKER • SYLVIA COOPER • PHYLLIS CURLENDER • ANN CUTROW • LILA DWARKIN • SALLY EDELIST • ELEANOR EINY • SUE ERLICH • PHYLLIS FELD • RUTH FEUERSTEIN • HELENE FEUERSTEIN • PAT FINE • SUSIE FREEDMAN • TAMAR FREEMAN • BOB FRIEDMAN • SHULAMITH FRIEDMAN • JEANIE GAYNOR • DORIS GERBER • MIDDIE GIESBERG • THELMA GINZLER • FANNIE GLUSKER • SHERRY GOLDENFELD • ANN GOLDENSON • JUDY GOLDSMITH • MIRIAM GOLDSMITH • DOROTHY GOREN • MURIEL GREEN • MINDY GROSS • SYLVIA GROSS • MARLENE GROSSMAN • RUTH HABER • HARRIET HACHER • HANNAH HANDMAN • HILDA HARDER • CONSTANCE HARRIS • HILDA HARTE • BARBARA HEITZ • ROBIN HERDAN • DORIS HILL • MIRIAM HOFFMAN • CONNIE HOMES • MURIEL HONIG • LOUISE JOHNSON • SYLVIA JOSEPH • NAT KALMAN • CHARLOTTE KAMENIR • SYLVIA KAPLAN • LOLA KARP • MYRTLE KARP • JOAN KLEINERMAN • ROSE KORTICK • SHAREL KRIMSKY • MOLLIE LEIFERT • PEARL LEVIN • LILLIAN LEVY • HANNAH LIPPERT • SYLVIA LIPTON • ELLEN MARGOLIS • BETSY MAZURSKY • PEARL NOVORR • RUTH NEBRON • MYRA NEUGASS • SYLVIA NEWMAN • ESTHER NOUROS • SOPHIE PATTERSON • STELLA POLLOCK • SYLVIA RABIM • JOY RABIN • DOROTHY RASKIN • RAE ROBBINS SARAH ROSENBERG • SUSAN ROTH • SARAH ROTHSTEIN SYLVIA RUBIN • MAXINE SALKIN • CLAIRE SCHNEIDER • SARA SCHOEN • JESSIE SCHWARTZ • JUNE SCHWARTZ CLARA SHAPIRO • PAULA SHATKIN • DINA SHIOD • LEA SHOLES • HARRIET SIEGEL • BEBE SIMON • EVELYN SIMON JEANETTE SIMON • HARRIET SOARES • RUTH STEELE • ROBERTA STRAUS • JOY TAUBMAN • PEARL TIRSHWELL • GLORIA TOLES • SHIRLEY TURTELTAUB • MILLIE TYNON • ANN VAN LEEWAN • PHYLLIS WAXMAN • RAMA WEITZMAN • H. WENKER • JACQUI WERNICK • ANNALIESE WOLFSON • THELMA WOLK • PRICILLA YABLON • REBECCA ZALOW

ACKNOWLEDGEMENTS

Bebe Simon, *Executive Editor-in-Chief*
Constance Harris, *Associate Editor*
Ruth Steele, *Literary Editor*
Barbara Kamilar, *Graphic Design & Production*
Carr Clifton, Marshall Safron, *Photography*
Color Media, *Special Graphic Effects*
Jerry Novorr, *Paper Cut Art*
Irv Hershman, *Index*
Sol Marshall, *Marketing*

Committee

Hilda Ashley	Robin Herdan
Lois Brenner	Muriel Honig
Sandy Candiotty	Charlotte Kaminer
Helene Feuerstein	Lillian Levy
Sherry Goldenfeld	Sylvia Lipton
Muriel Green	Paula Shatkin
Hannah Hamovich	Shirley Turtletaub

Special Thanks

Flora Mizrahi, *Typist*
Pearl Roseman, *Advisor*
Harvey Slayton, *Bread Baker for Cover Photo*
Jenny Wilkenson, *Food Stylist*
Staff of Los Angeles Jewish Family Service
Sandra King, *Executive Director*
Paul Castro, *Associate Director*

"Angels"

Ruth & Arnold Feuerstein
Helene & James Feuerstein
Betty & Marvin Hoffenberg
City National Bank
Columbia Savings & Loan
Great Western Bank
Hancock Savings Bank
I. Reinhard Memorial Fund

Our thanks to Hannah Hamovich
who inspired us to undertake this cookbook project.

*"And though your beginning was small,
your end will be great."*
JOB

In the beginning
comes the appetizer, featuring smaller portions
to stem immediate hunger, to stimulate taste, to
serve as a time-extender when served with drinks,
to pique the interest of the guest and to show the
creativity of the hostess.

Appetizers can be simple or as elaborate as mini-
meals. It all depends on what follows. If you are
fortunate it will be a good meal and, as the book
of Job predicts, "the end will be great."

PITA CRISPS
Serves 8

1 package split pita bread cut into strips or
  thinly sliced cocktail rye bread
¼ pound margarine, softened
¼ teaspoon marjoram
¼ teaspoon basil
¼ teaspoon garlic salt or powder

Spread pita or bread with butter or margarine. Sprinkle with mixed seasonings. Bake or broil until crisp.

CRISPY TORTILLA STRIPS

1 package flour tortillas (made with vegetable shortening)
oil for frying
powdered sugar
sugar-cinnamon mixture

Cut tortillas in ¾ inch strips. Heat oil for frying. With tongs, place tortilla strips in oil until golden on one side, turn on other side and remove to sheet lined, with paper towel. Sprinkle with powdered sugar or sugar-cinnamon mixture. Store in a tin.

WON TON CRISPS

1 package of square won ton
¼ pound margarine or butter
¼ cup Parmesan or Romano cheese, grated
1 large garlic clove, minced

APPETIZERS

Grease cookie sheet. Mix together margarine or butter, grated cheese and garlic. Spread mixture thinly on separated won ton, stacking them on top of one another. Slice stack in half diagonally and separate into individual pieces. Bake in 350° preheated oven until golden, about 6-10 minutes. Watch carefully to prevent burning. Remove from pan and store in tin.

If large square won tons are used, cut diagonally in 2 pieces. Can be used as a salad or soup accompaniment.

GARLIC-SESAME SPREAD
Serves 12

3 large cloves garlic, minced
2 tablespoons sesame oil
1 tablespoon honey
¾ teaspoon soy sauce
⅛ teaspoon cayenne pepper
¼ teaspoon grated orange zest
¼ teaspoon salt
12 hors d'oeuvre-size crackers
2 teaspoons snipped chives

Combine garlic, sesame oil, honey, soy sauce, cayenne pepper, orange zest and salt in small saucepan or microwaveable dish. Bring to boil on stove top or in microwave oven. Remove from heat.

Brush glaze on crackers. Sprinkle with chives. Arrange single layer on baking sheet. Bake on center rack of a 375° oven until deeply browned, about 6 minutes. Cool on rack. May be stored in an airtight container for 2 days.

SALSA DIP
Yields 3½ - 4 cups

1 large can (7 ounces) green chili salsa
I large can tomatoes
1 small can tomatillos, chopped (optional)
½ teaspoon whole or ground oregano (or more to taste)
1 small onion
1½ tablespoons vinegar
1 bunch cilantro, chopped

Process and combine all ingredients. Chill overnight to combine flavors. Serve with chips or crackers.

QUICK MIX GUACAMOLE
Serves 20

8 medium green onions
1 or 2 bottled, pickled, yellow chili peppers
4 large ripe avocados, peeled and cut into large pieces
salt to taste

In a food processor, using the steel blade, finely mince the green onions. Add chili peppers (seeds and liquid included) and process for 10 seconds. Add avocado pieces and process several seconds. Don't overprocess. Allow avocado to remain chunky. Season to taste with salt. Chill in air-tight container. Serve with tortilla chips.

Note: for a less spicy dip, omit chili pepper seeds.

APPETIZERS

GUACAMOLE WITH HOMEMADE SALSA
Serves 6-8

Salsa:
2 fresh green chilies, seeded and chopped
6 yellow chilies, seeded and chopped
2 ripe tomatoes, seeded and chopped
10 ounces stewed tomatoes
6 tablespoons corn oil
8 cloves garlic, minced
1 teaspoon dried oregano
3 teaspoons chopped fresh cilantro
salt, pepper

Guacamole:
4 ripe avocados, peeled and chopped
½ cup salsa, or more to taste
1 ripe tomato, seeded and chopped
1 scallion with top, finely chopped
cilantro sprigs (garnish)

Combine salsa ingredients, using care when handling chili peppers. (Wear rubber gloves to avoid skin irritation; remove seeds under cold running water; avoid getting any juice in eyes.)

Combine avocados, salsa, tomato, and scallion in a large bowl. Store covered in refrigerator until ready to serve. To serve, stir guacamole, transfer to a serving dish, and garnish with cilantro sprigs.

REFRIED BEANS OLE
Serves 10

2 cans refried vegetarian beans
4 ounce can chopped and drained jalepeno peppers
2 scallions, cut fine
1 cup grated Mozzarella cheese (or ½ cup grated Cheddar)
2 or 3 chopped Italian plum tomatoes
¼ cup chopped Italian parsley
¼ cup toasted pumpkin seeds

Place beans in a 2-quart shallow casserole. Layer the following: jalepeno peppers, scallions, plum tomatoes, Italian parsley, toasted pumpkin seeds.

Heat in 350° oven for 20 minutes. Serve with unseasoned corn chips.

MEXICAN DIP
Serves 12

1 can refried vegetarian beans
2 mashed avocados with lemon juice to taste
1 cup sour cream mixed with ½ package of taco mix
½ cup shredded Cheddar cheese
2 small tomatoes, diced
1 small can sliced black olives
¼ cup chopped red onion
¼ cup chopped parsley

Layer ingredients in large pyrex or quiche pan in the following order:
  1st layer;   beans
  2nd layer; avocado

APPETIZERS

3rd layer;   sour cream & taco mixture

Top with remaining 5 ingredients. Serve with chips.

ARTICHOKE CHEESE DIP
Serves 8

1 can (14 ounce) artichoke hearts, drained
½ cup grated Parmesan cheese
½ cup shredded Swiss cheese
¼ cup mayonnaise
½ cup sour cream
1 teaspoon Worcestershire sauce
¼ teaspoon mustard
dash pepper
chopped green chilies to taste (optional)

Preheat oven to 400°. Place ingredients in food processor and process until artichoke hearts are coarsely chopped. Spoon into a lightly greased 1 quart casserole. Bake 20 minutes. Serve with pita crisps or tortilla chips. May be refrigerated and reheated at 350°.

ARTICHOKE SPINACH DIP
Serves 8

1 6-ounce jar marinated, quartered artichoke hearts, drained
1 10-ounce package chopped, frozen spinach, defrosted and
  drained well
1 small jar diced green chilies
1 cup light mayonnaise
1 cup grated Parmesan cheese

Combine all ingredients and place in 2 quart greased casserole. Bake in 350° oven for 30 minutes. Serve with chips.

ARTICHOKE SQUARES
Serves 8-10

3 6-ounce jars marinated artichoke hearts
1 clove garlic, crushed
½ cup chopped onion
4 eggs
¼ cup seasoned bread crumbs
¼ pound sharp Cheddar cheese, grated
2 tablespoons minced fresh parsley
½ teaspoon dried oregano
½ teaspoon salt
½ teaspoon pepper
½ teaspoon Tabasco sauce
watercress or parsley sprigs

Drain the oil from one jar of the artichoke hearts and turn into a 12 inch skillet. Using moderate heat, gently heat the oil. Saute the garlic and onion in the oil for 5 minutes and set aside. Drain and discard the oil from the remaining artichoke hearts. Chop the hearts finely and set aside. In a medium sized bowl beat the eggs until foamy and blend in the bread crumbs, cheese, parsley, oregano, salt, pepper and Tabasco. Add the finely chopped artichoke hearts to the egg mixture and stir gently to blend. Add the onion and garlic. Mix well and spoon into a greased 9 x 9 inch pan. Bake in a preheated 325° oven for 30 minutes. Cool well before cutting into 2 inch squares. Before serving, place in a 325° oven for 10-12 minutes, then place on a warm serving plate garnished with watercress or parsley sprigs.

APPETIZERS

HOT CHEESE CHILI ON CHIPS
Serves 16

1 onion, peeled and finely diced
1 green pepper, finely diced
½ pound mushrooms, chopped fine
3 tablespoons margarine
1 cup Jack cheese, grated
1 cup Cheddar cheese, grated
½ small can chopped green chilies
round corn chips
1 teaspoon chili powder

Saute vegetables in margarine until soft, add mushrooms last in order not to overcook. Combine sauteed vegetables, chilies, cheese. Chill. One hour before serving, spread mixture on corn chips and sprinkle with chili powder. Bake on cookie sheet for 10 minutes at 350° and serve.

CHEESE-CHILE APPETIZER
Yield 42 squares

½ cup butter
10 eggs
½ cup flour
1 teaspoon baking powder
dash salt
1 can (8 ounces) green chilies, chopped
1 pint cottage cheese
1 pound Jack cheese, shredded

Melt butter in 13 x 9 x 2 inch pan. Beat eggs lightly in large bowl and add flour, baking powder and salt and blend. Add melted butter, chilies, cottage and Jack cheese and mix until just blended. Turn batter into pan and bake at 400° for 15 minutes. Reduce heat to 350° and bake 35-40 minutes longer. Cut into squares and serve hot. Recipe may be cut in half and baked in an 8 inch pan. Bake in jelly roll pan to serve larger amounts.

CHEESE PUFFS
Serves 8

1 cup milk
¼ cup butter or margarine
½ teaspoon salt
⅛ teaspoon pepper
1 cup all-purpose flour
4 eggs
1½ cups shredded Swiss or Gruyere cheese

Heat milk and butter in a 2 quart saucepan. Add salt and pepper. Bring to a boil. Add flour all at once, stirring constantly over medium heat until mixture leaves side of pan and forms a ball. Remove saucepan from heat. Beat in eggs one at a time until mixture is smooth and well blended. Beat in 1 cup of cheese. Using a large spoon, make 8 equal sized round mounds of dough in a circle on a greased baking sheet. Dough rounds should be touching. This step uses about ¾ of the dough. Using the remainder of the dough, place a small round ball of dough on top of each mound. Sprinkle puffs with remaining ½ cup shredded cheese. Bake on center shelf for about 55 minutes at 350° or until puffs are lightly browned and crisped.

APPETIZERS

BRIE EN CROUTE
Serves 8 - 10

1 frozen puff pastry sheet, thawed
Dijon mustard as needed
1 7-ounce round Brie
1 egg, lightly beaten
assorted sliced fruits and vegetables

Roll thawed puff pastry on floured board to slightly larger than cheese round. Spread Dijon mustard on center of pastry and place cheese on top of mustard. Bring edges of pastry up to cover about 1 inch of the top edge of Brie round. Tuck in edges of pastry so it adheres to cheese, cut off excess. Place on lightly greased pan and brush with half of beaten egg. Chill 1 hour and brush with remaining egg. Bake at 375° until golden, about 20 minutes. Remove from oven. Decorate with fruits and vegetables and serve in thin wedges on crackers.

MELTED BRIE WITH FRUITS
Serves 16

¾ cup chopped pitted dates
1 each, small apple, and small firm ripe pear, peeled,
  cored and diced
½ cup currants or raisins
½ cup chopped pecans or walnuts
⅓ cup rose wine or apple juice
1 wheel (2 pounds) ripe Brie, well chilled

In a bowl, mix dates, apple, pear, currants, nuts and wine. Set aside to soften fruit, about two hours. Cut Brie in half to make two round layers. Place 1 layer, cut side up, in a 10 inch shallow-rimmed baking dish (such as a quiche pan.) Spread with 2¼ cups of fruits. Top with second layer. Spoon remaining fruit into center of cheese. If made ahead, cover and chill up to two days. Bake uncovered in 350° oven until it melts at edges and center is warm, 25-30 minutes. Can be divided in half, using 1 pound wheel.

OLIVE, CHEESE AND CURRY
ON TOASTED MUFFIN
Serves 12

1 can chopped black olives (4½ ounces)
1 small onion, grated
1 cup shredded Cheddar cheese
½ cup mayonnaise
½ teaspoon curry powder
6 English muffins, toasted
1-2 tops of scallions (cut small)

Mix all ingredients and spread thickly on the toasted muffins. Cut into quarters. Bake in 450° oven 10 minutes. Note: May be frozen and reheated in 450° oven.

APPETIZERS

STUFFED CHEESE ROLLS
Serves 24

1 pound Tillamook cheese
1 small bottle pimiento stuffed olives, drained
2 hard cooked eggs, chopped
1 small onion, coarsely chopped
1 8-ounce can tomato sauce
¼ teaspoon Worcestershire sauce
salt and pepper to taste
24 small French rolls

Place filling ingredients in food processor and process until combined. Cut the top off rolls, reserve, and remove soft bread from rolls. Fill with cheese mixture and replace tops on rolls. Wrap each roll in waxed paper, twisting ends to secure. Place on baking sheet and heat at 350° for 20 minutes.

EGG SALAD AND CAVIAR SUPREME
Serves 10

15 eggs, hardboiled
1 small can black olives, chopped
½ teaspoon curry powder
mayonnaise to bind
1 pint carton sour cream
1 small jar caviar
parsley for garnish

Chop eggs finely. Add olives and curry powder with enough mayonnaise to bind. Pack in an 8 inch round ring mold sprayed with non-stick spray. Refrigerate overnight.

When ready to serve, place inverted plate over ring and turn right side up so that egg mixture slips out of mold. Spread sour cream over complete ring (top and sides). Sprinkle black caviar all around the top of the ring. Decorate center of ring with fresh parsley. Serve with crackers or thinly sliced black bread.

SPINACH BALL APPETIZERS
Yield 70 balls

2 packages frozen chopped spinach, drained well
2 cups herbed bread stuffing
2 large onions, finely chopped
5 eggs, well beaten
1½ sticks margarine
½ cup Parmesan cheese, grated
1 tablespoon garlic powder
1 teaspoon black pepper

Squeeze spinach well to drain all moisture. Combine all ingredients and mix well. Chill for 2 hours. Make walnut size balls, place on cookie sheet and bake 20-30 minutes at 350°. May be frozen unbaked on cookie sheet and placed in plastic bags in freezer. When ready to serve, remove from freezer, place on cookie sheet and bake at 350° for about 35 minutes.

Mustard Sauce:
1 tablespoon dry mustard
½ cup white vinegar
½ cup sugar
2 tablespoons orange juice
1 egg yolk

Mix mustard and vinegar in enamel pan and keep overnight. Add remaining ingredients and simmer until slightly thickened, about 5 minutes. May be refrigerated several weeks.

APPETIZERS

GLAZED ONIONS SPUMANTE

4 onions, sliced
¼ pound margarine
¼ cup red wine vinegar
2 tablespoons sugar
¼ cup grenadine

Saute onions in margarine, add wine vinegar and sugar, cook for 15 minutes over low heat. Add grenadine. Serve on sliced and toasted French bread or as an accompaniment to meat or poultry.

CONFETTI PATE
Serves 10

1 cup pecans
1 cup walnuts
1 cup sunflower seeds
¾ cup chopped onions
2⅓ cups water
½ cup chopped fresh cilantro
¼ cup chopped fresh parsley
½ cup grated carrots
½ cup grated zucchini
½ cup diced red bell pepper
1 each red, yellow and green whole bell peppers
red lettuce leaves, cooked asparagus, and artichoke hearts
  for garnish

Place first 6 ingredients in food processor and process 25-30 seconds. Pour mixture into medium-sized bowl. Stir in next 5 ingredients and chill. Hollow out bell peppers and stuff filling tightly. Slice in rounds and serve in tri-color combinations on lettuce leaves with asparagus and artichoke hearts.

MUSHROOM ALMOND PATE
Serves 8

3 tablespoons butter
1 cup almonds, slivered
½ cup fresh parsley
½ onion
1 clove garlic
½ pound mushrooms
1 teaspoon fresh thyme (or 1 tablespoon fresh rosemary)
½ teaspoon salt
½ teaspoon pepper
2 tablespoons dry vermouth or cognac

In a frying pan, melt 1 tablespoon butter over medium heat and saute almonds until golden brown. Remove to a bowl and wipe out pan. (Almonds can also be toasted in an enamel pan without butter, if desired.)

Chop parsley until very fine in a food processor. Set aside. Chop onion. Heat 2 tablespoons butter in pan and saute onions until soft and transparent. Chop garlic followed by the mushrooms with quick pulses (being careful not to overprocess). Add garlic and mushrooms to onions in pan and saute until liquid evaporates. Add thyme, salt, and pepper. Stir and remove from heat.

Reserve 2 tablespoons of almonds and process the rest until finely ground. Do not overgrind. Add mushroom mixture and vermouth, processing enough to blend. Add reserved almonds and all but 2 tablespoons of parsley. Pulse to incorporate. Press mixture into a crock or bowl and sprinkle with remaining parsley. Refrigerate several days to allow flavors to blend.

Serve with slices of crusty French bread and a sampling of flavored mustards. Best prepared 4-6 days in advance.

APPETIZERS

SPICY SPANISH EGGPLANT
Serves 24

1 medium onion, sliced thin
3 tablespoons olive oil
1 medium or large eggplant, sliced thin
½ cup red pepper, chopped
¼ cup red wine vinegar
¼ cup tomato sauce (or to taste)
1 tablespoon fresh or dry oregano, chopped parsley and
cilantro (optional)
¼ teaspoon ground pepper
2 cloves garlic, minced
¼ teaspoon chili powder

Heat 2 tablespoons olive oil and add onions. Saute until tender. Add the rest of oil and sliced eggplant and red pepper. Continue to saute until tender. Add vinegar, tomato sauce and seasonings. Simmer for 5 to 10 minutes, stirring until thick. Refrigerate and serve as appetizer with chips and crackers.

(If additional liquid is needed, broth can be used.)

RIKKI'S EGGPLANT MELANGE
Serves 6

2 medium eggplants
4 hard boiled eggs
4 very spicy pickles
2 tablespoons mayonnaise
1 bunch green onions
4 cloves garlic

Roast the whole eggplant over an open fire until soft. Blanch in cold water, peel, and mash with two silver forks. Chop eggs, pickles, and garlic very fine. Cut scallions into one inch dice. Blend all ingredients with enough mayonnaise to bind. Serve with pita bread quarters, plain or toasted.

BABA GHANOUSH
Yields 2½ cups

2 pounds eggplant (2 medium or 1 large),
*   whole and unpeeled*
¼ cup tahini (sesame paste)
¼ cup fresh lemon juice
1 large clove garlic, crushed
¼ cup finely minced onion
salt, if desired, to taste
freshly ground black pepper, to taste
1 tablespoon oil, preferably olive (optional)
2 tablespoons minced fresh parsley

Prick the eggplant in several places with a fork. Place it on a baking sheet, and broil it in a preheated broiler for about 20 minutes, turning the vegetable several times so that the skin chars on all sides. Let the eggplant cool. When the eggplant is cool enough to handle, cut it in half, scrape out the flesh into a bowl, discard the skin, and mash the eggplant with the tahini, lemon juice, garlic, onion, oil, salt, and pepper. Cover the mixture, and refrigerate it. Before serving, if desired, add minced parsley. Serve with pita, fresh or toasted, or as a dip for fresh vegetables.

VEGETABLE AND EGGPLANT CAPONATA
Yields 3 quarts

2 medium eggplants, cubed
2 large onions, chopped
½ cup olive oil
1½ cups celery, sliced
2 bell peppers (green or red) cut in 1 inch chunks
3 cloves garlic, chopped
2½ pounds peeled, seeded and chopped tomatoes or 1 can (28 ounces) chopped Italian tomatoes, drained
⅓ cup red wine vinegar
1 tablespoon sugar

3 tablespoons tomato paste
¼ cup fresh basil, chopped
¼ cup fresh oregano, chopped
½ cup parsley, chopped
1 teaspoon pepper, freshly ground, or to taste
¾ cup sliced, stuffed green olives
4 tablespoons drained capers
2 carrots, sliced thin
2-3 zucchini, sliced
½-1 cup pine nuts

Place cubed eggplant and onions in 5-6 quart pot in which oil has been heated and saute 5 minutes. Lightly brown pine nuts in olive oil and add to eggplant mixture. Add remaining ingredients and stir gently but thoroughly. Cover and simmer about 30 minutes, stirring occasionally. Remove cover and simmer for another 10 minutes or until thick. Serve at room temperature with chunks of Italian bread or as a salad spooned onto a bed of lettuce. Mixture will keep under refrigeration 3-4 weeks.

ZUCCHINI DELIGHT
Serves 12

3 cups grated zucchini
1 cup biscuit mix
½ cup onions, chopped
½ cup Parmesan cheese, grated
dash pepper and salt
½ teaspoon oregano
½ cup oil
2 eggs, slightly beaten
2 tablespoons parsley, chopped

Mix all ingredients together. Grease 9 x 13 inch pan. Bake in 350° oven for 35 minutes. Cut into squares. Can be used as an hors d' oeuvre or as an accompaniment to an entree.

HERRING APPLE DELIGHT
Serves 8

1 12-ounce jar wine herring
1 small apple (not Granny Smith)
1 small onion, chopped
½ can (8½ ounce) sliced or diced beets
about 2 tablespoons sour cream or yogurt
chopped walnuts for garnish

Cut up herring into bite size pieces. Peel and slice apple. Chop the onion. Cut up beets and use some of the juice. Add sour cream. Mix all ingredients together and chill.

Optional: sprinkle chopped walnuts on top.

APPETIZERS

MOTHER'S FESTIVE CHOPPED HERRING

32-ounce jar fat herring fillets
1 large red onion
2 peppers, green and red
1 handful of parsley
1 slice rye bread soaked in 2 tablespoons oil
2 tablespoons wine vinegar
1 large apple, pared and peeled
6 eggs, hard boiled and peeled
½ teaspoon cinnamon
½ teaspoon nutmeg
salt and ground pepper to taste
sprinkle of sugar (optional)
¼ cup fresh dill, chopped

Drain and wash herring. Set aside. In wooden bowl, chop onion. Add vegetables and continue to chop, then add herring, eggs, rye bread with oil and vinegar and chop until mixture is well blended. Add seasonings to taste and refrigerate. Sprinkle additional dill on top for garnish.

HERRING ANTIPASTO
Serves 15

1 jar (12-16 ounces) herring snacks in wine, including
  onions, drained and cut up
1 green pepper, diced
1 medium red onion, chopped
1 can (2½ ounces) chopped ripe olives
1 jar chili sauce (12 ounces)
1 jar (6 ounces) marinated artichoke hearts, drained
  and cut into small pieces.

32

Combine herring and onions with green pepper, red onion, olives, chili sauce and artichoke hearts. Place in a covered bowl and refrigerate at least 24 hours before serving. Garnish with chopped parsley or dill. Serve with French or Italian bread or crackers.

LOX AND CREAM CHEESE MOLD
Serves 10

1 envelope unflavored gelatin
¾ cup cold water
¼ cup heated half and half
½ cup sour cream
½ teaspoon Worcestershire sauce
¼ teaspoon Tabasco sauce
¼ teaspoon lemon juice
½ teaspoon chives
1 teaspoon dill
¼ teaspoon horseradish
1 4-ounce package cream cheese
¼ pound smoked salmon, cut up

Dilute gelatin in cold water and add to warmed half and half. Cool. Mix with all other ingredients. Spray or grease mold and line with wax paper. Spray or grease wax paper and fill with ingredients. Refrigerate.

APPETIZERS

SALMON TARTAR
Serves 12

1 pound smoked salmon
½ cup green onions with tops, chopped
1 or 2 tomatoes (depending on size), peeled and diced
½ cup cilantro, chopped
dash red pepper flakes or chili powder
½ cup parsley, chopped

Shred salmon with fingers into bowl. Add onions, tomatoes, cilantro and red pepper flakes. Mix well and let stand several hours in refrigerator. Drain if necessary and shape into a mound on serving platter. Sprinkle with chopped parsley. Serve with crackers, pita bread, etc.

SAVORY TUNA
Serves 8

1 can mushroom soup (10¾ ounces)
¼ pound Jack cheese, grated
½ pound Cheddar cheese, grated
1 can white tuna (12½ ounces)
1 can green chilies (7 ounces), seeded and chopped
  or if preferred, green chile salsa (7 ounce can) may
  be substituted
½ cup sliced black olives
½ cup white wine or sherry
¼ teaspoon coarse pepper
3 tablespoons capers, optional

Heat together mushroom soup and grated cheeses. Add remaining ingredients, continue to heat and serve in a bowl surrounded by crackers.

SARDINE ROLLUPS
Serves 8

2 cans sardines
1 (8-ounce) package puff pastry shells
mustard sauce

Drain sardines. Cut puff pastry into 8 triangles. Place whole sardines on wide end of triangle and roll up. Place on ungreased baking pan and bake at 375° for 12 to 15 minutes or until lightly browned. Serve with hot mustard sauce.

Hot mustard sauce:
½ cup sour cream
1½ tablespoons prepared mustard
½ teaspoon parsley flakes
salt
2 tablespoons butter or margarine

Combine sour cream, mustard, parsley flakes, salt to taste and butter. Heat, stirring occasionally. Do not boil.

MARINATED VEGETABLES
Serves 10

2 pounds carrots, sliced and cooked until crisp-tender
1 head cauliflower, cut into flowerettes, cooked until
* crisp-tender*
2-3 zucchinis, thinly sliced into rounds
1 small green pepper, thinly sliced
1 sweet red onion, peeled and thinly sliced

Combine all vegetables with marinade and refrigerate, covered, overnight.

Marinade:
1 10½-ounce can tomato soup
¼ cup oil
¼ cup sugar
½ cup red wine vinegar
1 teaspoon prepared mustard
1 teaspoon Worcestershire sauce
⅛ teaspooon salt
½ teaspoon pepper

Mix together until smooth.

Optional: Add salsa sauce or curry powder to taste.

CHICKEN ANTIPASTO
Serves 10

2 whole chicken breasts
3 cloves garlic
4 tablespoons margarine
1 can black olives
large jar green olives, pitted,
*   with pimientos*
1 can unmarinated artichoke
*   hearts, drained*
4 carrots
2 to 3 leeks
fresh parsley
½ pound mushrooms

Marinade:
½ cup extra virgin olive oil
¼ cup red wine vinegar
juice of half lemon
½ to 1 tablespoon oregano
1 to 2 tablespoons basil
white pepper to taste
Tabasco to taste
pinch of sugar

Mix ingredients in bowl.

Saute chicken in margarine and garlic until tender. Set aside. Slice chicken, artichoke hearts and olives with food processor. Put into bowl. Slice carrots and leeks with fine slicer on processor. Add chicken. Mince parsley with steel knife of processor. Add to mixture. Slice mushrooms by hand and set aside to add just before serving. Pour marinade over antipasto, mix well and chill for 2 hours.

DRUNKEN CHICKEN DRUMETTES
Serves 12

1 cup brown sugar
½ teaspoon dry mustard
¼ cup water
¼ cup gin
1½ teaspoons powdered ginger
¼ cup melted margarine
3 pounds chicken drumettes (meaty half of chicken wing)

Combine brown sugar, mustard, water, gin, ginger and margarine. Marinate chicken overnight in the refrigerator. Place on cookie sheet and bake at 350° for 45 minutes.

HOT SALAMI

1 12-ounce salami
cloves
1 jar jalapeno jelly
thinly sliced pumpernickel bread

Score salami with a knife. Stud salami with cloves. Cover with jalapeno jelly. Place in pan and bake in 300° oven approximately 3 hours. Discard fat from pan throughout baking. As fat runs off salami becomes hard. Slice and serve as an hors d'oeuvre with thin slices of pumpernickel bread.

Note: Mustard to cover may be substituted for jelly.

"While love is sweet, it is best with bread."
YIDDISH PROVERB

There's a world of wisdom here. We're talking basic and bread is that. Stone-age man started the process by baking flat breads (we translate that to tortilla, pita and matzoh, among others.) The Greeks went on to refine the flour and considered white quite superior. The Romans followed, as they were wont to do, keeping their idea of the choicest for the privileged and giving the coarse dark variety, that we so prize now, to the poor and the criminal.

Bread's the staple that many religions include in their rituals. For us, the matzoh is a potent Passover symbol and the braided challeh is Queen of the Sabbath table.

Now we invite you to sample the dough that we have raised to new heights.

CHEESE CRISP BISCUITS
Yields 2 dozen

1 cup flour
¼ cup butter or margarine
1 cup assorted grated cheese (Cheddar/Swiss)
⅔ cup dry rice crisp cereal
1 teaspoon Tabasco sauce
1 tablespoon caraway seeds

Mix all ingredients together and form into 2 long rolls. Cut into slices and place on cookie sheet. Bake in 350° oven for 12-15 minutes.

CHEESE BREAD
Serves 6

2 cups buttermilk biscuit mix
1 tablespoon sugar
1 teaspoon instant minced onion
¼ teaspoon oregano, crushed
¼ cup butter, melted
¼ cup white wine
½ cup shredded Cheddar cheese
1 egg, beaten
½ cup milk

Combine biscuit mix, sugar, instant onion and oregano. Add butter, wine, cheese, egg and milk. Beat until well blended. Spoon into well-greased 8-inch round baking pan. Bake at 350° for 25-30 minutes or until lightly browned.

BREAD

CHEESE CUSTARD BREAD
Serves 6-8

6 eggs, beaten
16 ounces cottage cheese (small curd)
1 cup milk
¼ teaspoon salt
1 cup biscuit mix
1 pound Jack cheese, diced
½ cube butter, melted

Blend all but butter. Pour ½ the melted butter into 9 x 13 inch pyrex pan. Pour rest of butter into cheese-egg mixture. Blend and pour into pan. Bake at 350° for 40-50 minutes or until golden brown. Let rest a few minutes. Cut and serve.

CHEESE-DILL BREAD

1 package dry yeast
¼ cup lukewarm water
1 cup cream-style cottage cheese, warmed
1 tablespoon dried onion flakes
2 tablespoons sugar
1 tablespoon margarine
2 tablespoons dill seed or dill weed
1 teaspoon salt
½ teaspoon baking soda
1 egg
2½ cups flour
melted butter
coarse salt

Dissolve yeast in lukewarm water. Add to warmed cottage cheese. Add onion flakes, sugar, margarine, dill, salt, soda, egg and flour; stir well. Knead dough on a lightly floured board. Let rise 2 hours.

Place dough in a greased 10-inch casserole or shape into a loaf and place in a greased loaf pan. Let rise 1 hour. Bake in a preheated 350° oven 40 to 50 minutes. When done, brush warm loaf with butter and sprinkle with coarse salt.

CUSTARD SKILLET BREAD
Yields 8 slices

2 tablespoons butter or margarine
1⅓ cups yellow cornmeal
2 tablespoons sugar
1 teaspoon baking soda
1 teaspoon salt, optional
⅓ cup sifted flour
1 cup milk
2 eggs, beaten
1 cup buttermilk
1 cup milk

Heat butter or margarine in 9 inch skillet or pan in preheated 400° oven. Sift together cornmeal, sugar, soda, salt and flour. Stir in 1 cup milk, eggs, buttermilk and mix well. Pour into skillet, then pour 1 cup of milk over top of batter. DO NOT MIX. Milk will settle to middle of bread to form a custard layer in the center. Bake until done, about 35 minutes. Don't overbake. Cut into wedges and serve hot with butter, honey, molasses or maple syrup.

BREAD

FARMHOUSE ZUCCHINI SPOONBREAD
Serves 8

1 pound zucchini, ends trimmed, coarsely grated
2 teaspoons salt
1 cup all purpose flour
¾ cup yellow cornmeal
2 teaspoons baking powder
1 cup buttermilk
2 large eggs
¼ cup butter or margarine, melted
½ cup Cheddar cheese, shredded
½ cup onion, minced
2 tablespoons green bell pepper, chopped (optional)

In colander, mix zucchini with salt and crush gently with your hands; set aside 30 minutes to drain. Rinse well under cool running water. With your hands, squeeze as much moisture from squash as possible. Lay squash out on towels and pat dry.

In a large bowl, mix flour, cornmeal and baking powder. Add buttermilk, eggs and melted butter; whisk to blend well. Stir in zucchini, cheese, onion and bell pepper. Pour mixture into buttered 9 inch square baking pan. Bake in a 425° oven until top is golden, about 30 minutes. Spoon onto plates.

SPOON BREAD SUPREME
Serves 6

1 cup white corn meal, sifted
1 teaspoon salt
½ teaspoon sugar
1½ cups boiling water
3 tablespoons butter, melted
3 eggs, separated (or use 2 ounces egg substitute and
  3 egg whites, beaten stiff)
1 cup buttermilk
½ teaspoon baking soda
1 carrot, coarsely grated
1 rib of celery, chopped
½ red pepper, chopped
1 teaspoon dried onion flakes
½ teaspoon black pepper
1 teaspoon baking powder

Optional:
¼ cup cilantro and parsley, chopped
1 cup Cheddar cheese, grated

To the meal, add salt and sugar; scald with boiling water. When lukewarm, add butter, well-beaten egg yolks and buttermilk with baking soda added to it. Mix thoroughly. Add grated carrot, chopped celery, red pepper, dried onion flakes, black pepper, and optional cilantro, parsley and Cheddar cheese. Add baking powder and fold in stiffly beaten egg whites. Pour into a well-greased pyrex dish and bake in preheated oven 350° for 40-50 minutes. Test for doneness in center of bread. Serve immediately.

BREAD

SOUTHWEST SPOON BREAD
Serves 8

1 can (20 ounce) cream-style corn
¾ cup milk
½ cup salad oil
2 eggs, beaten
1 cup cornmeal
½ teaspoon baking soda
1 teaspoon salt
1 can (about 2 ounce) chopped green chile, drained
1 cup grated Cheddar cheese

Mix corn, milk, oil and eggs. Stir in cornmeal, soda and salt. Gently fold in chiles and cheese.

Pour into a buttered 2-quart casserole. Bake, uncovered, in a preheated 400° oven 45 minutes.

BEST ONION ROLLS
Yields 18 rolls

Dough:
1 package active dry yeast
1 cup lukewarm water
2 tablespoons sugar
1½ teaspoons salt
¾ cup whole eggs (about 3)
6 tablespoons oil
4-5 cups all-purpose flour
1 egg, well beaten, for wash

Filling:
1 cup finely chopped onion

46

1 teaspoon salt
1 tablespoon poppy seeds
1½ teaspoons caraway seeds
1 cup dry bread crumbs
¼ cup oil

In a bowl, soften yeast in lukewarm water. Stir in sugar, salt, eggs, oil and enough flour to form a stiff dough. Knead on a floured surface until smooth and elastic, about 5 minutes. Place dough in a greased bowl and turn to grease top. Let rise, covered, in a warm dry place until doubled in bulk, about 1 hour. Punch down and knead on a floured surface and roll dough into an 18 x 24 inch oblong. Cut dough into 12-6 x 3 inch pieces. To prepare filling, mix all ingredients in a bowl. Spoon ¾ of the mixture over dough. Fold ⅓ of the dough over onions and fold ⅓ over again from the other side. Place rolls, seam side down, on a greased cookie sheet. Flatten rolls until they are 5 inches long. Cut rolls in half. Brush rolls with eggs wash and sprinkle with remaining onion mixture.* Let rise, covered, in a warm place until doubled in bulk, about 30 minutes. Bake rolls in a preheated hot oven, 400° for 15-20 minutes.

*The onion rolls can be frozen at this point. When ready to bake, place frozen rolls on a greased cookie sheet and let rise, uncovered, in a warm place until doubled in bulk, about 1 hour. Then bake as directed.

GREAT YEAST ROLLUPS
Yields 5 dozen

1 cake yeast (or 1 package)
½ cup lukewarm milk
4 tablespoons sugar plus 1 heaping teaspoon
1 cup butter, room temperature
2 egg yolks

BREAD

3¼ cups flour (or more)
2 tablespoons orange rind
¼ pound butter or margarine, melted
cinnamon, to taste
sugar, to taste
1 cup ground nuts
1 cup raisins
confectioners' sugar

Preheat oven to 375°. Use cookie sheet. Dissolve yeast in milk. Add 1 heaping teaspoon sugar. Let stand 25 minutes. Cream butter and remaing 4 tablespoons of sugar; add yolks. Add yeast, milk and orange rind and work in flour. Divide dough into 8 parts. Roll each part into an 8-inch circle. Brush with melted butter. Sprinkle with cinnamon, sugar, ground nuts and raisins. Cut in triangles (8 pieces) and roll from outside to center. Shape in form of a crescent. Let stand for 2 hours. Bake for 15 to 20 minutes until slightly browned. Before serving, sprinkle with confectioners' sugar.

FRENCH ONION BREAD
Yields 2 loaves

1 package dry yeast
¼ cup lukewarm water
1 envelope dry onion soup mix
2 cups water
2 tablespoons sugar
1 teaspoon salt
2 tablespoons Parmesan cheese, grated
2 tablespoons shortening
6-6½ cups sifted enriched flour
2 tablespoons cornmeal
1 egg white, beaten with fork with 1 tablespoon water

48

Dissolve yeast in lukewarm water. Simmer dry onion soup mix with 2 cups water, covered, for 10 minutes. Remove from stove. Add sugar, salt, cheese and shortening. Cool to lukewarm. Remove to large mixing bowl. Add yeast mixture; stir well until all yeast particles ar dissolved. Stir flour in gradually, mixing well after each addition. Knead mixture on floured board until smooth and elastic, about 5 minutes. Return to mixing bowl; cover with plastic wrap, cloth or plate.

Let rise until doubled, about 1½ hours. Punch down with fingers. Divide in half; cover and let mixture rest for 10 minutes. By hand, shape into 2 long loaves. Place on greased baking sheet that has been sprinkled with cornmeal. Cover with towel and let rise 1 hour. Bake in preheated oven at 375° for 20 minutes. With pastry brush, brush loaves with beaten egg white and water. Bake additional 10-15 minutes or until browned.

ONION PASTRY WITH TOMATO
Serves 8

2 cups flour
½ teaspoon salt
¼ cup butter
¼ cup vegetable shortening
3 to 4 tablespoons cold water
2 tablespoons olive oil
6 sweet onions, thinly sliced
salt, pepper
1 egg
½ cup whipping cream
3 tablespoons grated Parmesan cheese
1¼ pounds tomatoes, peeled and sliced

BREAD

Sift flour and salt into bowl. Add butter and shortening. Rub in fat with fingertips until mixture resembles crumbs. Mix in water, adding enough so dough forms soft, but not sticky ball. Press together lightly. Chill 15 minutes.

Heat 1 tablespoon oil in saucepan. Add onions and salt and pepper to taste. Press foil on top, cover with lid and cook very gently, stirring occasionally, until onions are very tender, 20 to 25 minutes. Remove cover and foil. Cook until all moisture is evaporated and onions are lightly caramelized. Taste to adjust for seasonings. Cool.

Grease baking sheet. Roll out pastry dough to 14 inch square. Place on baking sheet. Whisk egg with cream until mixed. Stir in cheese and pepper to taste. Spoon mixture evenly over pastry. Spread cooled onions on top. (If onions are warm, they will melt dough.) Top with tomato slices. Sprinkle with remaining 1 tablespoon oil and season to taste with salt and pepper.

Bake pastry at 400° until crisp and brown, 25 to 30 minutes. Serve warm or at room temperature. (Onion pastry is best eaten day of baking, but it can be kept up to 2 days in refrigerator. Reheat in low oven 10 to 15 minutes.) Cut in squares for serving.

Note: ½ teaspoon of dried red pepper flakes can be added to cream mixture if desired.

SWISS ONION RING
Serves 20

1 (1 pound) loaf frozen ready-dough or frozen, unbaked challah
2 cups shredded Swiss cheese
6 tablespoons melted butter or margarine

¾ *cup green onion, finely chopped*
2 tablespoons poppy seeds
¼ *teaspoon salt (optional)*

Let frozen dough thaw until pliable. (To thaw in microwave oven, place frozen dough in a plastic bag or cover with plastic wrap. Cook on LOW power for 6 minutes, rotating occasionally).

Mix together remaining ingredients.

Cut thawed loaf into 20 pieces (if using roll dough, cut each roll in half). Arrange half of dough pieces in bottom of greased ring mold or tube pan. Cover dough with half of cheese mixture. Top with remaing dough pieces.

Spread the remaining cheese mixture on top. Let rise until doubled. Bake in 375° oven for 25-30 minutes or until golden brown and it sounds hollow when tapped.

APPLESAUCE ORANGE NUT BREAD

1 large orange
½ *cup raisins*
1 cup applesauce
2 cups flour
2 teaspoons baking powder
2 teaspoons baking soda
½ *teaspoon salt*
1 cup sugar
½ *cup chopped nuts*
1 egg
2 tablespoons butter or margarine, melted

Remove seeds from orange and grind with raisins in a food

grinder or food processor. Add applesauce. Sift together flour, baking powder, soda, salt and sugar. Add to fruit mixture. Stir in nuts. Beat egg with butter and add to batter. Pour into greased 8 x 4 x 2½ inch loaf pan. Bake at 350° for 50 to 60 minutes. Remove from pan and cool on wire rack.

BANANA BREAD
Yields 2 loaves

2 cups sugar
1 cup butter or margarine
6 ripe bananas, mashed (3cups)
4 eggs, beaten
2½ cups cake flour
2 teaspoons baking soda
½ teaspoon salt

Cream together sugar and butter until light and fluffy. Add bananas and eggs, beating thoroughly. Sift together dry ingredients 3 times. Add to banana mixture. Mix until just combined. Divide equally into 2 greased loaf pans. Bake at 350° for 45 minutes to 1 hour or until firm in center and edges begin to separate from pans. Cool on rack 10 minutes before removing from pans.

ANOTHER BANANA BREAD
Yields 1 loaf

2 cups biscuit mix
¾ cup brown sugar, packed
¼ teaspoon soda
¼ teaspoon nutmeg
1 cup ripe banana, mashed

2 tablespoons light oil
2 eggs
1 cup walnuts, chopped
1 cup semi-sweet chocolate pieces

Preheat oven to 350°. Combine biscuit mix, brown sugar, soda and nutmeg in a small bowl. Beat together banana, oil and eggs until well blended. Stir into dry ingredients all at once, mixing only until blended. Stir in walnuts and chocolate pieces. Pour into a lightly greased 9 x 5 inch loaf pan. Bake for 40-50 minutes. (Test at 40 minutes with baking skewer for doneness.) Cool before serving.

PUMPKIN NUT BREAD
Yields 2 loaves

1 cup oil
3 cups sugar
3 eggs
1 teaspoon vanilla
3 cups flour
½ teaspoon salt
½ teaspoon baking soda
1 teaspoon baking powder
1 teaspoon cinnamon
½ teaspoon allspice
½ teaspoon nutmeg
½ teaspoon ground cloves
2 cups mashed, cooked, or canned pumpkin
1 cup chopped nuts

Beat together oil, sugar, eggs and vanilla until thoroughly blended. Sift together all dry ingredients. Stir into egg mixture. Add pumpkin and nuts. Divide equally into 2 greased 9 x 5 inch loaf pans. Bake at 350° for 1¼ hours.

BREAD

DATE AND NUT BREAD
Yields 1 loaf

¾ cup walnuts, chopped
1 cup pitted dates, cut-up
1½ teaspoons baking soda
½ teaspoon salt
3 tablespoons shortening
¾ cup boiling water
2 eggs
1 teaspoon vanilla
1 cup sugar
1½ cups all purpose flour, sifted

Mix walnuts, dates, baking soda and salt. Add shortening and water. Set aside for 20 minutes. Beat eggs in another bowl. Add vanilla, sugar and flour. Stir in date mixture. Pour into greased 9 x 5 x 3 inch loaf pan. Bake in preheated oven at 350° for 1 hour 5 minutes or until cake tester, inserted in center, comes out clean. Cool in pan 10 minutes. Remove from pan and finish cooling on wire rack. When cool, wrap in foil. Store overnight before slicing.

PRUNE BREAD
Yields 1 loaf

1 egg
1 teaspoon vanilla
1 teaspoon baking soda
1 cup boiling water
1½ cups prunes, chopped
1 teaspoon strong coffee
½ cup honey
2½ cups flour

BREAD

⅔ cup sugar
1 cup walnuts

Mix egg, vanilla, baking soda, water, prunes and coffee. Cover and let stand 20 minutes. Add remaining ingredients. Grease and flour 9 x 5 inch loaf pan. Bake 1 hour or longer until done.

SPICED PINEAPPLE ZUCCHINI BREAD
Yields 2 loaves

3 eggs
¾ cup oil
1½ cups honey
2 tablespoons vanilla
2 cup zucchini, grated
1 can (8 ounces) crushed pineapple, well drained
3 cups flour
1 teaspoon salt
1½ teaspoons baking powder
1 teaspoon baking soda
1½ teaspoons cinnamon
1 teaspoon nutmeg
1 cup walnuts, almonds or pecans, chopped

Beat eggs until light and fluffy. Add oil and honey. Continue beating until well blended. Stir in vanilla, zucchini and pineapple. Sift dry ingredients together. Stir into egg mixture along with nuts. Divide equally into 2 greased 9 x 5 inch loaf pans. Bake at 350° for 50 minutes.

BREAD

ZUCCHINI LOAF
Yields 1 loaf

3 eggs, beaten
3 cups zucchini, shredded
1 cup quick oatmeal
1 cup wheat germ
1¼ cups Cheddar or Jack cheese, shredded
2 cups fresh mushrooms, sliced
4 green onions, chopped
1 teaspoon mixed Italian herbs
½ teaspoon garlic powder

Combine all ingredients except ¼ cup cheese. Pour into 9 x 5 inch greased loaf pan. Top with reserved ¼ cup cheese. Bake at 350°-375° for 50-60 minutes.

STREUSEL-TOPPED
CRANBERRY PINEAPPLE BREAD
Yields 1 Loaf

2 cups sifted flour
1 cup sugar
1½ teaspoons baking powder
½ teaspoon baking soda
½ teaspoon salt
1 8¼-ounce can crushed pineapple
1 teaspoon grated orange zest
2 tablespoons melted butter or margarine
1 egg, beaten
½ cup chopped pecans
1½ cups coarsely chopped cranberries

Streusel Topping:
¼ cup sugar
3 tablespoons flour
1 tablespoon butter, chilled
¼ teaspoon cinnamon
pinch salt

Process topping until coarsely crumbled.

Sift together flour, sugar, baking powder, baking soda and salt. Discard 2 tablespoons pineapple syrup and mix remaining syrup and pineapple with orange zest, melted butter, and egg. Stir into dry ingredients just until moistened. Stir in pecans and cranberries. Turn batter into greased 9 x 5 inch loaf pan, then push batter into corners of pan leaving center slightly lower. Sprinkle with streusel topping.

Bake at 350° 1 hour or until wood pick inserted in center comes out clean. Remove from pan and cool. Wrap in foil and store overnight for best flavor and easy slicing.

WALNUT PLUM BREAD

1 (1 pound 13-ounce) can purple plums
½ cup butter or margarine
2 teaspoons baking soda
2 cups sifted flour
1 cup sugar
½ teaspoon salt
1 teaspoon cinnamon
½ teaspoon cloves
½ cup raisins
½ cup walnuts, chopped

BREAD

Drain plums, remove pits and mash or put through chopper or blender. In a saucepan combine plums with butter and heat until butter is melted. Remove from heat. Stir in soda, transfer to mixing bowl and let cool. Mixture will turn a grey color and foam. Cool to room temperature, then add flour, sugar, salt, cinnamon, cloves, raisins and walnuts. Mix well and turn into well greased 9 x 5 inch loaf pan. Bake at 350° 70 minutes or until center is firm when pressed lightly. Let cool 1 hour in pan, then turn out onto wire rack to cool completely. Serve warm or at room temperature.

CRUSTY SESAME BREAD
Yields 2 loaves

2 cups warm water
2 packages cake yeast
1 tablespoon sugar
½ teaspoon salt
5¾ cups sifted flour, approximately
1 egg white, beaten
1 tablespoon water
2 tablespoons sesame seeds

Pour warm water into a large bowl. Sprinkle or crumble in yeast, stirring until dissolved. Add sugar, salt and 3 cups flour. Add enough flour to form workable dough. Knead dough on floured board for about 5-7 minutes or until smooth ball is formed. Place ball in greased bowl, turning once to grease top of dough. Cover and let rise in warm place until doubled in bulk, about ½ hour.

Punch down and divide dough in half. Let rest 5 minutes. Shape each half into a ball. Place each ball 4 inches apart on a greased baking sheet. Slit top of loaves ¼ inch deep into a desired design. Cover and let rise in a warm place again, until slightly more than doubled in bulk, about ½ hour. Bake at 425° for 15 minutes. Remove from oven and brush with egg white which has been combined with water. Sprinkle with sesame seeds. Return to oven and bake an additional 20-25 minutes. Cool on wire rack.

OLIVE OIL AND BEER BREAD
Yields 2 loaves

1 package dry yeast
1 cup tepid light beer
4 scant cups sifted flour
1½ teaspoons salt
4 tablespoons olive oil

Dissolve yeast in beer. Mix flour and salt; add dissolved yeast and olive oil and mix to a soft dough. (Add an additional spoonful of beer if dough seems too stiff.)

On a lightly floured board, knead dough until it appears slick, smooth and very elastic (12-15 minutes). Place in an oiled bowl and cover with a towel. Put in a warm place until doubled in bulk.

Punch down dough or knead 2 minutes. Form into 2 loaves and place in greased loaf pans. (Or, if preferred, place in 1 large loaf pan.) Let rise again, covering with a towel. Bake in a preheated 375° oven 40-45 minutes. When done, bread will be brown and will make a hollow "thump" when tapped.

Turn out of pans onto the towel. If you like a soft crust, brush hot loaves with butter. Let cool.

BREAD

BEER BREAD

3 cups self rising flour
1 can beer (12 ounces)
3 tablespoons sugar
caraway, poppy or sesame seeds as desired
butter or margarine

Thoroughly combine all ingredients except butter or margarine. Pour into greased loaf pan. (pyrex is best, it is easy to see if bread is browned on bottom.) Bake at 350° to 360° for 40 minutes or until brown. Brush top of bread with butter or margarine just before baking is completed.

TWO-RAISIN CINNAMON ROLLS
Serves 12

½ ounce (2 packages)
  fast-acting yeast
½ cup warm water
1 cup room-temperature
  buttermilk
3 tablespoons sugar
2 teaspoons salt
4 cups all-purpose flour
4 egg yolks

8 ounces (2 sticks) very soft
  butter
½ cup butter, melted
½ cup sugar
1 tablespoon cinnamon
¾ cup golden raisins
¾ cup dark raisins
vanilla glaze or
  strawberry glaze

Dissolve yeast in warm water. In mixer with dough hook, combine yeast mixture, buttermilk, sugar, salt, flour and egg yolks. When dough is somewhat smooth, gradually add butter. On high speed, beat dough until smooth and elastic and sticky and pulling away from bowl, about 8-10 minutes. Put dough on sheet pan, cover and refrigerate 6 hours. Using flour to avoid sticking, roll out dough in rectangle. Dough should be ½ to ¾ inches thick. Brush dough with melted butter. Mix sugar and cinnamon together and sprinkle over buttered dough. Spread golden and dark raisins on top and roll dough lengthwise like a jelly roll, finishing with seam side down. Using sharp knife, slice roll into 2 inch sections. Place sections 1½ inch apart in greased 9 x 11 inch baking pan. Cover and let rise until double in bulk. Bake in preheated 350° oven for 15-20 minutes or until golden. Cool slightly in pan. Spread or drizzle either glaze atop warm rolls.

Vanilla glaze:
2¾ cups powdered sugar, sifted
½ vanilla bean, seeds only, crushed
2 tablespoons water
1 tablespoon vanilla extract

Whisk together all ingredients until smooth; cover until ready to use. Makes about 1 cup.

Strawberry glaze:
3 cups powdered sugar, sifted
4 tablespoons strawberry puree (grind 8 berries in a food processor)
2 tablespoons lemon juice

Whisk together all ingredients until smooth; cover until ready to use. Makes about 1½ cups.

BREAD

BLUEBERRY MUFFINS
Yields 24

3½ cups flour
½ teaspoon salt
⅔ cup sugar
4 teaspoons baking powder
4 eggs
½ cup melted butter
1½ cups milk
2 cups blueberries (fresh or frozen without syrup)

Sift together flour, salt, sugar and baking powder. In another bowl, beat eggs and stir in melted butter and milk. Quickly stir egg mixture into flour mixture, just until ingredients are combined.

Toss blueberries in a little flour to keep them from sinking to the bottom of the muffins, then fold into the batter.

Bake in small greased muffin tins at 450° for about 15 minutes or until skewer inserted in a muffin comes out dry. If you use tiny tea-muffin tins, they will be done in about 8 minutes.

BRAN MUFFINS
Yields 24

1 cup boiling water
1 cup bran cereal (dry)
1½ cups brown sugar, firmly packed
½ cup butter or margarine
2 eggs
2 cups buttermilk
2½ cups whole wheat flour

2 cups bran flakes
1 tablespoon baking soda
½ teaspoon salt
1¾ cups raisins or chopped dates or a combination

Pour boiling water over bran and set aside. Cream together sugar and butter until light and fluffy. Beat in eggs and buttermilk. Stir together flour, bran flakes, soda and salt. Add to creamed mixture, beating until just combined. Stir in softened bran, raisins and/or dates. Cover and refrigerate for 24 hours before using. Fill muffin tins lined with cup cake liners ¾ full with batter. Bake at 400° for 15 to 30 minutes depending on the size of the tins. This mix will keep refrigerated in a covered container for 6 to 8 weeks. Mix well and bake as many as needed at a time.

CRANBERRY MUFFINS
Yields 24

1 large egg
2 tablespoons oil
½ cup orange juice
1 cup sugar
2 cups flour
1½ teaspoons baking powder
½ teaspoon baking soda
2 teaspoons hot water
½ teaspoon orange extract
1 cup fresh whole cranberries
¾ cup walnuts, chopped

Beat egg, then add oil, orange juice and sugar. Stir together flour and baking powder. Add to egg mixture. Dissolve baking soda in hot water and add to mixture with orange extract. Stir in cranberries and nuts. Fill paper lined muffin pans ¾ full. Bake at 350° for 30-35 minutes or until golden brown. Immediately remove from pan and cool on rack.

BREAD

LOW FAT OATMEAL MUFFINS
Yields 40 mini or 20 regular size muffins

1 ½ cups dry sugar-free cereal
½ cup apple juice concentrate
1 egg white
½ cup nonfat milk or orange juice
3 tablespoons oil
1 large banana, mashed
½ cup dried plums or variety of dried fruits, chopped
2 tablespoons honey or ¼ cup brown sugar, packed
1 ½ cups all-purpose flour
½ cup dry oats
1 teaspoon ground cinnamon
1 teaspoon all-spice
1 ½ teaspoons baking soda
2 teaspoons baking powder
½ cup slivered almonds

Combine sugar-free cereal with apple juice in large bowl. Add egg white, nonfat milk, oil, banana, dried fruit, and honey. Mix well.

In another bowl combine flour, oats, cinnamon, all-spice, baking soda, and baking powder. Add this to first mixture, and mix well.

Line mini or regular size muffin tins with paper liners, and fill ¾ full with batter. Sprinkle almond slivers on top of each muffin. Bake at 350° for 20 or 30 minutes respectively.

NEW YORK CORN MUFFINS
Yields 12

2 cups corn meal

1 cup flour
1 cup sugar
1 tablespoon baking powder
dash salt
1 cup shortening
1 egg
1¼ cups milk
1 teaspoon vanilla

Combine corn meal, flour, sugar, baking powder and salt in large bowl. Cut in shortening until mixture resembles coarse crumbs. Beat egg and stir in milk and vanilla. Add to corn meal mixture, stirring just enough to moisten. Do not overbeat. Fill 12 muffin cups ⅔ full, or fill 11 muffin cups to the rim. Bake at 350°, 20 to 25 minutes or until golden. Cool thoroughly in muffin cups before loosening from pan or they will fall apart.

ORANGE MUFFINS
Yields 24

½ cup vegetable shortening
½ cup butter or margarine
3 cups flour
6 eggs
1 cup sugar
1 cup milk
½ teaspoon salt
3 teaspoons baking powder
1 cup orange juice
1 ounce roasted almonds, chopped
1 cup orange, peeled and diced (make sure orange is ripe and sweet)

BREAD

Mix flour, sugar, baking powder and salt together. Then beat in eggs, butter and shortening. Add orange juice and milk and mix well. Pour into muffin tin and sprinkle with almonds and orange. Bake at 375° for approximately 30 minutes.

SWEET POTATO MUFFINS
Yields 2-2½ dozen

¾ cup canned or cooked fresh sweet potatoes, mashed
¼ cup margarine
½ cup sugar
1 egg
¾ cup flour
2 teaspoons baking powder
½ teaspoon salt
¾ teaspoon cinnamon
¼ teaspoon nutmeg
½ cup milk
¼ cup pecans, finely chopped
1-2 tablespoons cinnamon sugar

Puree sweet potatoes in blender or food processor. Cream margarine and sugar. Beat in egg. Add sweet potatoes and mix well. Sift together flour, baking powder, salt and spices. Add alternately with milk and pecans only until just blended. Do not over mix. Fill small greased muffin tins completely. Sprinkle tops with cinnamon sugar. Bake at 400° for 25-30 minutes.

WHOLE WHEAT MUFFINS
Yields 1 dozen

1 cup white flour
1 cup whole wheat flour
3 tablespoons sugar
5 teaspoons baking powder
1 teaspoon salt
1 egg, beaten
¾ cup milk
4 tablespoons shortening, melted
½ cup raisins
½ cup chopped walnuts, optional

Combine and sift together the flour ingredients, sugar, baking powder and salt. Add the beaten egg and milk. Mix well. Add the melted shortening. Dredge the raisins in flour and add to the mixed batter. (½ cup chopped walnuts may be added) Fill well-greased muffin tins about ⅔ full. Bake in a hot oven 400° for 20 to 25 minutes. After 20 minutes, test with a cake tester or toothpick. If no dough adheres to the tester, the muffins are done. Serve hot.

BREAD

STUFFING BREAD
Yields 1 loaf

1¼ cups warm water (115°)
1 package active dry yeast
2 tablespoons plus 1 teaspoon instant toasted onions
1 tablespoon parsley
1 tablespoon sugar
1 tablespoon margarine, softened
1½ teaspoons poultry seasoning
1 teaspoon salt
3 cups all-purpose flour (approximately)
1 egg, beaten
½ teaspoon whole celery seed

Place warm water in large warm bowl. Sprinkle in yeast; stir until dissolved. Add 2 tablespoons instant toasted onions, parsley, sugar, margarine, poultry seasoning, salt and 1½ cups flour; blend well. Mix in enough additional flour to make very thick batter. Cover; let rise in warm, draft-free place until doubled in size, about 25 minutes. Stir batter down; turn into greased 1½ quart casserole. With floured hands, smooth top of dough in casserole. Fill large pan with very hot tap water (1 inch deep). Place casserole in water. Cover; let rise 25 minutes. Brush beaten egg on loaf. Sprinkle with remaining instant toasted onions and celery seed. Bake at 375° for 35 minutes or until done. Remove from casserole and cool on wire rack.

Sage advice as far as it goes
but what's cake for, if not to be eaten up? Cake
may not be as basic a food as bread (even though
legend tells us Marie Antionette thought
otherwise) but it is a necessity in its own right.

What's a "glazel tea" without a nice piece of
sponge cake, or a cup of coffee without coffee
cake with streusel? What's a birthday party
without a place to put the candles and what's a
special dinner without its crowning glory?

Yes, we do take cake. If the portion is too large,
ask for another fork and share it with a friend.

FRESH APPLE CAKE
Serves 10

2 cups flour
1 teaspoon salt
2 teaspoons baking soda
1 tablespoon cinnamon
1 teaspoon nutmeg
¼ teaspoon cloves
¼ cup butter
¼ cup oil
1 cup light brown sugar
¼ cup white sugar
4 cups diced apples
¾ cup white raisins
1 cup chopped walnuts
3 eggs

Grease and flour 9 x 13 inch cake pan. Sift together flour, salt, baking soda, cinnamon, nutmeg and cloves. Cream together butter, oil, brown and white sugar. Add eggs, one at a time to batter. Add sifted ingredients to the batter, followed by fruit and nuts. Bake in 350° oven for about 1 hour.

APPLE NUT BUNDT CAKE
Serves 12

3 eggs
2 cups sugar
¾ cup oil
½ cup nuts, chopped
1 teaspoon vanilla
4 Pippin apples, peeled and diced
2 cups flour

CAKE

1 teaspoon baking soda
1 teaspoon salt
2 teaspoons cinnamon or apple pie spice

Mix together eggs, sugar, oil, chopped nuts and vanilla. Add diced apples and blend well. Sift together flour, baking soda, salt and cinnamon. Add to egg-apple mixture and blend well. Pour into greased and floured bundt pan and bake at 350° for 1 hour 15 minutes or until cake tester comes clean.

APPLE SOUR CREAM CAKE
Serves 12

¼ pound butter
¼ cup sugar
1 egg
2 tablespoons water
1 cup flour
6 large tart apples, peeled, cored and thinly sliced
vanilla sugar or lemon rind

Topping:
2 egg yolks
2 tablespoons sugar
1 teaspoon flour
4 ounces sour cream
2 egg whites, stiffly beaten

Cream butter and sugar. Add egg, water and flour and work into smooth dough with hands. Refrigerate dough for 1 hour. Grease 9 inch springform and place thinly rolled out dough in circle and fit on bottom and sides of pan. Fill with apples and sprinkle with vanilla sugar or grated lemon rind. Cover with wax paper and bake approximately 15 minutes in 350° oven or until apples are soft.

For topping, combine egg yolks with sugar. Add flour and sour cream and fold in stiffly beaten egg whites. Pour mixture over apples. Return cake to oven for approximately 30 minutes or until topping is golden brown.

GERMAN APPLE CAKE
Serves 12

1 cup sugar
1 cup unsifted flour
4 tablespoons butter, cut into 4 pieces
1 teaspoon baking powder
1 teaspoon vanilla
1 large egg
4 large Pippin apples
3 tablespoons sugar
3 tablespoons melted butter
1 teaspoon cinnamon
1 large egg

Add first 6 ingredients to the bowl of the food processor. Process until mixture resembles cornmeal. Spread mixture in the bottom of a well-buttered 9-inch form pan.

Peel and seed apples. Slice in processor. Arrange apples in layers on top of the crumb mixture. Bake in preheated 350° oven for 45 minutes.

Meanwhile, add sugar, butter, cinnamon and egg to the bowl of the processor, using metal blade. Process until mixture is smooth and sugar dissolves. Spoon over apples and bake 25-30 minutes more or until top is firm.

CAKE

CHOCOLATE APPLESAUCE CAKE
Serves 8

¾ *cup sifted flour*
1 teaspoon baking soda
¼ *teaspoon salt*
¼ *teaspoon cloves*
1 teaspoon cinnamon
¼ *pound margarine*
1 cup sugar
2 eggs
½ *cup melted chocolate chips*
1 cup applesauce
½ *cup raisins*
½ *cup nuts (not almonds), chopped*
½ *cup chocolate chips*

Sift dry ingredients together. Cream margarine, sugar and eggs.
Blend in melted chocolate. Add dry ingredients alternately with
applesauce. Fold in raisins and walnuts. Line a 9 inch loaf pan
with wax paper. Pour in batter and top with additional chocolate
chips and chopped walnuts. Bake at 350° for 1 hour 15 minutes.

CHOCOLATE CAKE (NO FLOUR)
Serves 10

1 16-ounce package semi-sweet chocolate bits
5 eggs, separated
½ *cup sugar*
1 10-ounce package frozen raspberries, defrosted
1 4-ounce carton whipped topping

Melt chocolate bits over hot water in double boiler. Beat egg yolks and sugar with electric mixer until light and lemon colored. Add melted chocolate. Whip egg whites until stiff but still moist. Fold into egg yolk mixture. Pour into wax paper lined 8 inch springform pan. Bake at 325° for 45 minutes. Allow to cool. Turn cake out upside down onto serving platter. Peel off wax paper. Combine raspberries and whipped topping. Spread over cake.

FRENCH CHOCOLATE CAKE
Serves 10

1 pound milk or bittersweet chocolate
1 tablespoon water
1 tablespoon flour
1 tablespoon sugar
10 tablespoons soft butter
4 eggs, separated
sweetened whipped cream

Preheat oven to 425°. Melt chocolate with water in top of a double boiler over hot, not boiling, water. This is a critical step in the preparation and should be done very slowly. Remove melted chocolate from heat and stir in flour, sugar and butter. Beat yolks lightly and whisk into chocolate mixture gradually. Beat whites until they hold a definite shape but are not dry and fold into chocolate mixture. Overbeating or underbeating will ruin the cake. Beaten egg whites should be folded smoothly, quickly and easily into chocolated mixture.

Pour into 8 inch springform pan that has been lined with wax paper and bake 15 minutes. Turn off heat; open oven door leaving it ajar and allow cake to cool completely in the oven. If the center of the cake still feels soft, refrigerate 1-2 hours. Cake is best served at room temperature. Decorate with whipped cream.

CAKE

CHOCOLATE CHERRY CAKE
Serves 10

16 ounces chocolate chips
¼ cup butter
4 eggs
¾ cup sugar
¾ cup flour
¾ teaspoon baking powder
1 16-ounce can sour cherries, drained

Melt chocolate and butter in top of double boiler. Mix all other ingredients together except cherries. Combine with chocolate mixture. Add cherries. Bake in greased 8 inch springform pan in 375° oven for 40 minutes.

CHOCOLATE CHIP CHOCOLATE CAKE
Serves 10

1 package (2 layer size) dark chocolate cake mix
1 package (3¾ ounce) instant chocolate pudding
4 eggs
½ cup cooking oil
1 cup sour cream
½ cup warm water
1 16-ounce package semi-sweet chocolate morsels

Grease and flour bundt pan. In a large bowl, combine all ingredients except chocolate morsels. Beat for 3 minutes at medium speed of mixer. Add morsels and beat for 1 minute more. Pour batter into prepared pan. Bake at 350° for 55-60 minutes or until cake tests done. Cool in pan for 15 minutes. Turn out and continue cooling on wire rack.

Chocolate Glaze: (optional)
1 cup confectioners' sugar
2 tablespoons milk
2 tablespoons corn syrup
1 envelope pre-melted unsweetened chocolate

Combine all ingredients in a small bowl and beat until smooth. Use rubber spatula or a large spoon and put glaze on top of cake. The glaze will then run down the sides slowly.

CHOCOLATE CHIP COFFEE CAKE
Serves 10

¼ pound margarine
1 cup sugar
3 eggs
1 8-ounce carton sour cream
2 cups sifted flour
1 teaspoon baking powder
1 teaspoon baking soda
1 teaspoon vanilla

Topping:
½ cup brown sugar
6 ounces chocolate chips
½ cup walnuts, chopped

Cream margarine, sugar and eggs. Add sour cream and beat well. Sift flour, baking powder and baking soda and add to creamed mixture. Add vanilla. Pour half batter in greased and floured bundt pan. Sprinkle half topping mixture over batter. Pour remaining batter over this and swirl through. Finish with remaining topping. Bake at 350° for 45 minutes.

CAKE

CHOCOLATE MOUSSE TUNNEL CAKE
Serves 12-14

7 eggs, separated
½ cup unsweetened cocoa (sift before measuring)
¾ cup boiling water
1¾ cups sugar
1½ teaspoons baking soda
1 teaspoon salt
½ cup salad oil
2 teaspoons vanilla extract
½ teaspoon cream of tartar
1¾ cups sifted cake flour (sift before measuring)

In small bowl pour boiling water over cocoa, stir and cool ½ hour. Preheat oven to 325°. Sift flour with sugar, soda and salt. Add oil, yolks, vanilla and cocoa. Beat just until smooth. Sprinkle cream of tartar over whites. Beat at high speed until stiff peaks are formed. blend batter with whites. Bake in ungreased 10 inch tube for 60-65 minutes. Cool and remove from pan.

Chocolate filling:
3 cups heavy cream
1½ cups sifted (before measuring) confectioners' sugar
¾ cup sifted (before measuring) unsweetened cocoa
2 teaspoons vanilla extract
¼ teaspoon salt
1 teaspoon unflavored gelatin

Combine cream, sugar, cocoa, vanilla, salt; refrigerate 1 hour. Beat until stiff. Refrigerate again. Sprinkle gelatin over 2 tablespoons cold water to soften. Heat, stirring, over hot water to dissolve; cool.

Prepare cake:
Cut 1 inch slice crosswise from top of cake. With sharp knife, cut out

a cavity in cake leaving 1 inch thick walls around center, side and bottom. Carefully remove cake from this area (use removed cake for another dessert). Measure 2½ cups chocolate filling into small bowl; fold in gelatin. Use to fill cavity. Replace top. Frost top and sides with remaining filling. Freeze or refrigerate.

CARROT CAKE
Serves 12

1½ cups sugar
1½ cups oil
4 eggs
2 cups flour
2 teaspoons baking powder
1½ teaspoons baking soda
1 teaspoon salt
2 teaspoons cinnamon
2 cups raw grated carrots
1-8¾ ounce can crushed pineapple, drained
1 cup golden raisins
½ cup chopped walnuts

Mix together sugar, oil, and eggs. Beat well. Sift all dry ingredients and add to egg mixture. Add carrots, pineapple, raisins, nuts and mix well. Pour into greased and floured pyrex pan (9 x 13 x 2 inch) and bake at 350° for 35-40 minutes. When cool, sprinkle with powdered sugar.

CAKE

COTTAGE CHEESE CAKE
Serves 10

Crust:
½ pound butter
1 cup flour
½ cup sugar
1 egg yolk
⅛ teaspoon vinegar

Mix ingredients and press into springform pan.

Filling:
2 pounds creamed cottage cheese
½ pint sour cream
3-ounce package vanilla pudding
1 cup sugar
6 whole eggs, beaten until light
rind of one lemon

Mix together. Pour over crust and bake in 350° oven for 1½ hours. Refrigerate. This cake is best when 2-3 days old.

FILBERT LOAVES
Yields 2 loaves

¾ cup butter or margarine, softened
2¼ cups sifted flour
1 tablespoon sugar
1 cake yeast, finely crumbled
½ cup milk
3 eggs, slightly beaten
confectioners sugar

Nut filling:
2 cups filberts, ground
¼ cup butter, melted
1 cup sugar
1 teaspoon vanilla

Combine butter, flour, sugar and yeast with a pastry blender. Mix milk and eggs and add to flour mixture. Work together until dough leaves the side of the bowl. Divide dough in half and wrap each in waxed paper; place in a plastic bag and refrigerate overnight.

Next day, on a board that has been covered with confectioners sugar, roll each half of dough into a rectangle shape about ⅛ inch thick. Mix ingredients for nut filling and spread half evenly on each rectangle. Roll up dough as you would a jelly roll. Place on an ungreased baking sheet. Let rise 1 hour. Brush lightly with milk. Bake in a preheated 350° oven 40-50 minutes.

CAKE

MARZIPAN CAKE
Serves 10-12

Crust:
1¼ cups sifted all purpose flour
2 tablespoons sugar
1 egg
½ cup butter or margarine

Filling:
1 package (8 ounces) almond paste
¼ cup sugar
½ cup butter or margarine
3 large eggs
⅓ cup all purpose sifted flour
1 teaspoon baking powder
powdered sugar

For the crust: In a bowl, combine flour, sugar, and add whole egg with butter or margarine. Work into a dough until well blended and smooth. Line a buttered 10 inch springform pan with dough on bottom and 1½ inches up the sides of the pan.

For the filling: Work together almond paste and sugar until smooth and add butter or margarine. When smooth add eggs one at a time. Stir in flour mixed with baking powder and pour into crust. Bake at 350° for 30 minutes. Let cool for 10 minutes and unmold. Sprinkle with powdered sugar.

PUMPKIN-APPLESAUCE CAKE
Serves 16

½ cup margarine
¼ cup water
2 cups sugar
1 cup applesauce
1 pound can pumpkin
2 eggs
2½ cups flour
1 tablespoon baking soda

2 teaspoons salt
¾ teaspoon cinnamon
¼ teaspoon cloves
½ teaspoon nutmeg
½ cup walnuts, chopped
½ cup raisins, chopped
½ cup dates, chopped

Cream margarine, water and sugar. Add applesauce and pumpkin and beat thoroughly. Add eggs one at a time and beat after each addition. Sift all dry ingredients and add to egg mixture and beat approximately 3 minutes. Add nuts, dates and raisins, blending well. Pour batter into 2 greased and floured square or round 9 inch pans and bake at 350° for 35-40 minutes. Cool in pans on rack for 15 minutes and then remove from pans. Cool thoroughly.

PUMPKIN DESSERT
Serves 8-10

3 eggs
1¼ cups sugar
1 large can pumpkin
1 large can evaporated milk
2 teaspoons cinnamon
½ teaspoon ginger
1 teaspoon nutmeg
1 package yellow cake mix
1 cup nuts, chopped
1 cup margarine or butter, melted

CAKE

Whip eggs and sugar and add pumpkin, evaporated milk, cinnamon, ginger and nutmeg, mixing well. Pour into 9 x 13 inch pan. Sprinkle cake mix over batter, then the nuts. Drizzle melted margarine or butter over all and bake in 350° oven for 1 hour.

SWEET POTATO CAKE
Serves 10

1½ cups flour
2 teaspoons baking powder
1 teaspoon cinnamon
1 teaspoon ground cloves
1 teaspoon nutmeg
1 cup butter, softened
2 cups sugar
½ cup milk
4 ounces unsweetened chocolate, melted and cooled
4 eggs, beaten
2 cups chopped nuts
1½ cups mashed sweet potatoes

Sift together flour, baking powder and spices and set aside. Cream butter and sugar. Mix in milk, melted chocolate and eggs. Combine with sifted dry ingredients. Add nuts and mashed potatoes. Stir well. Pour into a greased and floured 10-inch tube pan. Bake in a preheated 350° oven 60 to 70 minutes.

TOFFEE COFFEE CAKE
Serves 10-12

¼ **cup sugar**
1 **teaspoon cinnamon**
2 **cups flour**
1 **cup sugar**
1½ **teaspoons baking powder**
1 **teaspoon baking soda**
¼ **teaspoon salt**
1 **teaspoon vanilla**
1 **cup sour cream**
½ **cup softened margarine**
2 **eggs**
3 **toffee bars (1⅛ ounces)**
¼ **cup margarine**

In a small bowl combine ¼ cup sugar and 1 teaspoon cinnamon and set aside. In large bowl combine all other ingredients, except toffee and ¼ cup margarine. Generously grease and lightly flour tube or bundt pan. Blend large bowl ingredients at low speed until moist and then beat at medium speed, approximately 3 minutes. Spoon ⅓ of the batter into pan then sprinkle with 2 tablespoons of sugar-cinnamon mixture. Pour another ⅓ batter and cinnamon-sugar mixture, then remaining batter and cinnamon-sugar mixture. Coarsely crunch toffee bars and sprinkle over top of cake. Melt ¼ cup margarine and pour over cake. Bake at 325° for 50 minutes. Cool upright for 15 minutes and remove from pan.

CAKE

UPSIDE-DOWN STREUSEL CAKE
Serves 8-10

4 eggs
¾ cup oil
¾ cup water
1 teaspoon vanilla
1 tablespoon butter extract flavoring
1 envelope whipped topping (dry)
1-3¾ ounce package vanilla instant pudding
1 package yellow cake mix

Streusel Mix:	Glaze:
½ cup sugar	**¾ cup powdered sugar**
2 teaspoons cinnamon	**1 teaspoon vanilla**
1½ ounces chopped	**1½ tablespoons milk**
pecans or walnuts	**1 teaspoon butter extract flavoring**

Beat eggs, oil, water, vanilla, flavoring, envelope of whipped topping, instant pudding and cake mix for 7 minutes. Spread ½ batter in greased and floured bundt pan. Mix sugar, cinnamon and nuts together and spoon half over batter. Pour over balance of batter and finish with remaining streusel. Marble slightly with knife. Bake at 350° for 50-60 minutes. Check outer edge with cake tester - it will look wet. Cool in pan about an hour. Before removing from pan, run knife around outer edge, pushing to loosen. Gently turn over and remove from pan. Mix glaze together and drizzle on top and sides of cake. Freezes well.

YOGURT COFFEE CAKE
Serves 8-10

½ cup butter or margarine, softened
1 cup sugar
2 eggs
2 cups flour
1 teaspoon baking powder
1 teaspoon baking soda
½ teaspoon salt
1 cup sour cream or unflavored yogurt
1 teaspoon vanilla

Cream butter and sugar. Beat in eggs one at a time. Sift together flour, baking powder, soda and salt; add to the butter mixture alternating with sour cream, beginning and ending with flour mixture. Add vanilla. Pour half the batter into a buttered square baking pan 9 x 9 x 2 inches, or a springform pan.

Topping:
⅓ cup brown sugar
¼ cup granulated sugar
1 teaspoon cinnamon
1 cup chopped nuts

Combine topping ingredients. Sprinkle half the mixture over the batter in pan. Add remaining batter and cover with remaining topping mixture. Bake in a preheated 325° oven 40 minutes or longer.

CAKE

OLD WORLD SPICE CAKE
Yields 20 pieces

2 cups water
½ cup oil
1 cup white raisins
3 slices lemon
1½ cups flour
1 cup sugar
¾ teaspoon baking soda
2 teaspoons baking powder
dash of salt
1 teaspoon ginger
1 teaspoon cinnamon
1 teaspoon nutmeg
1 tablespoon cocoa
3 eggs (2 large)
1 cup walnuts or pecans, ground
½ cup dry coconut, grated

Bring water, oil, raisins and lemon to a boil. Simmer for 10 minutes. Set aside to cool. Mix liquid with sifted dry ingredients. Add beaten eggs and fold in nuts and coconut. Line a jelly roll pan with wax paper. Pour on batter. Bake in 375° oven 20-30 minutes. Invert pan on rack. Peel off wax paper and cut into diagonal pieces.

POTICA (YUGOSLAVIAN COFFEE CAKE)

1 cup butter or margarine
½ cup milk
2 packages active dry yeast
¼ cup warm water

3 eggs, separated
2½ cups sifted flour
¼ teaspoon salt
¼ cup sugar
2 cups chopped walnuts
1 teaspoon cinnamon
3 tablespoons sugar
½ cup chopped pitted dates
¾ cup milk
1 cup sugar

Heat butter and ½ cup milk together until butter is melted. Cool to lukewarm. In a large bowl, dissolve yeast in the warm water and beat in egg yolks. Blend in milk and butter mixture. Sift in flour, salt and ¼ cup sugar. Beat until mixture is smooth and creamy in color. Cover bowl and refrigerate overnight. The following day, blend walnuts, cinnamon, 3 tablespoons sugar, dates and ¾ cup milk. Cook over medium heat, stirring until mixture thickens (about 10 minutes). Remove from heat and cool. Beat egg whites until stiff and slowly add 1 cup sugar, beating until meringue-like. Fold into the cooled walnut mixture. Remove dough from refrigerator and cut into 2 equal parts. Dust each with flour. Roll out each part of dough, one at a time, to make a circle 18-20 inches in diameter. Top rolled dough with half of the filling mixture, spreading it to within 1 inch of the edges. Carefully roll up dough, jelly-roll fashion. Place roll in well greased bundt pan. Roll out and fill second portion of dough in the same manner and place on top of the first roll. Allow to rise for 30 minutes. Bake at 350° about 1 hour or until a toothpick inserted in the center comes out clean. Cool for 5 minutes before turning out.

*"If hunger makes you irritable,
better eat and be pleasant."*
BOOK OF THE PIOUS, 13TH CENTURY

Take your hand out of the tin,
we spent a long time mixing, chopping and rolling
our cookies and bars and we want just a moment
more to savor the sweet smell of their baking and
to delight in the fine appearance of our
afternoon's work before they disappear.

How your family and friends will appreciate your
endeavors! Grandchildren will come running as
you dole out the tollhouse and claim a hug for
your prize-winning brownies.

Fancy or plain, when hunger calls and the sweet
tooth needs tending, a cookie or bar is a nice
"nosh".

BLACK 'N WHITE BARS
Yields 30 bars

6 tablespoons butter or margarine, melted
2 packages (1-ounce each) unsweetened liquid baking
  chocolate, or 2 1-ounce squares, best unsweetened
  chocolate
1 cup sugar
2 eggs
½ teaspoon vanilla extract
pinch salt
½ cup all-purpose flour
1 cup chopped walnuts, divided
½ cup chopped dates
¾ cup mini marshmallows
⅓ cup chocolate chips

Preheat oven to 425°. Line a 13 x 9 inch baking pan with foil; grease foil. In a small bowl combine melted butter or margarine and chocolate and set aside.

In mixer bowl combine sugar, eggs, vanilla and salt. Beat at high speed until light and fluffy, about 1 minute. Add chocolate mixture; beat well. Beat in flour. Stir in ½ cup walnuts and dates. Pour batter into prepared pan. Bake 12 minutes. Sprinkle with remaining walnuts, marshmallows and chocolate chips. Bake 2 minutes more. Cool in pan. Cut into 2 x 1½ inch bars.

COOKIES & BARS

BEVERLY HILLS COOKIES
Yields 30 cookies

2 egg whites
⅛ teaspoon salt
3 tablespoons sugar
½ teaspoon vinegar
½ teaspoon vanilla
½ heaping cup chopped walnuts
1 heaping cup chocolate chips, (melted)

Preheat oven to 350°. Grease a cookie sheet. Beat egg whites; add salt. Add sugar gradually and beat well. Add vinegar and vanilla and continue to beat well until egg whites hold their form and peak. Fold in nuts and chocolate. Mix carefully until all egg whites have disappeared. Drop by teaspoonful ½-inch apart. Bake for 8 minutes. *Do not* remove cookies from pan for 15 minutes.

DOUBLE CHOCOLATE
MARSHMALLOW BROWNIES
Yields 20

2 eggs
1 cup sugar
2 squares unsweetened chocolate
½ cup butter or margarine
1 teaspoon vanilla
⅔ cup flour
¼ teaspoon salt
½ teaspoon baking powder
¾ cup miniature marshmallows
½ cup semi-sweet chocolate chips

Beat eggs until fluffy and add sugar gradually. Melt butter and chocolate squares and add to egg mixture. Sift together flour, salt and baking powder. Add to chocolate mixture and beat well. Stir in chocolate chips and marshmallows and pour into greased and floured 11 x 7 x 2 inch pan. Bake in 350° oven for 25 minutes. (If doubling recipe, bake in 13 x 9 x 2 inch pan for 30 minutes.)

BROWNIES WITH FROSTING
Yields 16

½ *cup butter*
3 squares chocolate (3 ounces)
2 eggs, well beaten
1 cup sugar
½ *cup all purpose flour*
1 teaspoon vanilla

Place butter and chocolate in top of double boiler and heat until melted. Remove from heat and cool. Cream eggs and sugar and add to the cooled chocolate mixture. Add sifted flour and vanilla. Blend well and pour into a greased 8 inch x 8 inch pan. Bake at 350° for 25 minutes. Frost brownies while hot and cut immediately.

Frosting:
1 square chocolate (1 ounce)
1 cup powdered sugar
1 tablespoon butter
½ *teaspoon vanilla*
1 teaspoon cream

Melt chocolate over hot water. Remove from heat and add butter, sugar and cream. Blend in vanilla and frost.

COOKIES & BARS

CHOCOLATE MORSELS
Yields 24

Crust:
1¾ cups all-purpose flour
⅓ cup unsweetened
   cocoa powder
¼ cup sugar
pinch of salt
¾ cup (1½ sticks) butter,
   chilled and cut into small
   pieces
⅓ to ½ cup strong coffee,
   chilled

Filling:
12 ounces semisweet chocolate
   chips, melted
⅔ cup sugar
2 tablespoons (¼ stick) butter,
   melted
2 tablespoons milk
2 teaspoons coffee liqueur
2 eggs, room temperature
½ cup finely chopped toasted
   walnuts

Crust:
Sift flour, cocoa, sugar and salt into large bowl. Add butter and blend until consistency of coarse meal. Gradually mix in coffee. Knead dough briefly, then form into log. Wrap in plastic or aluminum foil and refrigerate several hours or overnight. Lightly grease tiny muffin pans (diameter of top of each cup should be about 1¾ inches). Cut the dough into 4 pieces. Working with ¼ of the dough at a time (keep remainder refrigerated), roll dough out into circle slightly less than ⅛ inch thick and 14 to 15 inches in diameter. Cut dough into circles using 3 inch round cutter. Gently press into prepared muffin cups. Repreat with remaining dough. Chill.

Filling:
Preheat oven to 350°. Combine chocolate, sugar, butter, milk and coffee liqueur in medium bowl and blend well. Add eggs and beat until smooth. Stir in chopped walnuts. Place 1 rounded teaspoon of filling into each muffin cup. Bake until filling is set, about 20 to 25 minutes. Let cool in pans 15 minutes. Transfer to wire racks and let cool completely.

CHOCOLATE DELIGHTS
Yields 36

1 cup shortening
¾ cup brown sugar, packed
¾ cup granulated sugar
1 teaspoon vanilla
2 eggs
½ teaspoon water
1⅓ cups flour
2 cups oats
1¾ cups walnuts, chopped
1 teaspoon baking soda
1 teaspoon salt
1 8-ounce package semisweet chocolate pieces

Cream shortening and sugars until fluffy. Beat in vanilla, eggs and water. Combine flour, oats, walnuts, soda and salt. Stir into egg mixture. Fold in chips. Roll into balls and press flat on ungreased baking sheet for small cookies, or make 2 inch balls and press flat for large cookies. Bake at 375° 10 minutes for small cookies or 15-20 minutes for large cookies or until firm.

CHOCOLATE "ANGEL" COOKIES
Yields 3 dozen

½ cup oil
4 squares unsweetened chocolate
2 cups granulated sugar
4 eggs
2 cups flour
2 teaspoons baking powder
½ teaspoon salt
2 teaspoons vanilla
1 cup powdered sugar

COOKIES & BARS

Melt chocolate and cool. Mix oil, chocolate and sugar. Blend in 1 egg at a time. Add rest of ingredients except powdered sugar. Chill overnight. Grease baking sheet. Drop by tablespoons on greased sheet. Bake for 10-12 minutes at 350°. Roll in powdered sugar.

VERY SPECIAL BROWNIES
Yields 20

4 ounces chocolate, unsweetened
½ cup butter or margarine
4 eggs
2 cups sugar
1 cup flour
1 teaspoon vanilla
1 teaspoon almond extract
12 ounces chocolate chips
⅔ cup white raisins

Melt butter or margarine and chocolate. Cream eggs and sugar well. Mix all other ingredients reserving about ⅓ of the chips. Spread dough in greased pan (9 inch x 13 inch). Sprinkle with remaining chocolate bits. Bake 25 minutes in preheated 350° oven being careful not to overbake. Slice in squares when cool.

CREAM CHEESE BROWNIES
Yields 20

3 tablespoons margarine
4 ounces semi-sweet chocolate squares
4 tablespoons margarine
6 ounces cream cheese
½ cup sugar
2 eggs, beaten
2 tablespoons flour
2 teaspoons vanilla
2 eggs, beaten
¾ cup sugar
½ cup flour
½ teaspoon baking powder
½ teaspoon salt
½ cup walnuts, chopped
1 teaspoon vanilla
¼ teaspoon almond extract

Melt margarine and semi-sweet chocolate squares in top of double boiler. Set aside to cool. Cream together beaten eggs, sugar, cream cheese, flour and vanilla. In another bowl, mix together eggs, sugar, flour, baking powder and salt, add cooled chocolate mixture, walnuts, vanilla and almond extract. Pour ½ of chocolate batter in greased and floured 9 inch square pan. Spread cream cheese mixture on top. Drop spoonfuls of remaining chocolate on top of cream cheese batter and bake 40-45 minutes in 350° oven or until edges begin to pull away. Cool in pan before cutting.

COOKIES & BARS

CHOCOLATE RUM BARS
Yields 24

Chocolate Bar Base:
4 ounces unsweetened
  baking chocolate
1 cup butter
4 eggs
2 cups granulated sugar
1 cup sifted flour
½ teaspoon salt
1 teaspoon vanilla

Filling:
½ cup unsalted butter
4 cups powdered sugar
¼ cup whipping cream
¼ cup rum
1 cup walnuts

Topping:
6 ounces unsweetened chocolate
3 tablespoons water
¼ cup butter

To make base, melt chocolate and butter over boiling water and let cool slightly. Beat eggs until light, adding granulated sugar gradually. When all sugar is beaten in, add chocolate mixture, flour, salt and vanilla. Beat 1 minute. Turn into greased and floured 9 x 15 inch pan. Bake in pre-heated 325° oven 25 minutes. Cool.

To make filling, beat butter and powdered sugar together, adding cream and rum gradually. When light and fluffy, add nuts. Mix well. Spread over base. Chill in refrigerator.

To make topping, melt chocolate pieces with water and butter over boiling water. Mix well. Pour over chilled bars. Chill and cut into 1 inch squares.

CHOCOLATE CHIP SQUARES
Yields 16

¼ *cup butter*
1 *cup brown sugar*
1 *egg*
½ *teaspoon vanilla*
1 *cup flour*
1 *teaspoon baking powder*
¼ *teaspoon salt*
1 *cup semisweet chocolate chips*
¾ *cup walnuts, chopped (optional)*
powdered sugar

Melt butter and add sugar, egg and vanilla. Beat until smooth. Sift together all dry ingredients and add to first mixture. Add chocolate bits and chopped walnuts. Spread in greased 8 inch pan and bake in a 350° oven for 30 minutes. Cut into squares. Sprinkle with powdered sugar when cool. May be frozen.

CHEWY GINGER SNAPS
Yields 8 dozen

1 *cup sugar*
¾ *cup butter or margarine*
1 *egg*
4 *tablespoons molasses*
1 *teaspoon ginger*
1 *teaspoon cinnamon*
1 *teaspoon salt*
2 *teaspoons baking soda*
2 *cups flour, sifted*
sugar

COOKIES & BARS

Cream sugar and butter. Add egg and beat until fluffy before adding molasses and dry ingredients. Form into marble-sized balls and roll in sugar. Flatten cookies with spatula and bake 1-inch apart on ungreased cookie sheets in 350° oven for 10-12 minutes. Cool on wire rack.

GRASSHOPPER STICKS
Yields 24

1½ cups sifted flour
2 cups sugar
¾ cup plus 2 tablespoons cocoa
½ teaspoon salt
1 teaspoon baking powder
1⅓ cups butter
4 eggs
2 tablespoons vanilla
2 tablespoons white corn syrup
2 cups sifted confectioners' sugar
4 tablespoons milk
4 tablespoons butter
1 teaspoon mint extract
1½ squares unsweetened chocolate, melted
    with 1½ tablespoons butter

Sift together flour, sugar, cocoa, salt and baking powder in bowl. Add butter, eggs, vanilla and corn syrup. Mix thoroughly. Spread batter in greased and floured 13 x 9 x 2 inch pan. Bake in preheated 350° oven for 40-45 minutes. Move sides away from pan. Combine confectioners' sugar, milk, butter and mint extract and heat well. Spread over cooled cake and allow frosting to set. Cut into bars. Using pastry brush, coat bars with melted chocolate and butter. Cool and let harden. Recut into bars.

L.A. MERINGUES
Yields 3 dozen

3 egg whites
¼ teaspoon cream of tartar
⅛ teaspoon salt
¼ cup granulated sugar
¾ cup sifted powdered sugar
⅔ cup gingersnap cookie crumbs
⅓ cup semisweet chocolate mini-morsels

Beat egg whites (at room temperature), cream of tartar and salt at high speed of an electric mixer until foamy. Gradually add granulated sugar, 1 tablespoon at a time, beating until soft peaks form. Gradually add powdered sugar, 1 tablespoon at a time, beating until stiff peaks form. (Do not underbeat.) Gently fold in cookie crumbs and mini-morsels. Drop mixture by tablespoonfuls onto wax paper-lined cookie sheets. Bake at 200° for 1½ hours or until dry. Turn oven off and let meringues cool in oven at least 12 hours. Carefully remove meringues from paper. Store in an airtight container.

TEATIME MACAROONS
Yields 24 cookies

1 (8-ounce) package almond paste
1 cup granulated sugar
⅓ cup egg whites
⅓ cup powdered sugar
2 tablespoons flour
3 teaspoons grated lemon or orange rind

COOKIES & BARS

Blend almond paste and granulated sugar. Add unbeaten egg whites, powdered sugar, flour, lemon or orange rind. Mix thoroughly. Drop by spoonfuls on cookie sheet covered with brown paper. Cover with a wet towel for 4 to 5 hours. Bake at 300° for 30 minutes. Remove from oven. Place brown paper with cookies on a damp towel. When paper is slightly damp, cookies can be removed. Place in airtight container when still warm to retain chewy flavor.

BUTTER HORNS
Yields 12 horns

2 cups flour
½ pound butter
1 egg yolk
¾ cup sour cream
¾ cup sugar
1 teaspoon cinnamon
¾ cup nuts, chopped
preserves

Work butter into flour with fingertips, add egg yolk and sour cream. Blend well; shape into ball. Sprinkle with added flour. Wrap in wax paper; chill several hours. Divide chilled dough into thirds. On lightly floured board roll one at a time into large circle about ⅛ inch thick. Combine sugar, cinnamon, nuts, raisins and any flavor preserves to taste. Sprinkle on rolled dough. Cut into 12 wedges. Roll up each section starting with widest part. Place on greased cookie sheet. Bake at 375° until lightly browned, 20 to 30 minutes.

CANDIED FRUIT CRISPS
Yields 3 dozen

½ cup plus 2 tablespoons sifted flour
1 cup mixed candied fruits
1 cup finely chopped blanched almonds
½ cup finely chopped blanched hazelnuts
5 tablespoons unsalted butter
½ cup firmly packed dark brown sugar
2 tablespoons light corn syrup
6 ounces semisweet chocolate, broken into small pieces
6 ounces white chocolate, grated (chill first to make
  this easier)

In a bowl, mix first 4 ingredients. In a large saucepan, combine 4 tablespoons butter, brown sugar and corn syrup. Place over low heat and stir until butter is melted and sugar dissolved (do not boil). Remove from heat and stir in fruit and nut mixture. Drop batter by scant teaspoons, 3 inches apart, onto nonstick baking sheet. Bake in a preheated 325° oven 10 to 12 minutes or until edges are light brown. Cool on baking sheet. Transfer to paper towels to absorb excess butter. In sauce pan melt semisweet chocolate and remaining butter over low heat. Using a small pastry brush, brush the bottoms of half the cookies with a thin layer of the dark chocolate. Cool chocolate-side-up on rack. In double boiler, melt the white chocolate (thin with a small amount of boiling water if necessary). Brush the remaining cookies with a thin layer of the white chocolate. Cool chocolate-side-up on rack.

COOKIES & BARS

CREME DE MENTHE SQUARES
Yields 20

1¼ *cups butter or margarine*
½ *cup unsweetened cocoa powder*
3½ *cups sifted powdered sugar*
1 *beaten egg*
1 *teaspoon vanilla*
2 *cups graham crackers, finely crushed*
⅓ *cup green creme de menthe*
1½ *cups semisweet chocolate pieces*

In heavy saucepan combine ½ cup butter and cocoa powder. Cook and stir over low heat until butter is melted. Remove from heat; stir in ½ cup of powdered sugar, egg and vanilla. Add graham crackers; stir until combined. Press onto bottom of ungreased 13 x 9 x 2 inch baking pan.

Melt ½ cup butter or margarine. In mixer bowl, combine melted butter and creme de menthe. Gradually add remaining powdered sugar, beating with electric mixer until smooth. Spread over chocolate layer. Chill in refrigerator for 1 hour. In heavy small saucepan, combine remaining ¼ cup butter and chocolate pieces. Cook and stir over low heat until melted. Spread over mint layer. Cover and chill 1-2 hours or until firm. Cut into small squares. Store in refrigerator 2 hours.

DATE NUT BARS
Yields 16

2½ *cups pitted dates*
½ *cup all purpose flour*
½ *teaspoon baking powder (double acting)*
⅓ *cup pecans*
⅓ *cup walnuts*
2 *tablespoons unsalted butter*

3 large egg yolks
½ teaspoon vanilla
whipped cream, slightly sweetened (optional)

Mix dates, flour, baking powder, nuts and butter. Process until the dates are chopped. Add to the mixture the egg yolks and vanilla (in a large bowl). Spread the mixture in the bottom of a buttered 8 inch square pan and bake at 300° for 25 minutes. Cool in the pan on a rack. Cut into 2 inch squares and serve with lightly sweetened whipped cream if desired.

PORT-DATE PINWHEELS
Yields 3-5 dozen

½ cup butter
½ cup sugar
½ cup brown sugar
1 egg, beaten
½ teaspoon vanilla
2 cups flour
½ teaspoon baking soda
1 teaspoon salt
port-date filling

Cream butter and sugars thoroughly. Add egg and vanilla and mix well. Sift dry ingredients together and add to creamed mixture, blending well. Chill. Divide dough in 2 and roll out ½ into rectangle ¼ inch thick. Spread with ½ filling. Roll up as for jelly roll. Repeat with remaining ½ of dough. Wrap rolls in wax paper and refrigerate several hours. Slice ¼ inch thick and place on greased cookie sheet. Bake at 400° for 8 minutes.

Port-Date Filling:
1 pound pitted dates, chopped

½ *cup sugar*
2 *tablespoons orange rind*
½ *cup port wine*
½ *cup walnuts, chopped*

In a saucepan combine dates, sugar, orange rind and port. Bring to boiling and cook, stirring constantly, until mixture thickens slightly. Cool. Add walnuts just before ready to spread onto dough. If mixture seems too thick to spread easily, thin with additional port.

RAISIN CHEESECAKE COOKIES
Yields 3 Dozen

⅓ *cup soft butter*
⅓ *cup brown sugar, packed*
1 *cup flour, sifted*
½ *cup raisins*
½ *cup walnuts or pecans, chopped*
1 *8-ounce package cream cheese (room temperature)*
¼ *cup granulated sugar*
1 *egg*
2 *tablespoons milk*
1 *tablespoon lemon juice*
½ *teaspoon vanilla*

Cream butter and brown sugar until fluffy. Add flour, raisins and nuts. Blend until crumbly. Set aside 1 cup of raisin mixture. Press remainder into an 8 inch (or 9 inch) greased square pan. Bake at 350°, 15 minutes or until golden at edges. Cool.

Mix together cream cheese and granulated sugar until smooth. Add egg, milk, lemon juice and vanilla. Beat until smooth. Spread mixture over baked crust. Sprinkle reserved raisin mixture on top. Bake at 350°, 25 to 30 minutes or until firm in center. Cool to room temperature. Cover and chill. Cut into bite size squares.

OATMEAL CRISPIES
Yields 3 dozen

¾ **cup granulated sugar**
½ **cup brown sugar**
½ **cup butter or margarine**
1 **tablespoon orange or lemon rind**
1 **egg**
½ **teaspoon vanilla**
¾ **cup flour**
½ **teaspoon salt**
½ **teaspoon baking soda**
1½ **cups quick oats**
½ **teaspoon cinnamon mixed with** ½ **teaspoon sugar**

In a large bowl of an electric mixer, blend ½ cup granulated sugar, brown sugar, butter, and rind. Add egg and vanilla and blend on high speed. Add flour, salt, baking soda and blend. Stir in oats. Shape lightly into walnut-sized balls and roll in cinnamon-sugar mixture. Bake at 350° for 10 minutes, until they start to brown.

COOKIES & BARS

NUT SQUARES
Yields 16

1 cup raisins
1 cup boiling water
1 teaspoon baking soda
1 cup sugar
2 tablespoons margarine, melted
1 egg
1½ cups all purpose flour
½ teaspoon baking powder
¾ teaspoon salt
1 cup nuts, chopped

Cover raisins with boiling water and baking soda and let stand overnight. Add rest of ingredients and mix. Bake at 350° in greased and floured 8 inch square pan. Bake approximately 30 minutes. Cut into squares.

OLD WORLD PASTRY BARS
Yields 4 dozen

¾ pound butter, softened
1¼ cups sugar
2 eggs
1 teaspoon vanilla
1 teaspoon salt
3¾ cups all-purpose flour, divided
1 cup chopped walnuts
1 (12-ounce) jar raspberry preserves or jam

Heat oven to 350°. In large bowl cream together butter and sugar until light and fluffy. Beat in eggs and vanilla until combined. In medium bowl mix salt with 3½ cups flour. Gradually add to butter mixture to form thick batter. Spread ¾ of the batter evenly over surface of a greased 11 x 17-inch jellyroll pan or cookie sheet with a rim. Spread jam in even layer on top. Sprinkle nuts evenly over all. Blend remaining flour with rest of dough. Crumble on top. Bake 35 minutes or until crust is golden brown. Cool completely and cut into bars.

OLD HAT HERMITS
Yields 40 bars

2 cups flour	*½ cup butter or margarine*
1 teaspoon ground cinnamon	*½ cup sugar*
¾ teaspoon baking soda	*2 eggs*
¾ teaspoon cream of tartar	*½ cup molasses*
½ teaspoon salt	*3 tablespoons chopped citron*
½ teaspoon ground cloves	*½ cup chopped raisins*
¼ teaspoon ground nutmeg	*½ cup currants*
⅛ teaspoon ground allspice	*¼ cup chopped walnuts*

Sift together flour, cinnamon, baking soda, cream of tartar, salt, cloves, nutmeg, and allspice. Set aside. Cream together butter and sugar in bowl until light and fluffy, using electric mixer at medium speed. Add eggs, one at a time, beating well after each addition. Blend in molasses.

Gradually stir dry ingredients into creamed mixture, mixing well. Stir in citron, raisins, currants, and walnuts. Spread mixture evenly in greased 13 x 9 inch baking pan. Bake at 350° for 20 minutes or until no imprint remains when touched lightly with finger. Cool slightly in pan on rack. While still warm, cut into 3 x 1 inch bars. Cool completely.

COOKIES & BARS

RASPBERRY MERINGUE BARS
Yields 24

2½ cups flour
5 eggs, separated
6 tablespoons sugar
1 cup sweet butter
1 tablespoon vanilla
¾ cup sugar
raspberry or other jam
1 tablespoon bourbon or sherry
3 cups finely chopped walnuts

Mix flour, egg yolks, sugar, butter and vanilla. Spread dough into greased 16 x 11 inch pan. Flatten and cover thickly with jam. Beat egg whites with ¾ cup sugar (added gradually) and bourbon (if desired). Fold in nuts and spread over jam. Bake at 350° about 45 minutes. Sprinkle with powdered sugar and cut into squares when cool.

PECAN FANTASY
Yields 24

Dough:
¼ pound butter, room temperature
¼ pound cream cheese, room temperature
1 cup flour

Mix all ingredients until a ball forms, and refrigerate for 2 hours.

Filling:
1 tablespoon butter or margarine, room temperature
1 egg
1 teaspoon vanilla

1 cup brown sugar
1 cup pecans, chopped

Preheat oven to 350°. Use 2 miniature muffin tins. Mix all ingredients together except pecans. Divide dough into quarters. Make 6 balls from each quarter. Place each ball in greased muffin tins, patting around to make a shell. Spoon filling into each shell about ½ full, not more than ¾. Sprinkle pecans over all. Bake for 15 minutes. Lower oven to 250° and bake 20 minutes longer. Cool in pan. Remove from pan and place in small fluted paper cups. Sprinkle with confectioners sugar.

SUGARLESS FRUIT BARS
Yields 16-25 bars

1 cup raisins
½ cup chopped apple
½ cup chopped dates
½ cup water
½ cup oil or margarine

Boil first 4 ingredients for 3 minutes, then add ½ cup oil or margarine. Cool. Add:

2 eggs, beaten
1 cup flour
1 teaspoon soda
¾ cup chopped nuts

Bake at 350° for 12-15 minutes on greased cookie sheets for cookies. Can also be baked in greased 9 x 9 inch pan for bars.

COOKIES & BARS

PINEAPPLE-APRICOT CHEESECAKE COOKIES
Yields 16

⅓ cup butter or margarine
⅓ cup brown sugar, packed
1 cup flour
½ cup walnuts, chopped
¼ cup granulated sugar
1 (8-ounce) package cream cheese, softened
1 egg
2 tablespoons milk
1 tablespoon lemon juice
1 teaspoon vanilla
¾ cup pineapple-apricot jam

Cream butter with brown sugar until light. Stir in flour and nuts until evenly blended. Reserve 1 cup for topping and press remainder into bottom of an 8 inch square pan.

Note: To facilitate removal and cutting of cookies, line the whole pan with foil.

Bake at 350° 12-15 minutes until lightly browned. Cool.

Blend granulated sugar with cream cheese until smooth. Add egg, milk, lemon juice and vanilla. Beat well. Spread crust with pineapple-apricot jam. Top with cream cheese mixture, spreading evenly. Sprinkle with crumb mixture, pressing lightly. Bake at 350° 25 minutes.

TURKISH DELIGHT ROLL
Yields 24

2 eggs
½ cup oil
½ cup sugar
1 orange, cut up
3½ cups flour
2 teaspoons baking powder
½ teaspoon salt
cinnamon
sugar
assorted glazed fruit, chopped
jam or preserves
¾ cup raisins
¾ cup chopped walnuts

In food processor, blend eggs, oil, sugar and cut up orange until liquified. Add flour, baking powder and salt. Knead until a soft dough is formed. Divide into 3 parts. Roll each on floured board. Sprinkle cinnamon and sugar on dough. Spread with jam, chopped nuts, raisins and glazed fruit. Roll up. Place on greased pan. Sprinkle additional sugar and cinnamon on top. Bake in 350° oven for 25 minutes, or until golden. Cut into diagonal slices.

"Honey and sweets brighten the eyes of man."
TALMUD

Just watch the crowd at the 'Dessert Table' as they eye the spread of jewel-like desserts. Desserts titillate and please us; even the lighter ones appeal.

On occasion we throw caution to the winds and indulge in the sensuality of a rich finale. Chocolate is a favorite ingredient in these desserts and for that we have to thank Columbus, who among other things, brought back the cocoa bean from the New World in 1502. It wasn't long before this treasure crept into our lives and became, literally and figuratively, the icing on the cake.

Enjoy the rich; we're poor too soon.

APPLE-RICOTTA PIE
LOW CAL
Serves 8

¾ cup grape-nuts cereal
2 large apples (e.g., Rome Beauty),peeled, cored
  and sliced thin
1 teaspoon grated lemon rind
1 teaspoon lemon juice
½ teaspoon cinnamon
1½ cups Ricotta cheese
⅓ cup sugar
1 egg white and 1 whole egg, lightly beaten
1 cup plain yogurt

Sprinkle the cereal on the bottom of a greased 8-inch springform cake pan. Arrange the apple slices over the cereal, and sprinkle them with the lemon rind, lemon juice, and cinnamon. In a medium bowl, combine the Ricotta, sugar, egg white and whole egg, and yogurt, mixing the ingredients with a spoon until they are smooth. Pour the mixture evenly over the apples. Bake the pie in a preheated 350° oven for 45 minutes. When cool, run a sharp knife around the form before removing the side.

SPIRITED BAKED APPLES
Serves 6

6 large baking apples
⅓ cup brown sugar
1 tablespoon pumpkin pie spice
2 tablespoons butter, melted
½ cup raisins
¼ cup chopped walnuts
2 tablespoons brandy
1 cup boiling water

DESSERTS

Preheat oven to 350°. Wash and core apples. With vegetable peeler, remove a ring off peel around the center of each apple to prevent skin from bursting while baking. Mix remaining ingredients together, except water. Fill apples; place in baking dish. Pour water around apples. Bake 1 hour or until fork tender. (Baking times vary with type of apple.) Serve warm with cream.

APPLE SLICES AU CHOCOLAT
Serves 16

¾ pound semisweet chocolate, chopped
6 tablespoons unsalted butter
3 tablespoons Madeira wine
5 large red and/or green apples, cored, cut into ½ inch
  wedges
1 lemon, halved

Line 2 large cookie sheets with waxed paper. Melt chocolate with butter in heavy saucepan over low heat, stirring until smooth. Mix in wine. Remove from heat. Place apples in large bowl. Squeeze juice from lemon over apples, toss gently, and drain. Skewer each apple slice with toothpick. Dip 1 slice into melted chocolate, shake off excess. Place on prepared cookie sheet. Repeat with remaining apples. Refrigerate until chocolate sets, about 1 hour. (May be prepared 2 hours ahead.) Remove toothpicks and serve.

CINNAMON BAKED APPLES WITH PECANS
Serves 6

1 cup Chenin Blanc wine
½ cup sugar
2 teaspoons ground cinnamon
6 apples, cored, with top third peeled
creme fraiche
⅔ cup finely chopped pecans
6 pecan halves
6 sprigs mint

Heat wine in saucepan over medium heat. Gradually add sugar and cinnamon and blend until dissolved. Stand apples in baking dish. Pour wine mixture over apples. Bake at 375° for 1½ hours, basting every 20 minutes, or until apples are tender. Remove from oven and cool. Arrange pool of ¼ cup creme fraiche on each of 6 dessert plates. Stand 1 apple in center of plate. Top with spoonful of remaining creme fraiche. Sprinkle with chopped pecans. Garnish with pecan half and mint sprig.

Creme Fraiche:
1 cup whipping cream
1 cup sour cream
1½ tablespoons powdered sugar
⅜ teaspoon vanilla

Gradually add whipping cream to sour cream. Add sugar and vanilla and whisk until thoroughly blended. Chill. Whisk again just before serving. Makes 2 cups.

DESSERTS

DEEP DISH APPLE PIE
Serves 8-10

Crust:
2 cups biscuit mix
5 tablespoons ice cold margarine
1 egg beaten with 5 tablespoons ice water

Put first 2 ingredients in food processor. Pulse serveral times until mixture resembles cornmeal. With machine running, add enough of the egg/water mixture to make a soft dough. Refrigerate.

Filling:
7 or 8 large Granny Smith apples, peeled and sliced
1 cup brown sugar
1/3 cup biscuit mix
2 teaspoons cinnamon
1/2 teaspoon nutmeg
juice and zest of 1 orange and 1/2 lemon
3 tablespoons apricot preserves
3 tablespoons brandy

Mix all ingredients together, pour over apple slices mixing well. Transfer to a 9 x 13 inch glass casserole. Roll out crust between wax paper and plastic wrap and cover apple slices. Flute edges and sprinkle crust with granulated sugar. Pierce crust with tines of fork. Cover top lightly with foil. Bake at 400° for 30 minutes, lower oven to 350° for 30 minutes more. Let cool 30 minutes in oven.

FRUITY APPLE PUDDING
Serves 6-8

½ *cup flour*
1 *teaspoon baking powder*
2 *eggs*
¾ *cup brown sugar*
1 *cup tart apples, peeled and diced*
½ *cup dates, finely chopped*
½ *cup pecans or walnuts, chopped*

Topping:
½ *cup cream*
½ *cup butter*
¾ *cup sugar*
1 *teaspoon vanilla extract*

Preheat oven to 325°. Butter and flour a baking pan (8 x 8 inches).

Sift together flour and baking powder. Set aside. Beat eggs and add sugar, beating constantly. Fold in flour. Add apples, dates, and nuts. Pour into baking pan and bake 40 minutes.

As the pudding bakes, prepare topping. Combine topping ingredients and heat until butter melts and sugar is dissolved, stirring constantly. Do not boil. Keep warm.

Remove pudding from oven and allow to cool slightly. Pour a small pool of sauce onto serving dishes. Scoop a portion of pudding on top and drizzle with remaining sauce.

DESSERTS

BAKED PEARS
Serves 6

½ cup water
juice and zest of 1 lemon
¼ cup port wine
1 cup sugar
1 sliced orange
6 slices lemon
2 to 3 tablespoons orange marmalade
6 Bosc pears
orange rind

Preheat oven to 350°. Put all ingredients, except pears, in a saucepan and cook down until strongly flavored and syrupy. Pour the mixture over the pears which have been placed upright in a pyrex dish, just large enough to hold them. Bake until tender, basting often.

APRICOT MOUSSE
Serves 8

1 large can apricots, drained (reserve liquid)
1 large can crushed pineapple, drained (reserve liquid)
1 large package apricot gelatin
1 cup (½ pint) whipping cream, or substitute
1 quart vanilla ice cream, softened

Combine apricot and pineapple liquids and bring to a boil. Add apricot gelatin to the hot mixture. Puree apricots and pineapple in blender. Pour into bowl with whipping cream, softened ice cream and hot mixture. Beat with whisk or beater and pour into serving dish. Refrigerate for 6 hours or overnight. Decorate with apricot halves.

RAVISHING FRUIT TART
Serves 8

1¼ cups all purpose flour
pinch of salt
5 tablespoons cold unsalted butter, cut into pieces,
  plus 2 tablespoons melted butter
1 egg, lightly beaten
1 package (7 ounces) marzipan, at room temperature
¾ pound small red plums (6 to 7), halved lengthwise
  and pitted
½ pound apricots (3 to 4), halved lengthwise and pitted
1 tablespoon sugar (optional)

Preheat oven to 400°. Butter 9½ x 1 inch tart pan with a removable bottom. In a medium bowl, combine flour and salt. Add cold butter and rub or cut it into flour until mixture resembles fine bread crumbs. Stir in beaten egg and gather the dough into a smooth ball. On a lightly floured surface, roll out dough into an 11 inch circle. Fit dough into prepared pan without stretching. Trim pastry level with the rim of pan by gently rolling your pin across the top. Roll the marzipan into a ball and then, on a lightly floured surface, roll out to form a 9 inch circle. Gently press marzipan onto the dough in pan. Cut each of the plum and apricot halves into 3 lengthwise wedges. Arrange plum and apricot in the pan, skin-side down, in alternating concentric circles. (The tart can be prepared to this point and refrigerated, covered, for up to 12 hours before baking.) Brush fruit with melted butter. If fruit is tart, sprinkle with up to 1 tablespoon sugar. Set the tart on a cookie sheet and bake in the middle of oven until fruit is tender and pastry crisp and nicely browned, about 45 minutes. Let tart cool to room temperature on a rack. Lift out onto a flat platter before serving.

DESSERTS

PECAN CRUST SURPRISE
Serves 10

1¾ cups pecan halves
¾ cup water
¾ cup sugar
about 7 tablespoons whipping cream
baked nut crust
chocolate sauce

Place pecan halves in a 9 inch pie or cake pan. Bake in a 350° oven until golden, 8-10 minutes. Shake occasionally. Meanwhile, in a 1½-2 quart pan, stir together water and sugar. Cook over medium-low heat, without stirring, until water turns clear, 12-15 minutes. Wash sugar crystals from pan sides with a wet brush as mixture boils. Increase heat to high and boil, uncovered, until syrup turns golden brown, 5 to 7 minutes. Remove from heat and gradually stir in 7 tablespoons cream (it will splatter) until blended. Sauce should be consistency of corn syrup. If too thick, add a little more cream. If too thin, stir over low heat until thicker. Gently mix pecans into warm caramel. Pour into baked nut crust and push nuts to arrange evenly; let cool. Drizzle warm chocolate sauce over tart. Cool until chocolate is firm. If made ahead, cover and store at room temperature up to 2 days. Cut into wedges.

Baked Nut Crust:
2 cups walnuts
½ cup blanched almonds
3 tablespoons sugar
6 tablespoons butter or margarine
1 teaspoon vanilla

Whirl 2 cups walnuts in a blender or food processor until finely ground but not powdery. Remove from blender. Add ½ cup

126

blanched almonds and 3 tablespoons sugar to blender or processor and whirl until powdery. In a bowl, cream together 6
tablespoons butter or margarine until fluffy. Add 1 teaspoon
vanilla and the ground nuts. Mix just until the dough holds
together. Press dough over bottom and sides of 9 inch tart pan
with removable rim. Bake in a 350° oven until golden, 20-25
minutes. Use warm or cool.

Chocolate Sauce:
2 tablespoons whipping cream
2 tablespoons semisweet chocolate, chopped
In a 1-1½ quart pan, stir 2 tablespoons each whipping cream and
chopped semisweet chocolate over low heat just until smooth.
Use warm.

GRAPEFRUIT FLUFF
Serves 8

4 grapefruit, medium
¼ cup rum
4 egg whites
½ teaspoon cream of tartar
¼ teaspoon salt
¼ cup brown sugar, firmly packed
1-10 ounce jar orange marmalade
½ cup shredded coconut

Cut grapefruits in half. Scoop out meat and membrane. Cover
grapefruit sections with rum. Marinate ½ hour. Beat egg whites,
cream of tartar and salt until foamy. Gradually beat in sugar until
stiff. Drain grapefruit, fold into meringue. Add marmalade. Pile
into grapefruit shells. Sprinkle coconut over top. Place on baking
sheet. Bake at 325° for 20 minutes or until lightly browned. May
be served warm or chilled.

DESSERTS

CELESTIAL COMPOTE
Serves 8

3 oranges, sliced
2 ripe pears
¾ pound green seedless grapes
1 can (1 pound, 13 ounces) whole peeled apricots, pitted
2 packages frozen peaches, thawed
1½ tablespoons finely shredded ginger
2 tablespoons cornstarch
orange juice to cover fruit
Kirsch or apricot brandy

Remove rind and pith sections from oranges. Reserve orange juice. Peel, core and slice pears. Mix orange segments and sliced pears with grapes, apricots, peaches and ginger. Blend cornstarch with a little orange juice and blend into fruit mixture. Add liqueur. Arrange in a 3-inch deep casserole dish and add orange juice. Bake uncovered at 350° for 1 hour. Serve hot or cold. Can be held for an hour or so in a warm oven.

LITCHI NUT FRUIT BOUQUET
Serves 8

2 11-ounce cans whole litchis
1 11-ounce can mandarin oranges
1´1-pound 4 ounce can pineapple chunks
1 medium Persian or Honeydew melon
½ cup Cointreau
¾ cup slivered blanched almonds

Place litchis and syrup in large bowl. Add drained oranges and pineapple chunks. Cut melon in half and seed. Scoop out balls. Save melon shell, if desired, for a serving container. Mix fruit with

128

Cointreau and refrigerate for several hours to blend flavors. Just before serving stir in almonds. Serve in crystal serving bowl or in chilled melon shell. Other fruits in season may be substituted.

RICE PUDDING
Serves 10

1 cup rice
2 cups water
1 cup milk
½ cup half and half
1¼ cups sugar
¼ cup butter
3 eggs
1½ cups softly whipped cream
1 cup raisins
cinnamon-sugar

Add rice to boiling water and cook until rice is soft and tender. Set aside. Combine ½ cup milk, half and half, sugar and butter in saucepan and bring to boil. Beat eggs with remaining milk in bowl. Slowly add cooked mixture to egg mixture in bowl, whisking to blend. Return mixture to saucepan and bring to boil, whisking constantly. Remove from heat and add cooked rice. Cool. Fold in whipped cream and raisins. Sprinkle cinnamon-sugar on top.

DESSERTS

FRUIT IN A RICE RING
Serves 6

¾ cup sugar
½ cup white rice
3¼ cups half and half
1 teaspoon vanilla extract
1 large egg
3 cups assorted fresh fruit, diced

Butter a 4 cup ring mold. Place ½ cup sugar and 1½ tablespoons water in a heavy saucepan and bring to a boil, stirring until sugar dissolves. Boil again without stirring, until the mixture turns a rich amber, about 8 minutes. Pour the caramel into the mold, set aside.

Place rice in a medium saucepan and cover with cold water. Bring to a boil and cook, uncovered, until water evaporates. Add vanilla to half and half and bring to a boil. Add to rice and simmer, stirring frequently, until most of the liquid is absorbed. Remove from heat.

Preheat oven to 325°. Blend together the egg and remaining ¼ cup sugar and stir into rice. Pack rice into the caramelized mold and cover with aluminum foil. Place the mold in another, larger pan that is the same height as the mold. Fill the larger pan half way with hot water and bake the rice for 30-40 minutes, or until a knife inserted in the center comes out clean. Place on a rack and let cool to room temperature, then chill for several hours. Dip the mold in hot water for about 1 minute, turn it onto a serving plate. Fill the center with diced fruit and berries.

DESSERT SOUFFLE
Serves 8

8 eggs, separated, room temperature
8 teaspoons sugar
6 cups fresh fruit, cut into pieces
Kirsh, enough to sprinkle over fruit
4 tablespoons brandy

Preheat oven to 350°. Use a 7½ inch x 12 inch oval oven proof casserole. Beat yolks until lemon colored; slowly add the sugar. Beat egg whites until stiff. Fold gently into the yolk mixture. Place the fruit into casserole and spoon meringue over the top, sealing it in. Bake for 15 minutes or until top is lightly browned. Heat brandy in a saucepan and pour over meringue. Ignite before serving.

PUMPKIN CUSTARD
Serves 8

2 egg whites and 1 egg, lightly beaten
2 cups pumpkin puree, drained if it is very moist
⅜ cup (6 tablespoons) packed brown sugar
2 tablespoons molasses
1 teaspoon cinnamon
½ teaspoon ground ginger
¼ teaspoon ground cloves
1 13-ounce can evaporated skim milk
2 tablespoons sherry

Preheat oven to 350°. In a large bowl, combine the ingredients in the order listed, whisking or beating them by hand until they are well mixed. Pour the mixture into a greased 1½ quart baking dish. Place the dish in oven, bake custard for 50-60 minutes or until custard has set and a knife inserted halfway between its center and side comes out clean.

PUMPKIN FLAN
Serves 6

1¼ cups sugar
1 cup canned pumpkin
¾ teaspoon cinnamon
¼ teaspoon ginger
¼ teaspoon nutmeg
½ teaspoon salt
1 14-ounce can evaporated milk
4 eggs, lightly beaten
¼ cup sherry

Heat 1 cup of the sugar slowly in a heavy iron skillet, stirring with a wooden spoon until melted and caramel colored. Pour into a 5 cup ring mold, rotating mold until bottom and sides are covered.

Combine pumpkin, remaining sugar, and spices. Add evaporated milk to beaten eggs and blend into pumpkin mixture. Stir in sherry. Carefully pour into the mold and place mold into a pan of warm water. Bake at 350° 45-50 minutes, do not overbake. Custard is done when a silver knife in center comes out clean. Cool out of oven and water, chill in refrigerator. To serve, run a spatula around side of mold and turn out onto a serving dish.

RASPBERRY SOUFFLE WITH FRAMBOISE SAUCE
Serves 12

1 envelope unflavored gelatin
2 tablespoons cold water
1 10½-ounce package frozen raspberries, defrosted
¾ cup sugar
1 cup egg whites (approximately 7-8 eggs)
1 cup heavy cream
raspberry Framboise sauce

Tear off a piece of waxed paper long enough to surround a one quart souffle dish. Fold paper in half lengthwise and brush one side with vegetable oil. With oiled side turned inward, tie the paper around souffle dish, extending it 2 inches above the rim. In a medium, stainless steel saucepan, soften gelatin in water. Puree and strain berries through a sieve. Add pureed berries to gelatin with the sugar and heat, stirring, until the gelatin and sugar have dissolved. Transfer to a large bowl and chill until cool but not jelled. Beat whites until stiff and fold into berries. Whip the cream and fold into berry mixture. Spoon carefully into the souffle dish. The mixture should rise above the rim. Chill overnight or freeze until several hours before serving. When ready to serve, remove collar and accompany with the following sauce.

Framboise Sauce:
1 10½-ounce package frozen raspberries, defrosted
¼ cup sugar
2 tablespoons Framboise (raspberry liqueur)

Puree and strain berries. Combine with sugar and Framboise liqueur.

DESSERTS

SUMMER LEMON SOUFFLE
Serves 10

1 envelope unflavored gelatin
¼ cup cold water
6 egg yolks
1 cup sugar
⅔ cup lemon juice
grated rind of 2 lemons
4 egg whites
1½ cups heavy cream
lemon slices
whipped cream

Tear off a piece of waxed paper long enough to surround a 1 quart souffle dish. Fold paper in half lengthwise and brush one side with vegetable oil. Tie the paper around the souffle dish with the oiled side turned inward and extending 2 inches above the rim.

Soften gelatin in the cold water. In a non-aluminum saucepan, beat egg yolks and sugar until thick and light. Stir in lemon juice and cook over low heat, beating steadily until thickened and hot, but not boiling. Mix in gelatin until dissolved and then lemon rind. Remove from heat and cool to room temperature, stirring occasionally.

Beat the 4 egg whites until stiff but not dry and fold into the cooled lemon mixture. Whip the cream and fold in. Slowly pour into the souffle dish. The mixture should rise above the rim. Freeze. When ready to serve, remove collar and decorate top with paper-thin lemon slices and additional whipped cream. A bowl of fresh blueberries is a pretty complement.

LEMON FLUFF MERINGUE
Serves 10

4 eggs, separated
½ cup sugar
grated peel and juice of 1 large lemon
1 cup whipping cream, whipped

Beat egg yolks with sugar, lemon peel and juice until light.
Cook and stir in double boiler over boiling water until thickened. Remove from heat and cool thoroughly. Fold in the
whipped cream. Turn into meringue crust and refrigerate at
least 2 hours to set.

Meringue Crust:
4 egg whites
1 cup sugar
1 teaspoon lemon juice
butter or margarine

Beat egg whites until stiff and glossy. Do not underbeat. Add
sugar, a tablespoon at a time. Add juice last. Butter 9-inch pie
plate generously. Spoon meringue mixture into pan and use
tablespoon to push up mixture, forming sides and bottom of
crust. Bake at 200° for 2 hours. Cool.

DESERTS

MERINGUES GLACEES
Serves 6-8

*3 egg whites at room
  temperature*
⅛ teaspoon salt
⅛ teaspoon cream of tartar

¾ cup sugar
½ teaspoon lemon juice
½ teaspoon vanilla
ice cream

Preheat oven to 300°. Add salt and cream of tartar to egg whites and beat until soft peaks form. Gradually add sugar and continue to beat until all sugar has been added and mixture is very stiff. Add lemon juice and vanilla. Drop by large rounded spoonsful onto cookie sheet lined with brown paper. Bake about 45 minutes. Remove to cake rack and cool. Split meringues in half and spoon ice cream on lower half; cover with top.

Alternate Fillings (Make depressions in meringues and fill)

Orange:
3 egg yolks
2 tablespoons sugar
⅛ teaspoon salt

*6 tablespoons undiluted frozen
  orange juice concentrate, thawed*
1½ cups whipped cream, whipped
2 tablespoons orange rind
6 orange sections

Beat yolks in top of double boiler. Add sugar, salt, orange concentrate. Cook, stirring, over boiling water until thickened. Remove from heat, add orange rind and chill. Fold in whipped cream. Spoon into meringues and chill 12-24 hours. Garnish with orange sections.

Strawberry:
1½ cups sliced strawberries
1 teaspoon grated lemon peel
¼ cup orange juice

¼ teaspoon salt
*½ cup unsifted
  powdered sugar*
1 cup whipping cream

Combine all ingredients except cream in blender or processor until pureed. Whip cream, combine with puree. Turn into a shallow pan and freeze until firm. Scoop into meringue shells and garnish with whole strawberries.

NUTTY MERINGUE TORTE
Serves 6 - 8

6 eggs, separated
1½ cups sugar
2½ tablespoons flour
1 teaspoon baking powder
3 cups walnuts or pecans, finely ground
2 cups whipped cream
whole walnuts for garnish

Preheat oven to 350°. Grease two 9 inch layer pans with removeable bottoms. Beat 6 egg yolks on medium to low speed of mixer, gradually adding sugar until light yellow and foamy. Sift together flour and baking powder and add gradually to egg mixture. Stir in ground nuts. Fold in 6 stiffly beaten egg whites. Divide batter between the 2 pans and bake for 25 -30 minutes. Cool in pans. Turn out carefully. Spread whipped cream between layers and over top and sides of cake to cover completely. Decorate with walnuts.

DESSERTS

CHOCOLATE TRUFFLES
Yields 3 dozen

7 ounces bittersweet chocolate, cut into small pieces
½ cup whipping cream
2 tablespoons butter
¾ cup powdered sugar, measured, then sifted
2 egg yolks
1-2 tablespoons dark rum or other flavoring to taste
unsweetened cocoa and/or coarsely chopped toasted nuts

Combine chocolate with cream and butter in top of double boiler over simmering water until melted. Add sugar and yolks and whisk until smooth. Remove from heat and add rum to taste. Place in flat glass dish and chill until workable, about 2 hours in refrigerator or 1 hour in freezer. Shape into small balls about 1 inch in diameter and roll in cocoa and/or nuts. Place in paper candy cups and refrigerate until firm.

CHOCOLATE DIPPED FRUIT
Serves 16

16 ounces semi-sweet chocolate pieces
6 tablespoons butter
½ teaspoon vanilla
fresh strawberries or dried fruits

Melt chocolate pieces in top of double boiler over hot water. Add butter and vanilla. Dip fruit 1 at a time, swirling to coat evenly. Place each piece on wax paper. Set in cool place to harden.

HOT CHOCOLATE SOUFFLE
Serves 8

8 ounces semisweet chocolate, chopped
1 cup whipping cream
6 egg yolks
1 teaspoon vanilla
2 tablespoons brandy
butter
10 egg whites
⅓ cup sugar
powdered sugar

Melt chocolate in cream in heavy saucepan over low heat, stirring constantly. Cook, stirring, until mixture is thick and just falls from spoon. Remove from heat. Beat egg yolks and add slowly to hot mixture until mixture thickens slightly. Stir in vanilla and brandy. Mixture may be kept covered at this point 3 -4 hours at room temperature.

Thickly butter 2 (1 quart) souffle dishes. Whip egg white until stiff. Add sugar and continue whisking until egg whites are glossy and form light meringue, about 30 seconds. Reheat chocolate mixture until hot. Add about ¼ of the meringue. Stir to combine. Add mixture to remaining egg whites. Fold together and place in prepared dishes, filling to within ¾ inch of rims. Souffles may be refrigerated up to 2 hours.

Bake souffles at 425° in lower third of oven until puffed, 15-18 minutes. Souffles should wobble slightly in the center. Sprinkle with powdered sugar and serve at once. Darker chocolate gives best results.

DESSERTS

CHOCOLATE MOUSSE
Serves 8-10

5 eggs
½ pound chocolate bits
5 tablespoons cold water
2 tablespoons rum

Separate yolks and whites of eggs. Place chocolate bits in saucepan with cold water. Cook, stirring until melted and smooth. Remove and gradually mix in beaten egg yolks and rum. Fold in stiffly beaten egg whites. Serve with whipped cream topping.

LIME PAPAYA COOLER
Serves 8

⅓ cup sugar
2 cups water
1 large papaya, halved, seeded, peeled and chopped
3 tablespoons fresh lime juice
freshly grated lime zest

Combine sugar and 2 cups water in a saucepan. Bring the mixture to a boil, stirring until sugar dissolves. Cool. Puree the papaya with lime juice and zest in a food processor. Add the syrup and blend well. Transfer the mixture to 2 metal ice cube trays without dividers, or a shallow metal pan and freeze. Stir and crush the lumps with a fork every 30 minutes for 2 - 3 hours or until mixture is firm but not frozen hard. Scrape with a fork to lighten the texture and serve in goblets. Makes about 1½ quarts.

STRAWBERRY SORBET
Serves 8

1 package (16 ounces) frozen strawberry halves
2 tablespoons Framboise liqueur (raspberry brandy)
1 teaspoon sugar

Thaw the strawberries partially and put in blender. Add the Framboise liqueur and sugar. Blend until smooth. Pour into any kind of container or mold, and freeze.

You may do the same thing with raspberries, boysenberries, etc. Add the liqueur which will complement the fruit.

KIWI ICE
Serves 8

1 cup sugar
1 cup water
9 ripe kiwis
¼ cup freshly squeezed lime juice

In a 2 quart saucepan over medium low heat, combine sugar and water and stir until sugar dissolves. Increase heat and boil 5 minutes without stirring to make a syrup. Remove from heat and set aside.

Cut 8 of the kiwis in half and remove pulp with a teaspoon. Puree pulp in processor, and stir together pulp, syrup, and lime juice. Turn into a freezer container, cover, and freeze until mixture begins to harden, about 1 hour. Remove from freezer and return mixture to a bowl, beat until smooth and light. Return to freezer until firm. Slice the remaining kiwi and use to garnish each serving.

DESSERTS

FRUIT ICE
Serves 8

1¼ cups water
1 cup sugar
⅛ teaspoon salt
juice of 1 large orange
juice of one large lemon
2 bananas, mashed
2 egg whites, stiffly beaten
½ cup chopped nuts

Bring ½ cup water to a boil with sugar and salt. Remove from heat and add remaining water, juices, and bananas. Pour into ice cube tray and freeze to soft consistency. Turn mixture into mixing bowl and beat thoroughly with electric mixer. Fold in beaten whites and nuts. Return to tray and freeze. Before serving you may beat the mixture again. If you do, add nuts just before serving.

PEACH SORBET
Serves 4

1 package (12 ounces) frozen peaches
2 tablespoons peach brandy
1 teaspoon sugar

Thaw peaches partially and process with brandy and sugar until smooth. Pour into a container or mold and freeze.

*"Throw a lucky man into the sea
and he will come up with a fish in his mouth."*
YIDDISH PROVERB

Some people will go to great lengths
to get a fresh fish. How we prize our fish so clear
eyed, red of gill, scales glistening, reposing on a
bed of crushed ice!

The demand for fish is high and the price is too,
but we still demand it and more and more of it,
as we learn how good it is for us and how light
and pleasing it can be when prepared the right
way.

We welcome the white fish from the Great Lakes,
the trout from Idaho, the roughy from New
Zealand, the salmon from Alaska and Norway,
the sea bass from Chile and Mexico and all the
other varieties that come swimming our way. The
operative words for us are "fins and scales". To
this we add wholesome, fresh and flash-frozen.

FISH STOCK (COURT BOUILLON)
Yield 2 quarts

butter or margarine
3 pounds trimming and bones of any white fish
1½ cups sliced celery
1 cup sliced leeks, green part only
10 sprigs parsley
3 thickly sliced carrots
3 teaspoons fresh lemon juice
1½ cups dry white wine
6 cups water

In heavy saucepan liberally coated with butter or margarine, combine all ingredients except water and wine. Cover and steam for about 5 minutes. Add the water and wine, bring to a boil, skim off the froth and simmer for 25 minutes. Strain and discard the solids and cool.

CIOPPINO
Serves 8

½ cup olive oil
2 onions, diced
1 tablespoon garlic, chopped
1 tablespoon parsley, chopped
1 tablespoon celery, chopped
1 tablespoon green pepper, chopped
2 cups solid pack tomatoes (with juice)
1 cup tomato sauce
1 tablespoon salt
fresh ground pepper
1 tablespoon paprika
½ cup sherry or Pernod
3 cups water
2 pounds assorted fish, cubed

FISH

Braise onions, garlic, parsley, celery, bell pepper in oil until golden brown. Add tomatoes, tomato sauce, salt, pepper, paprika and sherry or Pernod. Cook 15 minutes covered at medium heat. Add water. Cook slowly at a low simmer, covered 1 hour. Just before serving add fresh fish - adding the fish that has the longest cooking time first. Cook 10 to 15 minutes.

Use: halibut, red snapper, cod, fillet of sole.

FISH BLINTZES
Serves 6-8

Court Bouillon:
water
salt, to taste
peppercorns
4 celery tops
1 small onion, halved
2 carrots
½ lemon, sliced
3 cloves

Filling:
1½ pounds salmon and/or
  halibut
½ onion, sauteed
3 stalks celery, diced, sauteed
2 eggs
3 tablespoons minced parsley
½ teaspoon salt
dash pepper
dash thyme
dash basil
¼ pound margarine

Blintz Leaves:
1 cup flour
¼ teaspoon salt
3 eggs
⅔ cup water
1 tablespoon melted
  shortening

Cream Sauce:
4 tablespoons margarine
4 tablespoons flour
2 cups milk
sprinkle of thyme, dill,
  seasoned salt and pepper
3 tablespoons white wine
¼ cup grated Cheddar
  cheese
¼ cup capers
½ cup water chestnuts or
  fresh jicama, slivered
¼ cup sliced mushrooms,
  sauteed

Court Bouillon:
Combine bouillon ingredients and prepare enough bouillon to cover fish in pan. Cook bouillon for 20 minutes. Simmer about 20 minutes per one inch thickness or until fish flakes. Drain. Flake fish and mix with filling.

Blintzes:
Sift together flour and salt. Beat eggs until light. Beat in dry ingredients alternately with liquid, beating until smooth. Add shortening and mix well. Pour enough batter into a small lightly greased fry pan to distribute evenly over entire surface and cook over moderate heat until lightly brown. Turn bottom side up on wax paper. Place 2-3 tablespoons of filling on each leaf. Fold envelope style. Place melted margarine on flat cookie sheet and set blintzes, seam side down. Bake on both sides until brown in 350°-400° oven.

Cream Sauce:
Melt margarine, add flour, using medium heat. Add milk and stir until thick. Add remaining ingredients. Adjust seasonings to taste.

FISH

FISH PATTIES SUPREME
Serves 12

3 pounds fish (ground) - whitefish, sea bass, halibut
4 eggs, well beaten
½ cup cracker crumbs or potato flakes
½ cup milk
1 small onion, chopped, sauted
½ cup grated carrots
2 tablespoons oil to saute grated carrots
½ teaspoon seasoned salt
1 teaspoon thyme
½ teaspoon freshly ground pepper
1 teaspoon basil
¼ cup vegetable oil
½ cup parsley

Combine ground fish with eggs. Add cracker crumbs which have been mixed with milk, sauted onion, carrot and seasonings. Shape fish into patties. Brown patties lightly in oil or brown in 450° oven. Remove from oven and cover with sauce. Bake for 45 minutes.

Herbed Tomato Sauce:
2 tablespoons oil
½ onion, diced
1 green pepper, diced
½ yellow pepper, diced
½ red pepper, diced
1 26-ounce can plum tomatoes, with liquid
3 tomatoes, peeled and chopped
1 6-ounce can tomato paste
½ cup parsley
2 cloves garlic, crushed
½ teaspoon ground pepper

1 bay leaf
1 teaspoon fresh basil
seasoned salt to taste
¼ cup white wine
½ pound mushrooms, sliced and sauteed
1 ounce margarine or butter

Saute vegetables and add remaining ingredients. Cook sauce for 15 minutes. Reserve mushrooms for topping before serving.

FISH AND VEGETABLE MEDLEY
Serves 4

4 slices filet of sole, or other firm fish
2 stalks celery, sliced
1 green or red pepper, sliced
2 carrots, cubed or sliced
2 zucchini, sliced
½ cup margaine, melted
1 cup cornflakes, crushed
½ teaspoon seasoned salt
½ teaspoon lemon pepper

Saute vegetables in half of the margarine until tender. Dip fillets in remaining melted margarine, then in crumbs to which salt and pepper are added. Place vegetables in baking pan and put fish on top. Cover with foil. Bake at 350° covered, for 25 minutes. Uncover and bake for 10 more minutes.

FISH

LOW CALORIE FISH STEW
Serves 4

2 tablespoons olive oil
1 large sliced onion
2 cups cubed eggplant
1 medium green pepper, cut up
3 medium zucchini, cubed
1 large clove, minced
4 cups vegetable juice (tomato base)
¼ cup minced parsley
dash thyme
bay leaf
1 pound filleted fish, cut in 2 inch pieces

Heat oil in large saucepan. Add vegetables and cook gently until tender. Add juice, parsley, thyme and bay leaf. Simmer 5 minutes. Add fish and simmer 10 minutes.

MOUSSE STUFFED FISH
Serves 10-12

1 5-pound butterflied and boned white fish or salmon, lightly salted

Mousse Stuffing:
1¼ pounds fillet of fish (use sole or salmon to color contrast with boned fish)
¼ cup flour
1 teaspoon salt
½ teaspoon white pepper
2 egg whites
1½ cups light cream or milk

Rinse and pat dry fillets. Process in food processor. Add flour, salt and pepper. While processor is running add egg whites one at a time, then cream, 2 tablespoons at a time until well blended and stiff.

Fill whole fish with mousse and place in 9 x 13 inch pyrex dish. Cover loosely with waxed or parchment paper. Put pyrex dish into larger pan. Pour boiling water ¾ way up the larger pan. Bake at 375° for 50-60 minutes. Serve with sauce.

Sauce:
3 tablespoons butter or margarine
¼ cup flour
¾ teaspoon salt
1½ cups light cream or milk
⅓ cup dry white wine
2 tablespoons ketchup
2 egg yolks
2 cups sauteed mushrooms
juice of ½ lemon
parsley

Melt butter in medium pan. Remove from heat, stir in flour and salt. Gradually stir in 1 cup cream, stirring constantly. Reduce heat and simmer one minute. Add wine and ketchup. Beat yolks with ½ cup cream. Add mushrooms. Spoon over fish. Garnish with lemon and parsley.

FISH

POACHED FILLETS WITH
HERBED AVOCADO SAUCE
Serves 2

2 fillets of sole
1 cup dry white wine
½ cup water
1 teaspoon lemon juice
herbed avocado sauce
additional avocado slices for garnish

Roll fillets and secure with wood picks. Heat wine, water and lemon juice to boil in 2 quart saucepan. Reduce heat and place rolled fillets in water. Poach, covered, over low heat for 5 minutes. Remove with slotted spoon and chill fillets, if desired, in refrigerator. To serve, place rolled fillets on plate. Cover with herbed avocado sauce and if desired, garnish with avocado slices.

Herbed Avocado Sauce:
1 avocado, peeled and seeded
1 egg yolk
1 tablespoon tarragon vinegar
1 tablespoon lemon juice
½ teaspoon Dijon mustard
1 teaspoon dill weed, fresh or dry
1 teaspoon parsley, chopped
salt, pepper

Combine in blender, avocado, egg yolk, vinegar, lemon juice, mustard, dill weed and parsley. Blend until smooth. Season to taste with salt and pepper.

FISH FILLETS WITH HERBED RICE
Serves 4

*I pound fresh or frozen fillets, cut into 1 inch cubes and set
  aside*
1 package (7¼ ounce) herb flavored rice mix
2 tablespoons olive oil or salad oil
1 medium onion, chopped
¼ cup sliced mushrooms
1 clove garlic, minced or pressed
1 small green pepper, chopped
1 jar spaghetti sauce (16 ounces)
2 teaspoons dried basil
1 tablespoon Worcestershire sauce
¼ cup parsley

Prepare rice mix according to package directions and set aside.
Heat oil in frying pan, medium heat, add onion, garlic, sliced
mushrooms; stir and cook until onion is limp. Add the green
pepper, increase heat to medium high and cook, stirring, until
liquid is evaporated. Stir in spaghetti sauce, basil, Worcestershire
and fish cubes. Cover and simmer 6-8 minutes until fish flakes.
Stir in parsley. Spoon saucy fish mixture over rice.

FISH FILLETS DELUXE
Serves 4 - 6

1 pound haddock, whitefish or cod fillets
3 tablespoons sour cream
2 tablespoons Dijon mustard
½ cup dry bread crumbs
½ teaspoon dill weed
¼ teaspoon pepper
¼ cup butter or margarine

FISH

Remove and discard any skin from fish. Combine sour cream and mustard. Combine crumbs, dill weed and pepper. Spread fish with sour cream mixture; coat with crumbs. Cook in butter in large skillet over medium heat until golden brown and tender, about 10 minutes.

Note: If preferred use Italian seasoned bread crumbs in place of bread crumbs, dill weed and pepper.

FISH IN HERB SAUCE
4 Servings

4 fillets
1 cup dry Vermouth
1 large leek, cut into thin 6-inch strips
1½ cups evaporated skim milk
1 teaspoon dried thyme, crumbled
⅛ teaspoon white pepper
2 teaspoons lemon juice

Place fish and Vermouth in large skillet. Cover and simmer 10 minutes per inch thickness of fish. Add leek during last 5 minutes cooking time and cook, uncovered.

Remove fish and leeks from pan. Boil cooking liquid until reduced to about ¼ cup. Add milk and thyme and cook until reduced by about half, about 1 cup. Season with pepper adding lemon juice slowly, stirring constantly. Pour sauce over fish and serve.

FISH ITALIANO
Serves 4

1½ pounds fish
3 tablespoons butter
1 onion, sliced
½ cup mayonnaise
½ cup Parmesan cheese
3 tablespoons lemon juice
1 teaspoon Worcestershire sauce
½ teaspoon paprika
½ teaspoon oregano
2 tablespoons chopped parsley

Melt butter and pour in bottom of baking dish. Arrange sliced onions on melted butter. Top with fish. Combine all ingredients except parsley and pour over fish. Bake at 375° for 20 minutes. Before serving, sprinkle with parsley.

FISH PARMESAN
Serves 4

1½ pounds fillet of sole, or any thin white fish
salt
garlic
pepper
½ teaspoon oregano
1 can (8 ounces) tomato sauce
½ cup Mozzarella cheese, shredded
2 tablespoons Parmesan cheese, grated

Season fish with salt, garlic, pepper and oregano. Place in pyrex baking dish. Spread tomato sauce over fish. Sprinkle with cheeses. Bake at 425° for 15 minutes.

FISH

FISH TERIYAKI - (Microwave)
Serves 3-4

¾ cup soy sauce
½ cup sugar
1 teaspoon grated fresh ginger root
1 clove garlic, peeled and crushed
3 teaspoons sake (Japanese rice wine)
  or cooking sherry
1½ pounds fish fillets

In a shallow 2-quart heat-resistant, non-metallic baking dish combine soy sauce, sugar, ginger root, garlic and sake. Stir to combine well. Place fish fillets in sauce mixture and marinate for ½ hour. Heat uncovered on full power for 9 minutes, basting occasionally with sauce.

FISH WELLINGTON
Serves 4

2 pounds whitefish, sea bass or orange roughy
1 cup milk
1 package filo dough (6 leaves)
seasoned salt and/or dill, lemon juice, pepper to taste
1 package frozen spinach souffle, slightly thawed
melted butter or margarine

Soak fish in milk for ½ hour. Pat dry. Reserve milk. Defrost filo leaves and brush each leaf with melted butter. Place fish in dough, add seasoned salt, dill, lemon juice and pepper. Cut spinach souffle and distribute over fish. Wrap dough around fish, place on greased cookie sheet and bake in 350° oven for 30-40 minutes. Remove, put on platter and slice. Serve with the following cream sauce.

Sauce:
3 tablespoons margarine, melted
3 tablespoons flour
¼ cup grated Cheddar or Swiss cheese
1 chopped and peeled tomato

Heat reserved milk. Melt margarine and blend in flour. Add heated milk, stirring until it thickens. Add cheese and seasonings and continue stirring. Last, add chopped tomato. Continue cooking just until thoroughly heated.

HALIBUT WITH CAVIAR-LIME SAUCE
Serves 6

1 cup onion, minced
1 cup celery, minced
1 cup carrot, minced
4 tablespoons unsalted butter
¼ cup parsley, chopped
3 bay leaves
4 whole cloves
salt, freshly ground pepper
½ cup dry white wine
6 (6 ounce) halibut steaks
1 cup fish stock
¼ cup cream
2 teaspoons lime juice
2 teaspoons lemon juice
¼ cup black caviar
1 hard-cooked egg, sieved
2 tablespoons chives, minced

Saute onion, celery and carrot in butter about 10 minutes until vegetables are soft. Add parsley, bay leaves, cloves, and salt and

FISH

pepper to taste. Cook, uncovered, over low heat 15 minutes. Add white wine and simmer, uncovered, 5 minutes. Remove bay leaves, and puree mixture in food processor. Sprinkle halibut with salt and pepper, and poach steaks in fish stock in skillet until tender. Carefully remove steaks to platter. Add pureed vegetables and whipping cream to enough of the liquid for a desired consistency. Simmer, stirring constantly, 2 minutes. Add juices. Remove from heat and add 2 tablespoons caviar. Pour sauce over fish, and top each steak with 1 teaspoon caviar. Sprinkle with sieved egg and minced chives.

PESTO HALIBUT WITH TOMATO SAUCE
Serves 6

6 (¾ inch thick) pieces halibut fillet
3 cloves garlic
3 walnut halves
½ cup basil leaves
1 tablespoon olive oil
1 teaspoon grated Parmesan cheese
salt, pepper

Arrange halibut fillets on broiler rack. Combine garlic, walnut and basil in blender, and finely chop. Add oil in a stream, whirring until well blended and slightly thickened. Add Parmesan cheese and whir just enough to mix. Season with salt and pepper. Place halibut under broiler and broil until fish is opaque on top. Turn carefully. Brush thin layer of sauce over fish. Broil without turning, 3 to 4 minutes, or until fish is opaque and flakes when touched with fork.

Sauce:
6 medium-large ripe tomatoes, peeled and seeded
1 tablespoon olive oil

½ teaspoon finely chopped garlic
1 tablespoon finely diced roasted or fresh sweet red pepper
1 teaspoon mixed chopped herbs, oregano, basil or tarragon
4 Greek olives, minced
salt, pepper

Puree 5 tomatoes in food processor until smooth. Strain through fine strainer into saucepan. Add olive oil, garlic, red pepper, chopped herbs and olives. Season to taste with salt and pepper. Simmer over medium heat until sauce is reduced by half. Dice and add remaining tomato. Heat through only. Correct seasoning if necessary. Makes 2¾ cups.

ORANGE ROUGHY
IN ORANGE MINT YOGURT SAUCE
Serves 6

1½ pounds orange roughy fillets
1 teaspoon olive oil
½ teaspoon ginger root, minced or dried ginger
½ teaspoon garlic, minced
1 8-ounce carton plain nonfat yogurt
1 teaspoon orange peel, grated
1 teaspoon fresh mint leaves, minced
white pepper

Brush fish fillets with olive oil and sprinkle lightly with ginger and garlic. Broil 3 to 4 inches from heat source for about 5 minutes or until fish flakes when tested with fork. Meanwhile, stir together yogurt, orange peel and mint leaves. Season to taste with white pepper. Serve with fish.

FISH

RED SNAPPER WITH FRESH TOMATOES
Serves 4-6

2 pounds red snapper fillets
3 tablespoons butter
1 medium onion, chopped
1 clove garlic, minced
1½ tablespoons flour
⅔ cup dry white wine
2 green onions, chopped
4 tomatoes, peeled, seeded and coarsely chopped
1 teaspoon chopped parsley
⅛ teaspoon each basil and dill
¼ cup bread crumbs
2 teaspoons Parmesan cheese

Place fillets in well-buttered baking dish and season with salt and freshly ground pepper. Melt butter in saucepan. Add onion and garlic and saute for 5 minutes without browning. Stir in flour and add wine. Bring to boil and simmer for 5 minutes. Add tomatoes, green onions and herbs. Pour sauce over fish and sprinkle with bread crumbs and cheese. Bake uncovered at 350° for approximately 30 minutes.

POACHED SALMON VERMOUTH
Serves 4-6

1 whole salmon, 2½-3½ pounds
lemon juice
⅓ cup orange juice
¼ cup oil
dill
⅓ cup Vermouth

Wash and dry salmon. Place in double heavy foil. Add orange juice, lemon juice, oil, Vermouth, dill, pepper and salt. Wrap carefully so that all the liquids are retained. Place on cookie sheet and bake ¾ to 1 hour depending on size of fish.

To serve: Remove skin and dark meat (scrape off). If desired, the halves may be separated, center bone removed and the halves put together again.

SALMON SLICES BAKED IN SOUR CREAM
Serves 4

4 salmon steaks, 2 inches thick
1 teaspoon salt
2 cups sour cream
1 onion, finely chopped
2 tablespoons lemon juice
1 tablespoon fresh dill, chopped
parsley, chopped

Arrange steaks in a baking dish and salt lightly. Mix all other ingredients, except parsley, with sour cream and pour over fish. Bake at 350° for about 35 minutes. Sprinkle with chopped parsley.

FISH

SAUTÉED SALMON FILLETS WITH CHERVIL BUTTER SAUCE
Serves 4

4 6-ounce boneless salmon fillets with skin on
salt and freshly ground pepper to taste
2 teaspoons finely chopped fresh thyme or
  1 teaspoon dried
4 tablespoons butter
3 tablespoons chopped shallots
¼ cup dry white wine
2 tablespoons red-wine vinegar
¼ cup heavy cream
½ cup chervil leaves or fresh coriander, chopped
1 tablespoon fresh lemon juice
1 tablespoon corn or vegetable oil
4 sprigs fresh chervil for garnish

Sprinkle salmon with salt, pepper and thyme. Heat 1 tablespoon butter in a small heavy sauce pan. Add the shallots and cook briefly over medium heat, stirring until they are wilted. Do not brown. Add the wine and vinegar, bring to a boil and simmer until reduced to 5 tablespoons. Add the cream. As soon as it reaches a boil, turn the heat to low and whisk in the remaining 3 tablespoons butter, a little at a time. Add the chopped chervil and lemon juice. Blend well, season with salt and pepper. Keep warm.

Heat the oil over high heat in a nonstick skillet large enough to hold the fillets in one layer. Add the fillets skin side down. Cook about 3 minutes or until golden brown on one side. Turn the fish pieces and reduce the heat to medium. Cook until golden brown, about 2 to 3 minutes. Do not overcook. Keep warm. Distribute the sauce evenly over 4 serving dishes. Lay one fillet skin side up over the sauce on each plate and garnish with a sprig of chervil. Serve immediately.

MICROWAVE MAGIC SALMON
Serves 4

1½ pounds center cut salmon fillets
juice of one lemon
sprig of dill

Rinse fish well. Sprinkle with lemon juice and dill. Wrap each fillet carefully in plastic wrap making certain ends are well tucked in. Place in plastic bag. Microwave for 4 minutes at full power. Let cool before unwrapping. Remove skin and serve with lemon mayonnaise.

Lemon Mayonnaise:
1 cup mayonnaise
1 tablespoon Dijon mustard
¼ cup lemon juice
¼ cup fresh dill, chopped

For herb mayonnaise, add any of the following:
½ cup chopped chives
½ cup parsley
½ cup shredded basil

Add salt and pepper to taste.

FISH

PICKLED SALMON
Serves 10-12

2 cups white vinegar
1½ cups water
6 tablespoons sugar
2 tablespoons kosher salt
2 pounds salmon fillet (skin and bones removed)
6 bay leaves
2 white or yellow onions, sliced ¼ inch thick
2 tablespoons mixed pickling spices
sliced cucumbers and sour cream

Bring vinegar, water, sugar and salt to a boil. Let this mixture cool completely.

Cut the salmon into pieces approximately 1 x 2 inches. In a ceramic crock, glass bowl or plastic container, place a layer of salmon pieces, then a sprinkling of pickling spices and bay leaves, a layer of onions, then another layer of salmon and spices, continuing until you have used it all. Pour the cooked marinade over the fish. Cover and refrigerate 3-4 days.

Serve the salmon along with the marinated onions, sliced cucumbers and sour cream if desired.

POACHED SALMON IN
CHAMPAGNE DILL SAUCE
Serves 6

6 salmon fillets, 1 inch thick
3 tablespoons unsalted butter
3 tablespoons lemon juice
½ cup champagne
2 tablespoons chopped chives

Sauce:
¼ cup sour cream
1 tablespoon Dijon mustard
2 tablespoons lemon juice
1 tablespoon chopped chives
2 tablespoons snipped fresh dill

Bring salmon fillets to room temperature. Melt butter over low heat in a large skillet. Stir in lemon juice, champagne, and chives. Place fillets in skillet and baste. Cover and cook over low heat 10 minutes or just until fish cooks through. Whisk together sauce ingredients. Refrigerate until serving time. Serve salmon warm from the skillet with chilled sauce poured over each fillet.

FISH

POACHED SALMON AND DILL SAUCE
Serves 8-10

1 3-6 pound piece of salmon, bones and trimming
* for bouillon*
cheesecloth

Court Bouillon:
1 quart water
1 cup dry white wine
fish bones and trimmings
2 sprigs parsley
1 onion
1 slice lemon
1 teaspoon salt
2 cloves
4 pepper corns
1 bay leaf
pinch dry or fresh dill

Cucumber Dill Sauce:
1 cup sour cream
1 tablespoon minced dill
½ cup peeled and chopped
* cucumber*
1 tablespoon minced chive or
* green onion*

Combine all ingredients

Prepare court bouillon. Place all ingredients in pot and bring to rolling boil. Lower heat and simmer for 30 minutes. Cool and strain. Place bouillon in pan or poacher. Rinse fish and pat dry. Wrap in cheesecloth, leaving long ends overlapping the pot in order to facilitate lifting fish out when done. Lower fish into bouillon. Bring to boil. Turn heat down to simmer so that broth barely moves. Allow 7 minutes to the pound and when finished, let fish cool in broth (which will finish the cooking.) Lift fish using ends of cloth. Gently roll onto platter. Remove cheesecloth and peel off skin. Chill. Serve with cucumber dill sauce or spread sauce on salmon as topping.

SALMON AT THE SUMMIT
Serves 6

2 eggs
2½ teaspoons Dijon
  mustard
¼ teaspoon salt
2 tablespoons freshly
  squeezed lemon juice
¼ cup vegetable oil
¼ cup olive oil
6 cloves garlic, peeled

½ teaspoon freshly ground
  pepper
hot pepper sauce, to taste
2 pounds skinless salmon
  fillets
¼ cup dry white wine
1 large avocado, peeled
  and sliced
2 tomatoes, sliced

Preheat oven to 375°. In a food processor or blender, combine eggs, mustard, salt, and lemon juice. With the machine running, gradually add oils. Blend garlic, pepper, and hot pepper sauce. Check seasoning and add extra lemon juice, if desired.

Spread half of the sauce in a shallow baking dish (7 x 12 inches) and top with fish. Pour in wine and add remaining sauce. Top with alternating slices of avocado and tomato. Bake approximately 20 minutes.

FISH

SALMON LOAF SUPREME
Serves 6

1 can salmon (15 ounces), drained and mashed
½ cup cooked brown rice
1 cup spinach, cooked and drained
1 cup Ricotta cheese or tofu
2 tablespoons Parmesan cheese
2 eggs, beaten
½ to ¾ cup milk
2 tablespoons lemon juice
1 scallion, chopped
2 stalks celery, chopped
¼ cup fresh basil, minced
2 tablespoons melted butter or margarine
salt and pepper to taste

Add all ingredients to the drained and mashed salmon and pour into glass loaf pan or individual ramekins. Bake at 350° for 1 hour in loaf pan or 30 minutes in ramekins, until browned.

SALMON MOUSSE
Serves 12

1 8-ounce package cream cheese or 1 cup plain
   non-fat yogurt
1 can tomato soup
2 envelopes unflavored gelatin, softened in ½ cup water
1 small onion, finely chopped
1 cup celery, chopped
1 cup green pepper, chopped
1 16-ounce can salmon, drained or fresh cooked salmon,
   flaked

1 cup mayonnaise
¼ cup fresh dill, chopped (optional)

In a saucepan melt cream cheese in soup over low heat. Add softened gelatin, continue heating until gelatin dissolves. Add all remaining ingredients except mayonnaise. Allow gelatin mixture to cool slightly, then add mayonnaise. Pour mixture into greased, 9 cup mold. Chill until firm.

SALMON QUICHE
Serves 6

1 unsweetened pastry shell (9 inch), partially baked
1 can red salmon (1 pound), drained and skinned,
   reserve ¼ cup liquid from can
1 tablespoon butter
2 tablespoons minced shallots
4 whole eggs, beaten
2 tablespoons fresh dill
2 tablespoons sherry
⅛ teaspoon white pepper
1 cup cream, scalded

In a saucepan, heat butter and saute shallots. Blend for 20 seconds sauteed shallots, salmon, 4 eggs, dill, salmon liquid, sherry and pepper. Turn blender to low and add the scalded cream. Pour into pastry shell and bake at 375° for 25 to 35 minutes.

FISH

RICE AND SMOKED SALMON BAKE
Serves 4

3-4 cups fish stock or white wine
1 medium onion, finely chopped
4 tablespoons butter
2 tablespoons oil
1½ cups Arborio rice
⅓ cup heavy cream
⅔ cup smoked salmon, shredded
2 tablespoons parsley, chopped
½ cup Parmesan cheese, grated
2 tablespoons fresh dill, chopped
1 tablespoon capers
salt, if necessary, and freshly ground pepper

Heat the fish stock (or other liquid) and keep it simmering. In a heavy skillet or casserole, sauté the onion in half the butter and all the oil over medium heat until translucent. Add the remaining butter and when melted, add the rice. Stir with a wooden spoon until the rice is well coated. Add ½ cup simmering stock and stir over medium to low heat until the rice absorbs the liquid. Add another ½ cup stock and continue to stir and cook. Repeat, loosening any rice that sticks to the bottom of the pan. Regulate heat so rice doesn't brown or dry out too quickly and continue to add the stock. When the rice is more than half done (approximately 20 minutes), stir in cream and let mixture cook for a few minutes. Stir in smoked salmon and parsley. Continue cooking for 1 or 2 minutes. Stir in Parmesan, dill and capers. Add salt and pepper to taste.

SALMON SOUFFLE
Serves 8-10

3 onions, diced
¼ pound butter
½ pound low-salt lox
1 large can salmon (16 ounces)
12 eggs or egg substitute
1 pint milk
pepper

Saute onions in butter and put in 9 x 13 inch baking dish. Cut up lox and place over onions. Place drained and flaked salmon over this. Beat eggs with 1 pint milk and pepper and pour over all. Bake at 350° for 1 hour.

Optional: 1 pound sauteed mushrooms can be sprinkled on top.

SOLE WITH SPINACH
Serves 4

8 pieces fillet of sole
1 package frozen leaf spinach
⅓ cup grated Parmesan cheese
4 tablespoons butter
salt and pepper

Drain spinach well. Generously butter baking dish and place 4 fillets into dish. Cover with spinach and top with remaining fish. Sprinkle with cheese, salt and pepper and dot with butter. Bake for 30 minutes in 350° oven.

FISH

STUFFED SOLE GARNI
Serves 6

6 large fillets of sole
lemon juice
seasoned salt
12 thin slices of smoked salmon
2 tablespoons butter or margarine
½ small onion, diced
½ cup red pepper, diced
½ pound mushrooms, coarsely chopped
1 tablespoon dill
½ cup chopped parsley
½ cup Gruyere cheese, diced
¼ cup white wine

Marinate sole in lemon juice for 1 hour. Sprinkle with seasoned salt. Place 2 slices of smoked salmon on each sole fillet. Melt butter, saute onions, red pepper, mushrooms. Add remaining ingredients, except wine. Spread filling over salmon. Roll fillets and secure with toothpicks. Place in greased pyrex pan, rolled ends down. Sprinkle with wine. Bake uncovered for 30 minutes at 375°. Baste occasionally.

SOLE WITH BANANAS
Serves 4

4 6-ounce fillets of sole
salt and pepper
1½ tablespoons shallots, minced
2 cups dry white wine
1 cup fish stock
¾ cup lime juice
2 teaspoons curry powder

1 cup cream
2 egg yolks
2 cups cooked rice
1½ bananas, sliced

Sprinkle fillets with salt and pepper. Select a skillet large enough to hold fish in one layer. Sprinkle minced shallots, arrange fillets, add wine, fish stock, lime juice, cover with sheet of buttered wax paper and simmer over moderate heat for 7 minutes or until just opaque. Transfer fillets to a dish and keep warm. Stir curry powder into liquid and reduce over high heat to ½ cup. Add ½ cup cream and reduce liquid again to ½ cup. Beat egg yolks with remaining ½ cup cream and cook for 2 minutes over low heat.

Divide rice in 4 individual shallow flame proof dishes, arrange banana slices and then a fillet in each or use 1 low baking pan. Mask with sauce and broil for 3 minutes, or until sauce is lightly browned.

SEA BASS DIJON
Serves 4

4 slices sea bass
¼ cup lemon juice
¼ cup melted margarine
¼ cup white wine
3 tablespoons Dijon mustard
2 tablespoons capers

Marinate fish for 1 hour in lemon juice. Drain. Stir other ingredients; place fish in baking pan and pour the sauce over. Bake in 350° oven for 25 minutes and baste.

FISH

TUNA CASSEROLE WITH NOODLES
Serves 4-6

8 ounces green noodles
1 can tuna (7 ounces), drained
8 ounces mushrooms, sliced and sauted
½ cup pimiento strips
2 eggs, beaten
½ cup milk
1 teaspoon salt
¼ teaspoon pepper
½ teaspoon garlic salt
¼ teaspoon grated Parmesan cheese
¼ cup butter, melted

Cook noodles in rapidly boiling water until tender. Drain and rinse in cool water. Place in large bowl. Flake tuna and add to noodles with mushrooms and pimiento. Mix thoroughly. Combine eggs, milk and seasonings. Stir into noodle mixture. Pour into well greased 1½ quart casserole. Sprinkle top with Parmesan cheese. Drizzle butter over cheese. Bake at 350° for 25 minutes.

TUNA QUICHE IN RICE CRUST
Serves 4 - 6

1 package (6 ounces) herb rice mix
1 can white tuna (7 ounces), drained
¾ cup Swiss cheese, shredded
⅓ cup green pepper, chopped
⅓ cup green onion, chopped
4 eggs
1¼ cups milk
¼ teaspoon salt
dash pepper
¼ teaspoon Tabasco sauce

Cook rice mix as package directs. Cool. Generously butter a 10 inch pie pan. Form a high-standing crust with rice. Distribute tuna over crust. Sprinkle evenly with cheese, then green pepper and onion. Beat together eggs, milk, salt, pepper and Tabasco. Pour over tuna mixture. Bake, uncovered, in 350° preheated oven about 50 minutes or until set. Let stand 10 minutes before cutting.

"Meat is the prince of all foods."
TRACTATE PURIM

Meat has traditionally been the heart of the meal. A treat indeed if one could afford it. So special and such a delight was it considered that the "minhag" or custom is to include it (or at least poultry, its surrogate by Rabbinic law) in the Sabbath meal.

Although today's portions may be smaller and the cuts leaner, we still revel in meats' rich and satisfying flavor.

BLACK BEAN CASSOULET
Serves 8

1 pound black beans
3 tablespoons canola oil
3 cups chopped onions
2 tablespoons chili powder
1 tablespoon minced fresh jalapeno pepper
2 tablespoons minced garlic
1 teaspoon ground cumin
½ teaspoon oregano
fresh ground pepper, and salt (to taste)
1 quart water
¼ cup stone ground cornmeal
1 pound sliced, sweet Italian or Kielbasa sausage
¼ cup chopped cilantro
¾ pound chicken breast, cubed or stripped

Soak beans overnight. Bring to boil and cook for 2 hours. Drain and rinse. In Dutch oven, heat oil, add onions and saute until golden. Add chili powder, jalapeno pepper, garlic, salt, pepper, cumin, and oregano and cook until well blended. Stir in beans and water and bring to boil. Reduce heat, cover, and simmer for 2 hours or until done. Stir in cornmeal and simmer until thickened, adding additional liquid if necessary. Saute sausage and chicken cubes separately. Add sausage to casserole and layer chicken pieces on top. Preheat oven to 350° and bake casserole for 30-45 minutes until bubbly. Add some chicken stock if mixture seems too dry. Sprinkle cilantro on top. This dish may be served with grilled eggplant.

Grilled eggplant:
1 medium eggplant
¼ cup olive oil
¼ cup chopped parsley

MEAT

¼ - ½ cup Balsamic vinegar

Slice unpeeled eggplant in ¼ inch slices. Brush with olive oil and half of parsley. Grill, bake, or broil until brown on both sides. Sprinkle liberally with Balsamic vinegar and remaining parsley.

SAVORY RIB ROAST
Serves 6

1½ tablespoons Hungarian sweet paprika
1 tablespoon crushed black peppercorns
1 tablespoon coarse salt
1 tablespoon dried oregano, crumbled
1 tablespoon dried thyme, crumbled
2 teaspoons celery seeds
1 teaspoon cayenne pepper
2 tablespoons Dijon mustard
2 tablespoons grated onion
2 garlic cloves, pressed
1 4½-pound bone-in rib roast (small end), patted dry

fresh watercress
horseradish sauce (recipe below)

Mix first 7 ingredients in small bowl. Mix mustard, onion and garlic in another bowl. Rub mustard mixture over meat (not bones). Sprinkle with spice mixture. Cover and refrigerate overnight. Let stand 2 hours at room temperature before continuing.

Prepare barbecue (high heat). Spread hot coals to outer edges of barbecue. Place rectangular aluminum pan in center of coals. Place roast on rack above pan. Cover with grill lid and cook until meat thermometer inserted in center of roast registers 130° for medium-rare, about 1 hour 45 minutes. Cut off bones. Garnish roast with watercress. Serve with Horseradish Sauce.

Horseradish Sauce:
½ cup grated radishes (about 8 radishes)
3 tablespoons prepared horseradish
1 tablespoon Dijon mustard
1 teaspoon sugar
½ cup chilled non-dairy whipping cream, whipped to peaks
salt and pepper

BEEF BOURGUIGNON
Serves 4 - 6

2 pounds chuck, cubed
3 carrots, cut into ½ inch slices
1 cup celery, chopped
2 onions, sliced
2 cups canned tomatoes
1 cup tomato sauce
1 clove garlic
salt and pepper to taste
3 tablespoons minute tapioca
1 tablespoon sugar
½ cup wine (white or red)
½ pound mushrooms
1 pound small white potatoes

Combine all ingredients, reserving the mushrooms and potatoes. Roast covered at 250° for 3 hours. Add mushrooms and potatoes and cook covered 1 more hour.

MEAT

BRISKET OF BEEF WITH FRUITS AND SPIRITS
Serves 12

6-8 pound brisket (trimmed of fat)
1 package onion soup
1 bay leaf
1 teaspoon grated garlic (optional)

Cover a large sheet of heavy aluminum foil with ½ package onion soup. Place brisket on top of soup. Spread remaining ½ package of onion soup, 1 bay leaf and 1 teaspoon grated garlic (optional) over meat. Bring opposite diagonal corners of foil together. Seal.

Place sealed meat in oven (in pan), 325°, and cook for 4-5 hours until almost tender.

Sauce:
½ teaspoon Worcestershire sauce
1 tablespoon brandy
1 tablespoon lemon rind
2 tablespoons orange marmalade
1 teaspoon black pepper
½ teaspoon cinnamon
6 tablespoons dark brown sugar
⅛ teaspoon ground ginger
4 tablespoons honey
juice of lemon
2 cups dried apricots
2 cups prunes (pitted)
1 (12 ounce) bottle of beer

Remove meat and gravy from foil, cool and slice and place in serving casserole. Combine sauce ingredients and pour over meat in casserole; retaste for sweetness (add either more lemon juice, honey or both).

Should have from 3 to 4 cups liquid. Cover and bake at 350° about 45-60 minutes, until fork cuts meat. Serve from casserole.

BARBECUED BEEF BRISKET
Serves 8-10

1 cup ketchup
1 cup chili sauce
1 cup water
½ cup lemon juice
¼ cup brown sugar,
  firmly packed

1 tablespoon
  Worcestershire sauce
1 tablespoon Dijon mustard
1 package onion soup mix
  (1⅜ ounces)
6 pounds fresh beef brisket

In a saucepan, combine ketchup, chili sauce, water, lemon juice, brown sugar, Worcestershire sauce, mustard and onion soup mix. Simmer sauce mixture gently for about 10 minutes to blend flavors. Meanwhile, trim most of the outside covering of fat from the brisket, leaving just a thin layer. Wrap meat in foil adding some of the sauce. Bake at 325° for 3 hours. Then, place meat on the grill of a covered barbecue about 8 inches from medium-low coals. Cover barbecue, adjust the temperature-control dampers and cook until tender, turning and basting to brown evenly. To serve, cut meat across grain in very thin slices. Heat any remaining sauce and serve in a separate bowl to spoon over brisket.

MEAT

COMPANY BRISKET
Serves 8

5-6 pound brisket (double cut or single)
¼ cup melted margarine
salt, pepper, garlic salt, ginger (to taste)

Brush brisket with melted margarine; add ½ of the seasonings. Put meat under broiler just to brown for about 8 minutes. Turn meat over and repeat with more melted margarine and remaining seasonings.

Sauce:
5 onions sliced and sauteed in oil
1 16-ounce can tomato sauce
2 cups beef broth (use cubes and hot water)
1 28-ounce can stewed tomatoes or whole tomatoes
  with liquid
½ cup or more brown sugar
½ cup red or white wine
¼ cup lemon juice

Put meat in pan fat side up. Mix sauce ingredients and pour over brisket. Meat should be almost "drowning" in sauce. Bake at 300° at least 4-5 hours, until a fork goes in easily. Baste every ½ hour or so. Remove meat from gravy and refrigerate. Slice meat when cold. Pour gravy over and between slices. Reheat and serve. Best when made a day ahead.

MEAT

CAPE COD BRISKET
Serves 8

6 pounds first cut brisket
1 package onion soup mix
1 can (1 pound) whole cranberries

Line roasting pan with heavy foil, leaving enough foil to wrap securely. Place brisket on foil. Sprinkle soup mix and cranberries over meat. Seal ends tightly and roast in 350° oven for 3 hours until tender.

FAR EASTERN BEEF STEW
Serves 8

1 tablespoon grated fresh ginger
1 tablespoon ground turmeric
1 teaspoon ground cumin
½ teaspoon salt or to taste
freshly ground pepper to taste
4 pounds boneless chuck, fat removed, cut into 1-inch cubes
1 tablespoon vegetable oil
½ chopped onion
1 teaspoon chopped garlic
3 carrots, sliced
1 cup celery, sliced
1 cup peeled, seeded and diced tomatoes
¾ cup beef stock
½ teaspoon dried thyme
1 bay leaf

Combine ginger, turmeric, cumin, salt, pepper and sprinkle evenly over meat. Heat oil in a heavy casserole and brown meat, turning evenly for about 10 minutes. Discard fat. Add onion,

MEAT

garlic, carrots, celery, and cook for 5 minutes. Add tomatoes, beef stock, thyme, bay leaf and bring stew to a boil. Simmer and cook covered for 1 hour and 45 minutes or until meat is tender. Uncover casserole and continue cooking for 15 minutes, stirring gently until the gravy is reduced to the desired consistency.

HOT GLAZED CORNED BEEF
Serves 6-8

5 pounds corned beef brisket
3 large onions, sliced
2-3 cloves garlic, minced
6 cloves
3 bay leaves
1 tablespoon mustard
⅓ cup light brown sugar

Put beef in a Dutch oven or other heavy overproof casserole with a lid. Cover with cold water. Bring to a boil. Discard water and repeat, adding onions, garlic, cloves, and bay leaves. Cover pot tightly with lid and simmer gently, allowing 50 minutes per pound cooking time. Preheat oven to 350°. Remove meat from pot, drain, and place in a shallow pan, fat side up. Spread top of beef with mustard, and then pack on brown sugar with the back of a tablespoon. Bake 15 - 20 minutes or until well-glazed.

GROUND MEAT, SWEET AND SOUR
Serves 6

2 pounds ground meat
1 head cabbage, shredded
1 can whole cranberry sauce

1 bottle chili sauce

Layer ground meat and shredded cabbage in pyrex dish. Pour cranberry sauce and chili sauce over the top. Bake at 325° for one hour. Spoon over cooked rice or spaghetti.

MEATBALLS AND RICE NOODLES (MAIFUN)
Serves 6

oil
1 onion
2 stalks of celery
1 carrot
3 mushrooms
¼ cup oatmeal or potato starch
1 pound hamburger
1 egg
3 tablespoons tomato ketchup
dash pepper
¼ cup dry red wine
1 clove garlic
¼ teaspoon cinnamon
1 tablespoon powdered soup stock
2 cups maifun (rice noodles or sticks)
boiling water

Saute onion, celery, carrot, mushrooms in oil. Set aside. Mix hamburger with potato starch or oatmeal, egg and ketchup. Form into balls, saute and put into pot with all the remaining ingredients (except for noodles). Simmer for 35 minutes. While meat balls are simmering, pour boiling water over noodles, let sit for 10 minutes. Drain and cut through with scissors, add to cooked meat balls. Correct seasoning to taste.

MEAT

SNAPPY MEAT BALLS
Serves 4-6

2 pounds lean ground beef
1 egg
1 can (16 ounces) crushed pineapple (reserve juice)
salt and pepper to taste
½ teaspoon cloves
¼ teaspoon cinnamon or to taste
3 tablespoons brown sugar
3 tablespoons honey
2 tablespoons soy sauce
1 cup water
juice of 1 lemon
2 medium onions, chopped
4 ginger snaps
1 can (16 ounces) tomato sauce

Mix ground beef with egg, drained pineapple, salt, pepper, cinnamon and cloves. Form into medium sized balls and place in shallow roasting pan; cover and cook ½ hour. Uncover and add brown sugar, honey, soy sauce, pineapple juice, water, lemon juice, onions and ginger snaps. Cook uncovered 25 minutes until sauce is of desired consistency, basting occasionally. Serve with brown or white rice.

MEAT LOAF ELEGANTE
Serves 8

1 pound ground beef
1 pound ground veal
¼ cup uncooked oatmeal or potato flakes
½ grated onion
1 large grated carrot

2 eggs, beaten
1 teaspoon seasoned salt
½ teaspoon ground pepper
¼ cup ketchup or chili sauce (or salsa)
1½ cups cooked rice
½ onion, chopped
¼ cup parsley, chopped
1 medium apple, chopped
½ cup mushrooms
½ teaspoon basil
½ teaspoon thyme

Mix first 9 ingredients. Saute vegetables, apple, mushrooms. Mix with rice and herbs. In bottom of 9 x 13 inch baking dish, layer ½ of the ground meat mixture. Place rice mixture on top and top that with the remainder of the meat mixture. Bake in preheated 350° oven for 45-60 minutes.

Optional: ½ cup of mild salsa may be poured over top after ½ hour of baking.

2 pounds of veal or turkey may be substituted for the above combination.

MEAT

FLANK STEAK DIJON
Serves 4

3 pounds flank steak
4 tablespoons margarine
¼ cup scallions, chopped
2 tablespoons soy sauce
1 teaspoon Dijon wine mustard
dash of ground pepper
¾ cup dry sherry

For best results, the meat should be at room temperature before roasting. Preheat oven to 400°. Spread the flank steak with the 2 tablespoons softened margarine. Place on a rack in a shallow roasting pan and bake, uncovered, for 20 minutes. Meanwhile, saute the scallions in the remaining margarine until tender. Add the soy sauce, mustard and pepper. Stir in the sherry and heat just until boiling. When the meat has baked 20 minutes, pour the sauce over it and bake another 20-25 minutes to serve medium rare. Baste frequently. Remove from oven and let sit for 10 minutes, then carve into slices. Flank steak is sliced very thin across the grain.

FLANK STEAKS EXOTICA
Serves 6

1 medium onion, thinly sliced
½ cup olive oil
5 tablespoons lemon juice
2 tablespoons soy sauce
2 tablespoons fresh parsley, minced
1½ tablespoons fresh ginger, minced
1 tablespoon ground cumin
1 tablespoon chili powder

2 teaspoons dry Sherry
1 teaspoon turmeric
1 teaspoon dried oregano, crumbled
1 teaspoon pepper, coarsely ground
2 large garlic cloves, minced
4 pounds flank steaks
coarse salt
cilantro sprigs

Mix first 13 ingredients in large bowl. Divide marinade mixture between 2 large shallow baking dishes. Add steaks to dishes, turning to coat in marinade. Cover and refrigerate overnight, turning steaks occasionally.

Prepare barbecue (medium-high heat). Remove steaks from marinade. Strain marinade into heavy small saucepan. Season steaks with coarse salt. Grill steaks to desired degree of doneness, about 4 minutes per side for medium-rare. Transfer to platter. Let stand for about 5 minutes.

Meanwhile, bring marinade to boil. Cut steaks diagonally into thin slices. Pour some of marinade over. Garnish with cilantro and serve.

SAUCY FLANK STEAK
Serves 4

1½ pounds flank steak
3 tablespoons toasted sesame seeds
6 tablespoons soy sauce
3 tablespoons sesame oil
3 tablespoons sugar
2 cloves garlic, crushed
3 scallions, sliced
¼ teaspoon pepper

MEAT

Cut steak on bias into thin strips (semi-frozen meat slices easily). Mix all ingredients, marinate 2 hours. Broil until tender.

RED WINE SHORT RIBS
Serves 6

6 large short ribs of beef
1 tablespoon seasoned salt
1 teaspoon garlic powder
2 teaspoons Italian herbs
1 cup Burgundy

Place ribs, fat side up, in a shallow roasting pan. Combine remaining ingredients. Pour over ribs. Roast uncovered in a 325° oven 2½ hours.

BARBECUED LAMB RIBLETS
Serves 4

3 to 4 pounds breast of lamb, cut in ribets
4 cups hot water
1 teaspoon salt
½ teaspoon marjoram
⅛ teaspoon pepper
1 cup tomato catsup
¼ cup prepared mustard
¼ cup vinegar
⅓ cup molasses
¼ teaspoon liquid pepper seasoning

Brown riblets, a few at a time in large kettle. Drain off all fat, return meat to kettle. Add water, salt, marjoram and pepper. Simmer 40 minutes or until meat is tender. Drain. (Save stock to make soup another day.) Combine catsup and remaining ingredients in small bowl. Place riblets in single layer in large shallow pan. Spoon half the catsup mixture over the riblets. Broil 10 minutes, basting often, until meat is brown and glazed. Turn riblets and broil second side, basting with remaining sauce.

BARBECUED OR BROILED LAMB RIBLETS
Serves 4

1 16-ounce jar applesauce (unsweetened)
½ cup chili sauce
2 large garlic cloves, minced
2 tablespoons brown sugar
1 tablespoon lemon juice
1 tablespoon honey
1 tablespoon Worcestershire sauce
½ teaspoon salt
3 pounds lamb riblets, parboiled

Combine all ingredients except lamb. Bruch generously on riblets and grill 25-30 minutes, basting and turning frequently.

MEAT

LAMB SHANKS
Serves 6-8

8 lamb shanks, cracked
1 cup diced onion
1 clove garlic
2 tablespoons oil
1½ cups chopped tomatoes
½ cup green pepper, diced
1 cup celery, diced
½ cup catsup
2 tablespoons brown sugar
1 teaspoon dry mustard
2 cups consomme
1 teaspoon Worcestershire sauce
2 slices lemon
bay leaf, basil and thyme

Brown onion and garlic in oil and add all other ingredients except the shanks. Stir until blended and simmer 10 minutes. Place shanks in open pan in 400° oven to brown. Pour sauce over meat. Bake slowly (300°-325°) for 4 hours, basting often.

MOROCCAN LAMB IN RAISIN SAUCE
Serves 4 - 6

olive oil
2 onions, sliced
4 pounds lamb, cubed
½ cup dry red wine
salt, pepper, garlic, curry to taste
½ box golden raisins

Cover bottom of pan with a bit of olive oil. Add wine, sliced onions, cubed lamb and spices to taste. Cover pot and cook over slow flame until lamb is almost done (very soft). Add raisins and simmer 15 minutes.

Optional: Add slivered almonds or use dried fruits such as pears and apricots.

MEAT

OSSO BUCCO
Serves 6-8

6 pounds veal shanks
¼ cup flour
½ teaspoon salt
¼ teaspoon black pepper
½ cup olive oil
1 medium onion, minced
1 medium carrot, minced
1 stalk celery, minced
2 cloves garlic, minced
1 cup dry white wine
1 cup beef broth
2 1-pound, 13-ounce cans tomatoes, drained
½ teaspoon basil
½ teaspoon rosemary

Gremolata: *2 teaspoons grated lemon peel*
               1 garlic clove, minced
               3 tablespoons parsley, chopped

Have veal shanks sawed into 2 inch pieces and secure each with string. Coat shanks with flour seasoned with salt and pepper. Heat ¼ cup olive oil in heavy skillet. Add shanks, a few pieces at a time and brown well on all sides. While veal is browning, saute onion, carrot, celery and garlic in remaining ¼ cup oil in large casserole or Dutch oven. Cook, stirring occasionally, until vegetables are tender. When veal is browned, arrange on top of vegetables. Place wine, beef broth, tomatoes, basil and rosemary in pan used to brown veal and cook, stirring to loosen any bits and pieces of meat that may have stuck to pan. When mixture boils, incorporate scrapings from bottom of pan, then pour over veal. Cover casserole. Bake at 325° 1½ hours or until veal is very tender. Remove veal to warm platter. Remove strings. Remove fat from surface of pan juices and ladle juices over veal. Sprinkle top with Gremolata and serve with rice, pilaf or pasta.

ROMANIAN TONGUE WITH OLIVES
Serves 8

1 fresh beef tongue
3 tablespoons margarine
2 onions, chopped
1 clove garlic, minced
2 tablespoons flour
½ cup tomato sauce
½ cup dry white wine
2 tablespoons vinegar
½ teaspoon pepper
1 bay leaf
½ teaspoon powdered ginger
1 cup ripe olives

Place tongue in deep saucepan with water to cover and boil until tender (about 3 hours.) Drain, reserving 1½ cups stock. Remove skin and slice tongue into ¼ inch slices. Set aside. Melt margarine, add onions and garlic. Saute 5 minutes stirring carefully. Add flour and mix until smooth. Combine 1½ cups stock, tomato sauce, wine and vinegar. Add to onion mixture gradually, stirring until boiling point is reached. Add pepper, bay leaf, ginger, olives and tongue. Cook over low heat for 15 minutes. Correct seasoning, adding salt if necessary.

MEAT

SALAMI-EGG BAKE
Serves 12

2½ cups salami, chopped
½ cup onion, finely chopped
2 tomatoes, diced
½ cup green pepper, diced
1 teaspoon salt
¼ teaspoon pepper
12 eggs, slightly beaten (or egg substitute)

Mix ingredients thoroughly. Pour into shallow pan about 9 x 13 x 2 inches. Bake in a 350° oven for about 10-12 minutes or until set. Cut into 12 pieces.

ROAST VEAL DIJON
Serves 4

1 small, boned, rolled veal shoulder
½ cup melted margarine
1 8-ounce jar Dijon wine mustard
1 10½-ounce can consomme or 2 tablespoons dried soup
   mix in 10 ounces of water
¼ cup sherry
dried tarragon to taste (optional)
arrowroot or flour (optional)

Preheat oven to 300°. Place meat in a shallow roasting pan. Blend melted margarine and mustard and pour over meat, covering all sides. Roast 2-3 hours. (During the last hour, baste every 20 minutes with a mixture of consomme and sherry.) The meat will carve more easily if you wait 20 to 30 minutes after removing it from the oven, keeping it warm with a loose cover of foil. Make a gravy of the pan juices, thickening, if necessary, with arrowroot or flour. Pass gravy separately with chopped parsley sprinkled on top.

Optional: Marinate veal for a day before cooking. Use a bit of oil, 1/4 cup lemon juice, 1/4 cup white wine, 2 crushed garlic cloves, 1 tablespoon of dry herbs (or 1/4 cup fresh) such as basil, thyme, oregano, salt and pepper. Pour over meat, cover and refrigerate.

VEAL FLAMENCO
Serves 8-10

4 pounds boneless veal, cubed
1/4 cup margarine
1/4 cup olive oil
16 small white onions, peeled
2 teaspoons sugar
2 canned pimientos, chopped
4 carrots, cubed
1 8-ounce can tomato sauce
2 cups dry white wine
1/2 teaspoon salt
minced parsley

Saute veal cubes in mixture of margarine and olive oil. Transfer meat to casserole. Add onions and sugar and cook over low heat until onions are lightly browned. Add pimientos, carrots and saute briefly. Add tomato sauce, white wine, salt and simmer 5 minutes. Add sauce and vegetable to meat in casserole (may be frozen or refrigerated at this point). Return to room temperature before proceeding. Bake at 350° about 3 hours or on top of stove at lowest possible heat until meat is tender. Sprinkle with minced parsley.

MEAT

VEAL a l' ORANGE
Serves 6-8

finely grated peel of 2 oranges
grated peel of ½ lemon
1 teaspoon Dijon-style mustard
1 teaspoon dry chicken bouillon (use powdered bouillon
* or mashed bouillon cube)*
3 pounds boned veal shoulder rolled and tied
½ teaspoon salt
1 tablespoon all-purpose flour
2 tablespoons margarine
½ cup white wine
¼ cup Grand Marnier or other orange liqueur
juice of 2 oranges

Orange Sauce:
1 tablespoon cornstarch
juice of 2 oranges
¼ cup non-dairy whipping cream

fresh parsley sprigs and thinly sliced fresh orange
* for garnish*

Mix together grated orange and lemon peels, mustard, and chicken bouillon. Spread over veal to coat and let stand at room temperature 2 hours. Preheat oven to 350°.

Gently scrape coating from meat and pat meat dry with paper towels. Sprinkle veal lightly with salt and flour. In a skillet, brown roast quickly on all sides in margarine over medium-high heat. Transfer veal to a shallow baking pan and roast 15 minutes. Remove from oven; add white wine, Grand Marnier, and orange juice. Return to oven and continue roasting 1 hour or until tender, basting with pan juices several times. Remove to a carving platter and keep warm.

To prepare Orange Sauce: Combine cornstarch with orange juice; blend until smooth. Pour into hot roasting pan, stirring constantly and scraping up browned bits from the bottom. Bring the mixture to a boil over direct heat. Reduce heat to low and add non-dairy whipping cream, stirring to make a thin sauce.

To serve, thinly slice the veal and arrange in an overlapping pattern on a serving platter. Surround with parsley and orange slices. Pour some of the Orange Sauce over the meat and pass remainder.

VEAL 'N VERMOUTH
Serves 4

¼ pound fresh mushrooms, sliced
3 tablespoons margarine
1 tablespoon olive oil
1 pound scallopini of veal
1 teaspoon garlic salt
1 lemon, thinly sliced
¼ cup dry Vermouth
1 tablespoon fresh parsley, chopped

Saute mushrooms in margarine in heavy frying pan until deep golden; remove and reserve. Add olive oil to pan and brown veal quickly and lightly. Sprinkle with garlic salt during browning. Place lemon slices over veal; add Vermouth. Allow to boil rapidly scraping pan juices and tossing veal to coat with pan gravy. Add mushrooms and toss to heat through. Sprinkle with parsley to serve.

MEAT

VEAL STEW PRIMAVERA
Serves 8-10

2 tablespoons vegetable oil
4 pounds lean veal, cut into 1½ inch cubes
1 teaspoon salt
ground pepper to taste
1½ cups onion, chopped
1½ cups dry white wine
2¼ cups chicken stock
1 pound ripe tomatoes, peeled, seeded and cut into
* ½ inch cubes (about 2 cups) or 1 can stewed tomatoes*
1 bay leaf
½ teaspoon dried thyme or 4 sprigs fresh thyme
¼ cup parsley
4 celery stalks, sliced into ½ inch wide pieces
1 pound carrots, cut into 1½ inch lengths
1 pound small zucchini, cut into 1½ inch lengths
1 eggplant, peeled and cubed (about 3 cups)
¼ cup chopped fresh parsley for garnish

Heat oil in large cast iron pot and brown the veal well on all sides. (If the pot is small, brown the meat in 2 batches.) Add salt, pepper, onion and brown lightly. Add garlic and cook briefly. Do not brown. Add wine and stir. Add stock, tomatoes, bay leaf, thyme and parsley and simmer for 1 hour. Add celery and carrots and cook for 15 minutes. Add remaining vegetables, stir and cook uncovered for the last 10 minutes to reduce the gravy. Skim the surface to remove any fat. Remove bay leaf. Garnish each serving with parsley.

"When the barley is gone from the jar, strife comes lurking at the door."
YIDDISH PROVERB

You can't live on love alone. Remember to stock the pasta, grains and rice and you will always have the basis for a good meal and harmony at home.

Now we know that carbohydrates don't make you fat (watch the sauces); on the contrary, they satisfy without enlarging (some moderation is in order).

Splendid one-dish meals can be based on pasta and rice. Whole countries testify to that. Look at Italy, India and China. Better yet, look back to your mother or grandma. They knew how noodle kugel could anchor (or maybe sink) a meal!

COLORFUL FRIED RICE
Serves 5

4 tablespoons peanut oil
1 egg
2 teaspoons water
1¼ cups sliced fresh shiitake or button mushrooms
1¼ cups small broccoli florets
1¼ cups red bell pepper, chopped
1½ tablespoons minced peeled fresh ginger
¼ cup green onion, thinly sliced (about 5)
3 cups cold cooked long-grain white rice
  (about 1½ cups uncooked)
3 tablespoons soy sauce
additional sauce

Heat 1 tablespoon oil in heavy large nonstick skillet over medium heat. Beat egg with water until well blended. Pour into skillet, tilting to spread egg to thin 10-inch round. Cook until golden and flecked with brown spots, about 1 minute. Release edges and turn "pan-cake" over. Cook until second side is done, about 30 seconds. Transfer egg pancake to work surface and cut into ½ inch wide, 2 inch long strips.

Heat remaining 3 tablespoons oil in same skillet over high heat. Add mushrooms, broccoli, red pepper and ginger. Stir until vegetables are just tender, about 3 minutes. Add green onions and cook 1 minute longer. Add rice and 3 tablespoons soy sauce to skillet. Cook until mixture is thoroughly blended and heated through, stirring almost constantly. Mix in egg strips and season generously with pepper. Pass with additional soy sauce.

PASTA & RICE

ARMENIAN RICE PILAF
WITH APRICOTS AND ALMONDS

¼ cup margarine
1 onion, chopped
⅛ teaspoon ground saffron
¼ teaspoon ground cloves
1½ cups long-grain white rice
3 cups chicken stock or canned broth
½ cup dried apricots, quartered (about 3 ounces)
¼ cup dried currants
½ cup slivered almonds (about 2 ounces), toasted
salt and pepper

Melt margarine in heavy medium saucepan over medium heat. Add chopped onion, ground saffron and cloves and saute 5 minutes. Add rice and stir to coat grains. Mix in stock, dried apricots and currants. Bring to boil. Reduce heat to low. Cover and cook until rice is tender and liquid is absorbed, about 15 minutes. Fluff rice with fork. Add slivered almonds and season to taste with salt and pepper.

BARLEY AND WILD RICE PILAF
6 Servings

4 teaspoons olive oil
1 cup chopped onion
1 cup pearl barley
½ cup wild rice
3 garlic cloves, minced
3 cups water
2 teaspoons salt
1 large red bell pepper, seeded and cut into ½ inch dice

1 cup thinly sliced mushrooms
3 garlic cloves, thinly sliced
1 cup snow peas, julienne

Heat 2 teaspoons olive oil in heavy, large saucepan over low heat. Add chopped onion and saute about 10 minutes. Add barley, wild rice and minced garlic and stir well. Add water and salt and bring to boil. Reduce heat, cover and simmer mixture until grains are tender and water is absorbed, about 1 hour.

Heat remaining oil in large heavy skillet over low heat. Add red pepper and saute about 5 minutes. Add mushrooms and sliced garlic and cook 5 minutes. Add snow peas. Combine vegetables with grains and serve. May be held in warm oven for up to 1 hour.

CONFETTI RICE CASSEROLE

1½ cups cooked brown rice
1 onion, chopped
½ green or red pepper, chopped
½ cup parsley, minced
¼ cup cilantro, minced
7 ounces tofu
1 8-ounce can redicut tomatoes, with or without salsa
1 tablespoon basil and/or oregano
salt and pepper
1 cup Mozzarella cheese, grated

Combine the above ingredients, saving the cheese for the last 10 minutes. Place in a greased 2-quart casserole. Bake at 350° for 50 minutes.

Optional: Chopped broccoli or spinach may be added to mixture.

PASTA & RICE

CHINESE FRIED RICE
4-6 Servings

4 cups cooked rice
¼ cup vegetable oil
2 eggs, lightly beaten
½ cup frozen peas
½ cup water chestnuts, sliced
2 mushrooms, finely chopped
2 tablespoons tamari sauce
1 teaspoon soy sauce
1 teaspoon sesame oil
2 scallions, sliced

Heat oil in deep skillet or wok. Add rice and stir-fry about two minutes. Make a well in the center of the rice, add the eggs, and stir constantly until scrambled. Add remaining ingredients, mix well. Taste and adjust seasonings.

Note: Any vegetables you wish may be used, including carrots, peppers in place of, or in addition to, ingredients called for.

HOLLYWOOD RICE
Serves 12

4 cups water
3 cups long grain rice
3 cups each, low fat Cheddar and Monterey Jack cheese
3 cups hot salsa
3 cups frozen kernel corn
2 cups sour cream (may use light)

Place water and rice in 4 quart heavy casserole. Cover, bring to boil and cook 20 minutes. Cool. Reserve 1 cup each, Cheddar and Monterey Jack cheeses, 1 cup salsa, 1 cup corn. Stir together remaining ingredients and rice. Turn mixture into 4 quart, 2 inch high ovenproof casserole. Top with remaining cheeses, corn, and salsa. Bake uncovered at 350°, 30 minutes until heated through.

CURRIED APRICOT RICE
Serves 8

⅓ **cup mayonnaise**
⅓ **cup plain yogurt**
2 cloves garlic, minced
2 teaspoons lemon juice
2 teaspoons curry powder
½ **teaspoon ground cumin**
1 small jalapeno pepper, finely chopped
1 teaspoon salt
1½ **cups dried apricots, chopped**
½ **cup tart green apple, peeled and diced**
½ **cup celery, chopped**
½ **cup peanuts, chopped**
½ **cup green onions, sliced**
2 tablespoons cilantro, finely chopped
4 cups hot cooked long-grain rice

Combine mayonnaise, yogurt, garlic, lemon juice, curry powder, cumin, pepper and salt. Toss together remaining ingredients and stir gently into hot rice. Add mayonnaise mixture and blend lightly. Chill before serving.

PASTA & RICE

LENTIL RICE STEW
Serves 4-6

3 tablespoons dried green split peas
3 tablespoons dried brown lentils
4 onions, chopped
1 tablespoon oil
4 cups water
1½ cups cooked rice
¼ teaspoon turmeric powder
1 teaspoon pepper
2 tablespoons cilantro leaves, chopped, or
　1¼ teaspoons coriander
2 tablespoons parsley, chopped
3 cloves garlic, crushed
¼ inch fresh ginger root, peeled and ground, or
　1 teaspoon ginger powder
salt to taste
2 tablespoons garbanzo beans
2 to 4 tablespoons lemon juice

Cover the dried peas and dried lentils in water, soak for 4 hours or overnight.

In a skillet, over a low heat, soften the onions in oil. Add water and simmer until about 2 cups of liquid remain. Add soaked lentils and peas. Cook 2 to 3 hours. Drain.

In a large pan, mix together the lentils and peas, onions, cooked rice, turmeric, pepper, cilantro, parsley, garlic, ginger root, salt, and garbanzo beans. Heat. Add lemon juice before serving. May be served hot or at room temperature.

LUSCIOUS RICE PUDDING
Serves 6

1 cup water
½ cup short grain white rice
½ vanilla bean, split
salt
2 cups milk
1 cup heavy cream
½ cup sugar
2 eggs
½ cup raisins
½ teaspoon cinnamon

Bring water to boil in heavy saucepan. Add rice, vanilla bean and salt. Cook 10 minutes. Add milk and cook over very low heat, until rice is tender. Preheat oven to 350°. Butter a shallow 1½ quart baking dish. Combine sugar, cream , eggs and raisins, then fold in rice mixture. Remove the vanilla bean and pour rice mixture into the baking dish. Sprinkle with cinnamon. Place the baking dish into a larger pan in the oven. Pour boiling water into the larger pan to a depth of 1 inch. Bake 30 minutes, or until pudding is firm and the top is golden brown. Cool on a wire rack. Serve at room temperature.

PASTA & RICE

PEPPER AND RICE CASSEROLE
Serves 8

1½ cups brown and wild rice, cooked
2 tablespoons powdered vegetable stock
2 cups Mozzarella cheese, sliced thin
1½ cups spaghetti sauce
2 tablespoons oil or margarine
1 large onion, minced
1 red pepper, thinly sliced
1 green pepper, thinly sliced
½ cup parsley, minced
2 tablespoons oregano
8 ounces fresh mushrooms, sliced

Place cooked rice, prepared with powdered vegetable stock, in bottom of pie pan as in a pie crust. Layer half of sliced cheese and pour over one half of the spaghetti sauce. Sprinkle fresh minced parsley and oregano over sauce. Sauté onion, peppers, mushrooms and place half over sauce. Cover with remaining vegetables and remaining sauce. Layer the rest of cheese on top and bake at 350° uncovered for 45 minutes.

NOODLES 'N RICE
Serves 10

¼ pound margarine
8 ounces fine noodles
1 cup instant rice
1 can sliced water chestnuts
½ pound sliced mushrooms
½ pound pea pods
1 can chicken broth (unsalted)
1 packet onion soup mix mixed with 1 cup water

1 tablespoon soy sauce

Melt margarine and add noodles and rice. Brown. Add rest of ingredients. Bake covered for 45 minutes at 350°.

RICE-NOODLE MELANGE
Serves 8

1 tablespoon chili oil
2 tablespoons sesame oil
2 tablespoons olive oil
1 large onion, diced
2 carrots, sliced
1 red and 1 green pepper, chopped
2 Japanese eggplants, sliced
2 cups broccoli, chopped
1 cut string beans
2 zucchini, chopped
½ cup parsley, chopped
½ cup cilantro, chopped
4 tablespoons soy sauce
½ teaspoon ground pepper
16 ounces wide rice noodles

Heat oils, saute onion, add and saute remaining vegetables. Add remaining ingredients, except for noodles. Add rice noodles that have been cooked for 5 minutes in salted water, and then drained and rinsed in cold water. Heat and serve.

PASTA & RICE

RICE NOODLE GUMBO
Serves 8

1 tablespooon sesame oil
2 tablespoons olive oil (or more as needed)
1 red onion, chopped
2 carrots, chopped
1 red and 1 green pepper, chopped
2 Japanese eggplants, sliced
2 cups broccoli, chopped
2 stalks celery, chopped
½ cup parsley, chopped
½ cup cilantro, chopped (optional)
4 tablespoons soy sauce
½ teaspoon ground pepper
1 tablespoon grated fresh ginger
½ teaspoon chili oil (to taste)
8 ounces ribbon rice noodles cooked in boiling salted water
* according to directions; drained and rinsed in cold water*

Heat oil, saute onions, add vegetables and stir until tender. Add remaining ingredients including rice noodles. Heat and serve.

THREE STAR RICE
Serves 6-8

6 tablespoons butter
1 large onion, chopped
3 cloves garlic, finely chopped
1 teaspoon each - ground cloves, cardamon
* and cinnamon*
1½ cups rice, uncooked
1 cup seedless raisins
½ cup fresh mint leaves, finely chopped

½ cup fresh coriander or cilantro leaves
½ teaspoon ground ginger
pinch of saffron
3 tablespoons lemon juice
½ teaspoon salt
½ cup toasted pine nuts
3½ cups water

In a large saucepan heat the butter and saute the onion and garlic until the onion is golden brown. Stir in the cloves, cardamon, cinnamon and rice. Continue to saute for several minutes. Add the raisins, mint, coriander, ginger and saffron, stirring well. Add 3 ½ cups of water, lemon juice and salt and bring to a boil. Stir with a fork just once and lower the flame. Cover and cook about 20 minutes over a low flame until the liquids are absorbed. Remove from heat and let stand 15 minutes. Fluff with a fork, garnish with nuts and serve hot.

TOFU/RICE SALAD
Serves 6

1 pound quick cooking brown rice
3 bunches green onions, chopped
1 bunch celery, chopped
1 cup mayonnaise
⅓ cup sweet pickle relish
1 8-ounce package tofu
dill to taste
1½-2 cups Red Flame seedless grapes, sliced

Cook rice according to package directions. Cool. Toss with chopped onions and celery. Mix together mayonnaise and sweet pickle relish. Drain tofu well and chop fine. Combine all ingredients and chill.

PASTA & RICE

RICE AND VEGETABLE-STUFFED
CABBAGE BAKED IN WINE
Serves 6-8

1 large head green cabbage
½ teaspoon ground cumin
salt
freshly ground black pepper
2 onions, minced
olive oil
3 cloves garlic, crushed
1 ½ cups finely minced parsley
2 eggs, beaten
1 cup cooked brown or white rice

1 cup cooked peas
1½ cups cooked garbanzo beans
½ teaspoon saffron
3 carrots, sliced
2 onions, sliced
1 whole garlic clove
¾ cup dry white wine
¾ cup vegetable broth

Remove tough outer leaves of cabbage. Wash and shred leaves. Set aside. Cook head of cabbage in large pot of boiling water 10 minutes. Drain in colander and let cool. Gently peel off leaves and spread on paper towels. Sprinkle with cumin and salt and pepper to taste.

Saute minced onions in 2 tablespoons olive oil until tender, about 5 minutes. Transfer to large mixing bowl. Add to bowl crushed garlic, parsley, eggs, rice, peas, garbanzo beans and shredded cabbage leaves. Add saffron and mix thoroughly with hands. Taste to adjust for seasonings.

Take large piece of cheesecloth and place 4 to 5 of largest cabbage leaves in circle at center so that bottoms of leaves overlap. Place stuffing in center at point where leaves overlap, then cover with remaining leaves. Pull up corners of cheesecloth and tie tightly with piece of string to form firm, melon-shaped ball.

Saute carrots, sliced onions and whole garlic in 2 tablespoons olive oil in deep roasting pan 5 minutes. Add wine and broth. Place stuffed cabbage on top of vegetables. Cover with foil and bake at 350° ½ hour, checking to make sure liquid doesn't evaporate. Cabbage is done when knife slides through ball easily.

To serve, place cabbage ball on warm, shallow serving dish. Slice in large wedges. Pour cooking juices over each slice. Note: Serve with sprouted wheat or other hearty bread.

WILD RICE STUFFING
WITH RAISINS AND PINE NUTS
Serves 10

½ cup golden raisins
5 tablespoons Tawny Port
2 small onions, finely chopped
2 carrots, peeled, finely chopped
2 celery stalks, finely chopped
2 cups wild rice
1 teaspoon dried rosemary, crumbled
1 bay leaf, crumbled
½ teaspoon dried thyme, crumbled
3 cups chicken stock or canned broth
½ large Granny Smith apple, peeled, finely chopped
½ cup toasted pine nuts

Combine raisins and Port in small bowl. Let stand 1 hour at room temperature.

Saute onions, carrots and celery in skillet until tender, about 12 minutes. Mix in rice, rosemary, bay leaf and thyme. Add stock. Cover and simmer until rice is tender and liquid is absorbed, stirring occasionally, about 1 hour 15 minutes. (Can be made 1 day ahead. Cover, chill. Bring to room temperature before continuing.)

Preheat oven to 350°. Mix raisin mixture, apple and pine nuts into stuffing. Season with salt and pepper. Transfer to baking dish. Cover and bake until hot, about 20 minutes.

VEGETARIAN BROWN RICE
Serves 6

4 medium-size dried Chinese mushrooms
boiling water
½ pound tofu, cut into ½-inch cubes
2 tablespoons soy sauce
1 tablespoon sesame oil
1 to 2 cups salted or unsalted peanuts, cashews, chopped
* walnuts, or pecans*
8 scallions (white and crisp green parts), sliced into rounds
¼ cup oil
6 stalks bok choy or other Chinese cabbage, sliced on
* thediagonal into ¼-inch strips*
½ cup sliced water chestnuts
4 cups cold cooked brown rice
1 tablespoon hoisin sauce
2 tablespoons soy sauce
4 eggs slightly beaten (or egg substitute)
soy sauce and sesame oil to pass at the table

Place the mushrooms in a small heatproof bowl. Add enough boiling water to cover the mushrooms completely. When they are soft (in about 15 minutes), cut the mushrooms into thin slivers, discarding the stems.

Mix tofu with soy sauce and sesame oil. Place the tofu, nuts, and scallions in separate serving bowls.

In a wok or 12-inch skillet, heat ¼ cup of oil until it is moderately hot, 350-375°. Add bok choy and mushroom slivers, stir constantly for half a minute, then mix in water chestnuts. Now add the rice, stirring to coat grains with oil. When rice is hot, blend in the hoisin and soy sauces; finally, stir in slightly beaten eggs mixing thoroughly. The eggs will coat rice and will cook quickly from the heat of the rice. Serve the hot rice with its accompaniments.

COMPANY ORZO
Serves 4

1 cup orzo (rice-shaped pasta, available at specialty
  foods shops and many supermarkets)
¼ teaspoon crumbled saffron threads
2 teaspoons freshly grated orange zest
2 tablespoons fresh orange juice
3 tablespoons olive oil
⅓ cup dried cherries (available at specialty foods shops)
2 tablespoons slivered almonds, toasted lightly
1 scallion, sliced thin diagonally
3 cups water

In a saucepan boil the orzo in 3 cups boiling water with the saffron for 8 minutes, or until it is al dente, drain it, and refresh it under cold water. In a bowl stir together the zest, the orange juice, and salt to taste, add the oil in a stream, whisking, and whisk the dressing until it is emulsified. In a bowl toss the orzo, drained well, with the dressing and stir in the cherries, the almonds, and the scallion. Serve the orzo at room temperature.

PASTA & RICE

COUSCOUS 4 U
Serves 4

1 ½ tablespoons unsalted butter
½ teaspoon salt
1 cup couscous
⅓ cup pine nuts, toasted lightly
¼ cup minced fresh parsley leaves
⅓ cup thinly sliced scallion
1 tablespoon white wine vinegar
1 ½ cups water

In a saucepan combine the butter, the salt, and 1½ cups water, bring the liquid to a boil, and stir in the couscous. Let the couscous stand, covered, off the heat for 5 minutes, fluff it with a fork, and stir in the pine nuts, the parsley, the scallion, and the vinegar. The couscous may be made 6 hours in advance and kept covered and chilled. Reheat before serving.

ISRAELI COUSCOUS
Serves 8

¾ cup vegetable oil
1 ½ pounds lamb, cubed
3 pounds chicken, cut up
3 large onions, chopped
3 large tomatoes, chopped
1 large green pepper, sliced thin
freshly ground pepper to taste
2 teaspoons turmeric
2 teaspoons kosher salt
½ teaspoon allspice
1 cup water
10 ounces fresh or frozen peas, cooked

1 pound chick-peas, cooked
1 package frozen artichoke hearts
½ pound bulgur wheat, cooked

Heat oil in deep oven-proof pot. Add lamb and chicken, brown. Remove meat, saute onions; add tomatoes and cook 10 minutes. Add green peppers, spices and water. Return meat. Cover and bake 1 hour at 350°. Add peas, chick-peas and artichoke hearts. Cook ½ hour more or until done.   Place bulgur wheat on large serving platter and spoon meat mixture over it.   Let stand 5 minutes to blend.

ITALIAN POLENTA
Serves 6-8

1 cup cornmeal
1 cup cold water
2 cups boiling water
1 teaspoon salt
¾ to 1 cup milk
1 tablespoon butter
pinch fine herbs
pinch minced garlic
pinch nutmeg
Parmesan cheese and melted butter for top

Mix cornmeal and cold water in pot suitable for microwave oven. Add boiling water and salt. Microwave 3 to 4 minutes uncovered, stirring occasionally (2 to 3 times). Remove from oven. Cover for 2 minutes. Add milk, cheese, butter and herbs. Blend. Pour into buttered dish. (Can be done ahead.)

To serve, bake covered 325° about ½ hour or until hot. Sprinkle on Parmesan cheese (freshly grated if possible) and some additional melted butter before serving.

PASTA & RICE

BAKED GNOCCHI
Serves 8-10

1 stick (½ cup) unsalted butter, cut into bits
1 cup water
1 cup plus 2 tablespoons milk
1 tablespoon salt
½ teaspoon freshly ground black pepper
½ teaspoon freshly grated nutmeg
2½ cups all-purpose flour, sifted
8 large eggs
1 cup heavy cream
¾ cup plus 2 tablespoons freshly grated Parmesan

In large saucepan combine butter, water, milk, salt, pepper, and nutmeg. Bring the mixture just to a boil, stirring until the butter is melted, and add the flour, all at once, stirring briskly with a wooden spatula until the mixture pulls away from the side of the pan and forms a ball. Transfer the mixture to a large bowl, let it cool for 5 minutes, and stir in the eggs, 1 at a time, incorporating each egg completely before adding the next.

In another large saucepan bring 6 inches of salted water to a simmer. Drop walnut size ovals of the paste into the water, a few at a time, simmer them uncovered, for 5 to 7 minutes, or until they are cooked through, and transfer them as they are cooked with a slotted spoon to a large bowl of ice and cold water. Transfer the gnocchi with the slotted spoon to a large colander and let them drain well. Arrange the gnocchi in one layer in a buttered 2 quart gratin dish, pour the cream over them, and sprinkle the gnocchi with the Parmesan. Bake the gnocchi in the middle of a preheated 425° oven for 10 minutes and broil them under a preheated broiler about 4 inches from the heat for 1 to 2 minutes, or until they are browned lightly.

NOODLES IN ADVANCE
Serves 6-8

1 (8-ounce) package noodles
4 tablespoons butter or margarine
½ cup slivered almonds
3 tablespoons poppy seeds
2 tablespoons lemon juice
dash cayenne pepper
butter or margarine

Cook noodles and drain. Melt butter, add almonds, and brown quickly. Add poppy seeds and lemon juice. Place noodles in ovenproof dish in which they will be served. Pour the butter mixture over the noodles and toss gently. Sprinkle lightly with pepper. Dot with butter. Cover with aluminum foil. This can be done well before guests arrive. Bake in 400° oven for 30 minutes.

NOODLE PUDDING WITH BROCCOLI
Serves 6

8 ounces medium width noodles
1 package frozen chopped broccoli (10 ounces) thawed and drained
3 eggs, beaten
1 cup non-dairy creamer
1 envelope onion soup mix
2 ounces melted margarine

Cook noodles, drain and set aside. Mix broccoli, eggs, soup mix and non-dairy creamer. Add noodles and margarine and bake at 350° for 45 minutes to 1 hour.

SPINACH NOODLE SALAD
Serves 8

1 package spinach noodles, cooked until just tender; drain
1 bottle Italian salad dressing
2 2-ounce jars sliced pimientos, drained
1 small can sliced black olives, drained
1 cup sliced fresh mushrooms
1 small green pepper, cut into thin slices
2 cups raw broccoli flowerettes
2 cups raw zucchini cut into thin rounds
grated Parmesan cheese, as desired

Place cooked noodles, cut if desired, in large mixing bowl. Gently toss with dressing. Mix in vegetables. Add cheese to taste. Toss. Cover and refrigerate overnight to combine flavors.

BEST YET NOODLE PUDDING
Serves 15 - 20

1 pound medium noodles, cooked and drained
½ cup butter
7 eggs, beaten
1 cup sugar
3 cups milk
2 cups small curd cottage cheese
2 cups sour cream
1 cup sliced apples
1½ teaspoon vanilla
1 cup golden raisins
lemon juice to taste

Topping:
½ cup cornflake crumbs

1 teaspoon cinnamon
1 teaspoon sugar
butter

Place hot noodles in large mixing bowl. Stir in butter until melted and noodles are well coated. Add all remaining ingredients except ingredients for topping. Spoon into large greased baking pan. Cover and refrigerate overnight. Combine crumbs with cinnamon and sugar. Set aside. When ready to bake, dot noodle pudding with butter. Top with crumb mixture. Bake at 350° for 1 ½ hours.

Optional:
Omit the milk and 1 egg and add 2 large green apples, peeled and grated.

SAVORY ORIENTAL NOODLES
Serves 4

water
1 tablespoon peanut oil
½ pound Chinese egg noodles
1 tablespoon sesame seed oil
1 cup bean sprouts

Boil water, adding enough for the noodles. Add the peanut oil to the boiling water and boil noodles for 3 to 5 minutes. Stir occasionally. Drain and rinse in cold water. Cut noodles into 6-inch pieces. Mix noodles with sesame seed oil, set aside. Rinse bean sprouts, drain on paper towel to dry. Set aside.

Sauce:
2 tablespoons tahina
2 tablespoons dark soy sauce

1 tablespoon brewed tea
½ tablespoon red wine vinegar
½ tablespoon chili oil
½ tablespoon sesame seed oil
½ teaspoon sugar
1 clove garlic, minced
1 teaspoon ginger root, freshly ground
2 scallions, chopped

In a bowl, mix tahina, soy sauce and tea and blend thoroughly. Add vinegar, sesame and chili oils, sugar, garlic, ginger and scallions. Combine all ingredients well. When ready to serve, add bean sprouts to the noodles. Mix sauce once again and pour over noodles. Toss until coated.

Variations: Substitute 1 cup sliced chicken (white part only), for bean sprouts. Substitute all tahina for equal parts of tahina and peanut butter. Blend both together thoroughly.

THAI NOODLES AND ASPARAGUS
IN PEANUT SAUCE
Serves 6

Peanut Sauce:
1½ tablespoons minced ginger root
1 tablespoon minced garlic
1 tablespoon red wine vinegar
1 tablespoon brown sugar
6 tablespoons chunky peanut butter
¼ cup soy sauce
2 tablespoons Chinese chili paste
1 teaspoon sugar
2 tablespoons vegetable oil
½ cup vegetable stock

3 green onions, minced

Combine ingredients and process well until dressing is creamy. Do not refrigerate. Blend well again before pouring over noodles and asparagus.

Noodles and Asparagus:
8 ounces linguine or spaghettini
1 pound asparagus
5 tablespoons sesame seeds, toasted
4 scallions, cut into 2 inch julienne
2 small pickling cucumbers, peeled
1 cup carrots, shredded

Cook pasta in boiling water until al dente, drain and place in large bowl. Add sauce and 4 tablespoons sesame seeds. Toss well. Arrange asparagus, scallions, carrots and cucumbers over the top and sprinkle with remaining sesame seeds. Serve at room temperature.

PASTA SALAD
Serves 8-10

1 pound package fusili pasta, cooked and drained
1 9-ounce package frozen peas
cucumber, red onion, Italian tomatoes and bell pepper,
  chopped in desired amounts
black olives and pimiento, chopped (optional)
Italian salad dressing
pepper
herb seasoning to taste

Toss pasta and vegetables with dressing. Add pepper and herb seasoning. Cover and chill at least 4 hours.

PASTA & RICE

PASTA PESTO
Serves 6-8

1 pound narrow noodles
1 cup fresh basil leaves, washed and dried
2 large garlic cloves, peeled and chopped
½ cup pine nuts
½ cup olive oil
½ cup grated Parmesan cheese
⅛ cup grated Romano cheese
¼ cup cream
salt and pepper to taste

To make pesto sauce, combine basil, nuts and garlic in blender; add oil. Shut off motor and add cheeses, salt and pepper. Cook noodles in water according to package instructions. Save 2 tablespoons of the pasta water and mix with pesto sauce. Add ¼ cup cream. Drain noodles. Stir in pesto sauce and mix well.

BROCCOLI PESTO LINGUINE
Serves 6-8

2 cups small broccoli florets
½ cup coarsely chopped basil leaves
2 large cloves garlic, chopped
¼ cup pine nuts, toasted
½ teaspoon salt, ¼ teaspoon pepper
¾ cup extra virgin olive oil
½ cup grated Parmesan cheese
1 pound linguine, cooked al dente

Place broccoli in processor. Add basil, garlic, pine nuts, salt, pepper and oil. Process until smooth. Add cheese. Serve over hot pasta.

Note: This pesto is milder than one made with all basil leaves, you may want to add more basil. Pesto can be refrigerated in a tightly covered jar for a week covered with a thin film of oil.

PASTA WITH PESTO SAUCE, MACADAMIA NUTS
AND ROASTED PEPPERS
Serves 4

3 cups loosely packed fresh basil leaves (about 2 ounces)
1 cup olive oil
¾ cup roasted macadamia nuts (3 ounces)
6 garlic cloves, minced
1¼ cups freshly grated Parmesan cheese (about 5
   ounces)
2 large red bell peppers
1 pound linguine
2 tablespoons olive oil
chopped macadamia nuts
additional grated Parmesan

Puree first 4 ingredients in processor. Transfer sauce to large bowl. Stir in 1¼ cups Parmesan cheese. Season pesto to taste with salt and pepper. (Can be prepared 1 week ahead. Transfer to jar. Pour enough additional oil over pesto to cover completely. Cover and refrigerate. Pour off extra oil before using.)

Char peppers over gas flame or in broiler until blackened. Wrap in paper bag and let steam 15 minutes. Peel and seed; slice peppers thinly.

Cook linguine in large pot of boiling salted water until just tender but still firm to bite, stirring occasionally. Drain well. Return to same pot and mix with 2 tablespoons olive oil. Add all ingredients.

PASTA & RICE

TUNA-TOPPED PASTA
Serves 2

3 tablespoons olive oil
1 8- to 10- ounce 1-inch-thick fresh tuna steak
3 large garlic cloves, minced
1 anchovy fillet, chopped
1 16-ounce can Italian tomatoes with juices
6 ounces spaghettini
¼ cup chopped pitted imported brine-cured olives (such
*   as Kalamata)*
¼ cup chopped fresh Italian parsley

Heat 1 tablespoon oil in heavy medium skillet over medium-high heat. Season tuna with salt and pepper. Add tuna to skillet and sear until almost cooked through, about 3 minutes per side. Transfer tuna to plate. Reduce heat to medium. Add remaining 2 tablespoons oil, garlic and anchovy to skillet and saute until fragrant, about 1 minute. Add tomatoes and cook until reduced to sauce consistency, breaking up tomatoes with back of spoon, about 12 minutes.

Meanwhile, cook pasta in large pot of boiling salted water until just tender but still firm to bite. Drain well. Transfer pasta to large bowl.

Add olives and parsley to sauce and simmer 1 minute. Cut tuna into ¾ inch pieces and add to sauce with any accumulated juices. Simmer until tuna is just cooked through, stirring frequently, about 1 minute. Season sauce to taste with salt and pepper. Spoon sauce over pasta and toss to coat.

PASTA SALAD WITH ROASTED EGGPLANT, PEPPER AND PINE NUTS
Serves 8

2 pounds eggplant (1 large eggplant)
3 tablespoons red wine vinegar
2 large green peppers, cut in half and seeded
4-5 plum tomatoes, chopped
6 ounces medium sized pasta, cooked and drained
⅓ cup finely minced parsley
6 tablespoons olive oil
3 cloves garlic, finely minced
⅛ teaspoon hot pepper sauce
2 tablespoons toasted pine nuts
black pepper to taste

Trim eggplant and cut in half lengthwise. Place on broiler pan lined with aluminum foil and broil 2 inches from heat, skin side up, for 5 minutes. Turn over and sprinkle with 1 tablespoon of vinegar. Add the green pepper halves, skin side up. Continue to broil for 15 minutes until the surfaces of both vegetables are charred and blistered. Remove eggplant and peppers and let cool. Peel eggplant and cut into ¾ inch cubes. Rub off the skin of the peppers and cut into ½ inch pieces. Put in a large bowl along with chopped tomatoes, drained pasta and parsley. Toss gently. In a small bowl, mix remaining 2 tablespoons vinegar, oil, garlic and hot pepper sauce. Pour over salad and toss again. Sprinkle with pine nuts and fresh black pepper. Serve at room temperature.

PASTA & RICE

PASTA ET AL
Serves 6-8

½ cup finely chopped parsley leaves
1 garlic clove, minced
2 medium onions, minced
4 radishes, minced
2 carrots, minced
1 large leek, minced (white part only)
⅓ cup basil leaves (fresh) or 1 teaspoon dried
3 tablespoons butter
3 tablespoons oil
1 cup finely chopped radicchio
4 tomatoes, peeled and diced
2 small zucchini, sliced
1 cup clear vegetable broth
½ cup sliced green pepper
1 (1-pound) box linguine, cooked according to package directions
freshly grated cheese

Combine parsley, garlic, onions, radishes, carrots, leek and basil. Heat the butter and oil in a large pot. Add vegetable mix and simmer until soft. Add the radicchio, tomatoes, zucchini and broth. Simmer, covered, for ½ hour. Add the green pepper and simmer a few minutes more. Serve heated over hot linguine with lots of freshly grated cheese.

HEAVENLY ANGEL'S HAIR
Serves 8

1 pound capellini (angel hair pasta)
3 tablespoons unsalted butter, cut into bits and softened
1½ cups freshly grated Parmesan

232

1½ cups heavy cream
½ teaspoon salt, or to taste
¾ teaspoon white pepper

In a large kettle of boiling salted water, cook the pasta for 4 minutes, or until it is al dente, drain it well, and return it to the kettle. To the kettle, add the butter, tossing the pasta well, stir in the Parmesan, cream, salt, and pepper, and spread the mixture evenly in a buttered 13 x 9 inch baking dish or 8 buttered 1-cup ramekins. Bake the flan in the middle of a preheated 400° oven for 20-30 minutes, or until the top is golden. Serve the flan cut into squares or, if using ramekins, unmold the flans carefully onto dinner plates.

FETTUCCINE PRIMAVERA
WITH MARINARA SAUCE
Serves 8

Sauce:
5 cups tomato sauce
2 cups water
½ cup dry red wine
3 cups finely chopped onions
2 cloves garlic, minced
1 teaspoon dried oregano, crushed
1 teaspoon dried basil, crushed
¼ teaspoon rosemary, crushed
¼ teaspoon thyme, crushed
1 dried bay leaf, crumbled
freshly ground black pepper, to taste
½ teaspoon salt
½ teaspoon sugar

PASTA & RICE

Pasta:
1 cup pine nuts
1 pound fettuccine, cooked
8 cups fresh vegetables (cauliflower, broccoli, carrots,
*   zucchini, etc.)*
2 cups freshly grated Parmesan cheese
fresh basil (chopped and whole leaves for garnish)

Combine all sauce ingredients and bring to a boil. Reduce heat and simmer 2 hours uncovered. (Makes 1 quart.)

Toast pine nuts in a 350° oven until lightly browned, about 10 minutes. Watch carefully to avoid burning. Set aside.

Cut vegetables into florets or julienned pieces. Steam until crisp-tender. Drain and refresh immediately with cold water. (Reheat pasta and vegetables by dipping into boiling water when ready to serve.)

For each serving, place 1 cup pasta on a warm serving plate and top with hot marinara sauce. Add 1 cup vegetables and sprinkle with ¼ cup cheese. Top with 2 tablespoons pine nuts and garnish with chopped basil and 1 whole basil leaf.

MANICOTTI
Serves 4-6

1 package manicotti noodles
2 tablespoons extra virgin olive oil
1 12-ounce carton Ricotta cheese
2 packages frozen, chopped spinach, thawed and drained
1 tablespoon garlic powder
1 teaspoon nutmeg
1 teaspoon pepper

3 cups spaghetti sauce, bottled or homemade
sliced mushrooms
mixed Italian seasoning
4 ounces grated Parmesan cheese

Cook noodles al dente according to package directions. Add olive oil to cool water and let noodles rest. The oil will prevent the noodles from sticking together. Combine Ricotta cheese, spinach, garlic powder, nutmeg and pepper. Stuff cheese mixture equally into cooked noodles. Place filled pasta in greased 9 x 13 inch casserole dish. Cover with sauce, mushrooms and sprinkle with Italian seasoning. Top with Parmesan cheese. Cover with foil and bake at 350° for 45 minutes. Uncover and bake an additional 15 to 30 minutes.

RAVIOLI WITH PESTO CREAM SAUCE
Serves 4

3 tablespoons butter
½ cup sliced mushrooms
2 tablespoons minced garlic
2 cups packed fresh spinach leaves
1 cup half and half
¼ cup chopped drained oil-packed sun-dried tomatoes
1 9-ounce package ravioli with basil and cheese
   or cheese tortellini
½ cup freshly grated Parmesan cheese (about 1½ ounces)
salt and pepper
¼ cup chopped fresh basil or 2 teaspoons dried, crumbled
3 tablespoons toasted pine nuts

Melt butter in heavy large skillet over medium heat. Add mushrooms and garlic and saute until mushrooms are tender, about 5 minutes. Add spinach and cook until wilted. Add cream and sun-dried tomatoes and boil until thickened to sauce consistency, stirring occasionally, about 6 minutes.

Meanwhile, cook ravioli in large pot of boiling water until just tender but still firm to bite. Drain.

Add ravioli and grated Parmesan cheese to sauce in skillet and stir over medium heat until heated through. Season to taste with salt and pepper. Mix in basil and toasted pine nuts.

BEST GUEST LASAGNE
Serves 12

8 ounces lasagne noodles
2 10-ounce packages frozen spinach, chopped
3 cups thick spaghetti sauce (from a mix, canned or
*   homemade)*
4 eggs
2 cups creamed cottage cheese
6 tablespoons minced green onion
2 tablespoons minced parsley
1½ teaspoons salt
1 pound Mozzarella cheese, thinly sliced
½ cup shredded Parmesan cheese

Cook noodles according to package directions adding 2 tablespoons butter or oil to water; drain. Cook spinach according to package directions; drain thoroughly. Cover bottom of 13 x 9 x 2 inch dish with thin layer of sauce. Beat eggs in medium bowl; blend in cottage cheese, spinach, green onion, parsley and salt. In baking dish, layer in order half the following: noodles, cottage cheese mixture, Mozzarella slices and sauce. Repeat with remaining ingredients topping with noodles, sauce and Parmesan cheese. Bake at 350°, 35 minutes or until bubbly. Let stand 10 minutes or more before cutting.

SPINACH LASAGNA
Serves 4-6

1 cup onions, chopped
8 ounces fresh mushrooms, sliced
1 tablespoon oil
4 cups tomatoes, crushed
1 can tomato paste (6 ounces)
1 teaspoon garlic powder
½ teaspoon salt
⅛ teaspoon pepper
1 teaspoon parsley flakes
1 teaspoon oregano, crushed
1 tablespoon Worcestershire sauce
1 package frozen, chopped spinach, thawed and drained
1 pound Ricotta cheese
¾ cup Parmesan cheese
1 package (8 ounces) lasagna noodles
12 ounces Mozzarella cheese

Saute onions and mushrooms in oil in a large saucepan. Add tomatoes, tomato paste, garlic powder, salt, pepper, parsley, oregano and Worcestershire sauce. Simmer uncovered for 30 minutes or until mixture thickens. In a small bowl combine spinach, Ricotta and Parmesan cheeses. Arrange ½ of the uncooked noodles in the bottom of an oiled baking pan. Top with ½ of tomato sauce, ½ or the spinach mixture and ½ of the Mozzarella cheese. Repeat the layers. Cover with foil and bake at 350° for 40 minutes. Remove foil and bake an additional 15 minutes. Remove from oven and let stand for 15 before cutting.

PASTA & RICE

LASAGNA SURPRISE
Serves 8

2 large green peppers
3 large red peppers
1 pound eggplant
3 zucchini, trimmed
1 jar (15 ounce) marinara sauce
4 flat anchovy fillets
1 clove garlic, crushed
⅓ cup olive oil
1 container (15 ounce) part-skim Ricotta cheese
1 package (8 ounce) Mozzarella cheese, shredded
salt and pepper to taste

Halve, core and seed peppers. Place skin side up on baking sheet; brush lightly with salad oil. Broil 3 to 4 inches from heat until blackened, about 10 minutes. With tongs, transfer peppers to plastic bag; close bag tightly. Let stand 10 minutes.

Meanwhile, pare eggplant; cut crosswise into ¼-inch-thick slices. Spread in a single layer on clean baking sheet. Set aside. Cut zucchini lengthwise into ¼-inch-thick slices. Arrange in a single layer on another baking sheet. Brush eggplant and zucchini lightly with salad oil; sprinkle with ½ teaspoon each pepper and salt, dividing evenly. Broil vegetables until browned on both sides, about 4 minutes in all. Set aside.

Preheat oven to 375°. Remove skin from peppers; cut each half lengthwise into 3 slices. Set aside.

In bottom of 12 x 8 x 2-inch baking dish, spread ¼ cup marinara sauce. Top with eggplant, overlapping slices slightly. In a small bowl, mash anchovies with garlic and olive oil to form a paste; spread ⅓ of mixture over eggplant. Spread half the ricotta on top;

sprinkle with ⅓ of Mozzarella. Spread ¼ cup sauce on top; arrange peppers evenly over sauce. Dot with half of remaining anchovy mixture and the remaining Ricotta; sprinkle with half of Mozzarella; spread ¼ sauce on top; arrange zucchini, overlapping slightly over all. Dot with remaining anchovy mixture. Cover with remaining sauce; sprinkle with remaining Mozzarella. Bake 45 minutes, until hot and bubbly.

TOFU LASAGNA
Serves 4-6

1 box of lasagna noodles, cooked (7 ounces)
1 onion, chopped
2 stalks celery, diced
1 red pepper, diced
2 tablespoons oil
1 container tofu
½ cup Ricotta or N.Y. pot cheese, mixed together
*   with tofu*
1 teaspoon ground pepper
1 teaspoon oregano (or Italian herbs)
½ teaspoon seasoned salt
½ cup of prepared spaghetti sauce

Topping:
½ cup grated Jack or Cheddar cheese
½ cup grated Mozzarella cheese
1½ cups spaghetti sauce

Sauté vegetables in oil. Make alternate layers lasagna noodles, vegetables and tofu-cheese mixture. After final layer of noodles, pour spaghetti sauce over all and add grated cheese topping. Bake 1 hour in 350° oven in 12 x 8 inch pan.

PASTA & RICE

ZUCCHINI LASAGNA
Serves 8

Tomato sauce:
2 cups chopped onion
3 large cloves garlic
3½ cups Italian tomatoes,
    undrained and mashed
2 6-ounce cans tomato paste
2 cups water
2 tablespoons dry sherry
2 tablespoons olive oil
1 bay leaf
½ teaspoon salt
¼ teaspoon pepper
½ teaspoon oregano
¼ teaspoon basil

Noodles:
1 8-ounce package lasagna
    noodles, cooked
5-6 zucchini sliced
16 ounces Ricotta cheese
1 cup low-fat cottage cheese
1 cup Parmesan cheese
¾ pound Mozzarella cheese,
    sliced
2 tablespoons fresh parsley
½ teaspoon basil
¼ teaspoon thyme
¼ teaspoon rosemary

Sauce:
Saute onion and garlic in oil for 1-2 minutes. Add sherry, simmer until water evaporates. Mix tomatoes, tomato paste, water and seasonings. Add to saucepan and simmer uncovered 1 hour, stirring occasionally. Sauce should be thick. Makes 6 cups. Can be doubled and frozen.

Noodles:
Mix together Ricotta, cottage cheese, herbs and seasonings. In 10 x 13 inch pan, alternately layer noodles, cheese, herbs and seasonings, sliced zucchini, tomato sauce, and Mozzarella. Repeat twice with Parmesan on top. Bake in 350° oven for 45 minutes until bubbly.

SUN DRIED TOMATO SPAGHETTINI
Serves 6

1 pound spaghettini
¼ cup oil
1 large onion, chopped
3 ribs celery, chopped fine
3 carrots, chopped fine
4 cloves garlic, minced
1 28-ounce can tomatoes, undrained
¾ cup sun dried tomatoes in oil, chopped or cut
1 cup dry white wine
¼ cup fresh basil, julienne
2 tablespoons grated Parmesan cheese

Heat oil in large, heavy saucepan. Add onion, celery, carrots, garlic and saute 20 minutes. Stir in canned tomatoes, sun dried tomatoes and wine, simmer for 1 hour uncovered. Stir occasionally. Process sauce on pulse mode until blended but not smooth. Pour over hot pasta, garnish with basil. Serve with fresh grated Parmesan cheese.

PENNE FOR TWO
Serves 2

1 pound Swiss chard, stems cut from the leaves and the stems
  and leaves chopped separately
⅛ teaspoon dried red hot pepper flakes, or to taste
3 large garlic cloves, sliced thin
2 tablespoons olive oil
½ cup water
salt and pepper to taste
1 cup drained canned tomatoes, chopped
½ pound penne or other tubular pasta

¼ **cup freshly grated Parmesan plus additional as an accompaniment**

Rinse and drain separately the Swiss chard stems and leaves. In a large heavy skillet cook the red pepper flakes and the garlic in the oil over moderate heat, stirring until the garlic is pale golden; add the stems and ¼ cup of water, and cook the mixture, covered, for 5 minutes, or until the stems are just tender. Add the leaves with the remaining ¼ cup water, salt and pepper to taste and cook the mixture covered, for 3 minutes, or until the leaves are tender.

While the chard is cooking, in a kettle of salted boiling water boil the penne until it is al dente and drain it in a colander. In a large bowl toss the penne with the chard mixture and ¼ cup of the Parmesan and serve it with the additional Parmesan.

CHEESE BAKE
Serves 6

Batter:	Filling:
1 cup margarine	1½ pounds cottage cheese
½ cup sugar	3 tablespoons margarine,
4 eggs	melted
1½ cups flour	1 egg
4 tablespoons baking powder	2 tablespoons sugar
1 tablespoon salt	

Put half of batter on bottom of pan, (make sure it's not liquidy); flatten out. Put cheese filling in middle, then batter. Bake at 325° for 1 hour until it's a little brown on top. It comes out like a very fluffy cake with cheese melted in it.

This is a side dish, not a dessert.

POULTRY

"If a pauper dines on a chicken,
either he is sick or the chicken was."
YIDDISH PROVERB

Times change.
Chicken is no longer the exclusive province of the affluent. Poultry is now readily available, well priced, low in cholesterol (minus the skin) and as always, delicious. The big problem is which great recipe to try first. So go catch a free-wheeling range-bird (our ancestors had the right idea) and start cooking the whole or its parts.

ALMOND CHICKEN STIR FRY
Serves 4-6

1 cup whole almonds
3 tablespoons peanut oil
½ cup chopped scallions
4 boneless chicken breasts, skinned and sliced
8 ounces bamboo shoots, drained
6 ounces water chestnuts, drained
1 English cucumber, thinly sliced
½ cup chicken stock
2 teaspoons dry sherry or Chinese cooking wine
1 teaspoon grated ginger root
1 teaspoon soy sauce
½ teaspoon cornstarch
1 tablespoon water
dash salt
dash red pepper

Preheat oven to 400°. Place almonds in a shallow pan and brown in oven, stirring often, 12 to 15 minutes. Chop half the almonds. Set aside.

Heat oil in wok until oil just begins to smoke. Add scallions and stir fry 1 minute. Add half the chicken; stir fry 1 minute. Add remaining chicken and repeat. Stir in bamboo shoots, water chestnuts, and chopped almonds, tossing mixture 1 minute. Repeat with cucumber.   Add stock, sherry, ginger, and soy sauce. Stir and heat 1 minute.

In a small bowl, mix cornstarch with a tablespoon of water. Stir mixture slowly into wok. Add salt and pepper, and stir until liquid thickens, about 2 minutes. Turn onto a warmed serving platter and top with whole almonds. Serve over rice or noodles.

POULTRY

CHICKEN MARENGO
Serves 6-8

6 chicken breasts, skinned, boned and cut into bite-size
  pieces
½ cup flour
1 teaspoon tarragon
salt and pepper to taste
2 tablespoons margarine
2 tablespoons oil
½ cup white wine
1 16-ounce can chopped tomatoes
12 mushrooms, sliced
1 2-ounce can sliced black olives
1 small clove garlic, minced
fresh parsley (for garnish)

Combine flour with tarragon, salt and pepper. Coat chicken pieces with flour mixture. Heat oil and margarine and brown chicken. Place pieces in casserole. Add wine, tomatoes, mushrooms, olives, and garlic. Bake covered in 350° oven for 20 minutes. Remove cover and bake additional 20 minutes.

CHICKEN BITES EN BROCHETTE
Serves 16

vegetable cooking spray
¼ cup minced onion
½ teaspoon crushed, dried red pepper
2 tablespoons brown sugar
½ teaspoon coarsely ground black pepper
3 tablespoons white wine vinegar
3 tablespoons low-sodium soy sauce
3 tablespoons dry sherry
4 pounds boned, skinned chicken breasts
2 small red bell peppers, each cut into 16 (1-inch) pieces
2 teaspoons sesame seeds, divided

Coat a small skillet with vegetable cooking spray; place over medium heat until hot. Add minced onion and crushed red pepper; saute 3 minutes or until tender. Remove from heat. Stir in brown sugar, black pepper, white wine vinegar, soy sauce, and sherry. Set aside.

Place each piece of chicken between 2 sheets of heavy-duty plastic wrap. Flatten to about ¼-inch thickness, using a meat mallet or rolling pin. Cut chicken into 64 (1-inch) pieces; place in a bowl. Add onion mixture; toss well. Cover and marinate in refrigerator 3 hours, stirring occasionally.

Drain chicken, reserving marinade. Thread 4 chicken pieces and 2 bell pepper pieces onto each of the 16 (8-inch) wooden skewers. Place 8 skewers on a rack of a broiler pan coated with cooking spray; place rack on a broiler pan. Brush with reserved marinade, and sprinkle evenly with ½ teaspoon sesame seeds. Broil 3 to 4 inches from heat 2 minutes. Turn skewers, brush with marinade, and sprinkle evenly with ½ teaspoon sesame seeds. Broil an additional 2 minutes or until chicken is done. Repeat procedure with remaining ingredients. Serve warm.

POULTRY

CHICKEN BREASTS WITH
CHUNKY PEANUT SAUCE & ORIENTAL SALAD
Serves 4

2 boneless chicken breast halves
2 tablespoons soy sauce
1 tablespoon vegetable oil
1 teaspoon minced fresh ginger
2 green onions (white and green parts, sliced)

Place chicken in small baking pan. Pour soy sauce and oil over it. Sprinkle with ginger. Turn to coat. Let stand 20 minutes. Preheat oven to 450°. Roast chicken until just cooked through, about 20 minutes. While chicken is cooking, prepare sauce.

Sauce:
6 tablespoons chunky peanut butter (do not use freshly ground or old-fashioned style)
½ cup low-salt chicken broth
1 tablespoon brown sugar
1 tablespoon soy sauce
1 ½ teaspoons minced fresh ginger
1 teaspoon chili paste with garlic

Combine peanut butter, broth, sugar, soy sauce, ginger and chili paste in heavy small saucepan. Simmer sauce until smooth and slightly thickened, whisking frequently, about 2 minutes.

Arrange chicken breasts on plates. Mound Oriental salad along side. Spoon sauce over chicken; spoon small amount of sauce atop salad. Sprinkle chicken and salad with green onion.

Oriental Salad:
4 ounces spaghettini or rice noodles
2 broccoli stalks, cut into small florets

248

2 tablespoons Oriental sesame oil
1½ tablespoons soy sauce
1 tablespoon balsamic or red wine vinegar
2 green onions, chopped

Cook spaghettini in large pot of boiling salted water until almost done, stirring occasionally. Add broccoli and cook until pasta and broccoli are just tender but still firm to bite. Drain. Rinse with cold water and drain well. Transfer pasta and broccoli to large bowl. Add all remaining ingredients and toss to coat thoroughly.

CHICKEN MARSALA
Serves 4

1 pound chicken breasts, boned
½ teaspoon seasoned salt
1 teaspoon paprika
2 tablespoons dried tarragon leaves
⅓ cup Marsala wine

Season chicken. Broil until golden brown. Soak tarragon leaves in Marsala wine while chicken is broiling. Spoon 2-3 tablespoons on each chicken breast. Return to oven and bake at 350° until wine has evaporated, basting occasionally until chicken becomes browned.

Can be made ahead of time and reheated in a covered, greased dish with a little added wine and water.

POULTRY

CHICKEN WITH PEANUTS IN HOT SAUCE
Serves 4

2 chicken breasts, skinned, boned and cubed
marinade (see below)
sauce (see below)
1 tablespoon oil
2-3 dashes dried red pepper flakes
6 scallions, sliced into one inch pieces
½ pound sliced mushrooms
½ cup salted, roasted peanuts

Marinade:
1 egg white
1 tablespoon tamari (or soy) sauce
1 tablespoon cornstarch
1 tablespoon water

Sauce: to be assembled before stir frying
1 teaspoon sugar
salt to taste
1 teaspoon cornstarch
1 tablespoon tamari (or soy) sauce
1 teaspoon white vinegar
1 teaspoon sesame oil
2 tablespoons water

Mix marinade ingredients, add cubed chicken and refrigerate for 30 minutes. Assemble sauce (must be done prior to stir-frying.) Heat skillet until hot. Add oil and pepper flakes. Stir-fry chicken until opaque. Add scallions and mushrooms and stir-fry 1-2 minutes. Add prepared sauce to pan and quickly stir-fry until sauce thickens and coats chicken. Add peanuts. Serve immediately over rice.

HERBED STUFFED CHICKEN BREASTS
Serves 6

3 whole boned chicken breasts
1-8 ounce package herb-seasoned stuffing
1 small onion, diced
½ cup diced celery
3 eggs, beaten
½ cup margarine
1 can chicken consomme
½ cup sliced mushrooms

Make a stuffing by sauteing onion and celery in margarine, adding mixture to bread crumbs along with whatever margarine remains in saute pan. Add eggs and mix with fork. Can be prepared a day ahead up until this point. Place stuffing on breasts and wrap skins to hold like a ball. Place in greased shallow pan, skin side up. Heat consomme and pour over breasts. Roast uncovered 1 hour in 350° oven. Baste about 3 times. Add mushrooms for the last 15 minutes.

MUSHROOM STUFFED CHICKEN BREASTS
Serves 4

4 chicken breasts, boned, skinned and halved
mushroom filling (recipe below)
¼ cup margarine
1¼ cups breadcrumbs, seasoned with:
1 teaspoon oregano
½ teaspoon basil
½ teaspoon thyme

Pound chicken breast halves between layers of plastic wrap until ³⁄₈ inch thick. Place mushroom filling on each piece. Roll, tuck in edges and fasten with toothpicks. Coat chicken rolls with melted margarine, roll in bread crumbs and bake at 350° for 45 minutes. Uncover and bake 15 minutes longer or until brown.

Mushroom Filling:
Saute 2 tablespoons each, chopped onion, celery and ¼ pound sliced mushrooms, in 2 tablespoons margarine until soft. Mix with ¼ teaspoon salt and ¼ teaspoon pepper, 1 tablespoon lemon juice, ⅓ cup blanched and slivered almonds.

CHICKEN SESAME
Serves 6

6 chicken breasts, boned and halved
¼ cup flour or corn meal
1 egg yolk
¼ cup soy sauce
¼ cup sesame seeds, toasted
2 tablespoons fresh ginger, grated
2 tablespoons sesame oil
2 tablespoons corn oil

Combine egg yolk and soy sauce. Coat chicken with flour or corn meal and dip into egg mixture. Dip in sesame seeds and sprinkle with ginger. Saute chicken in oils until brown. Bake in 350° oven for about 30 minutes. Pour sauce over chicken and bake at 325° for 10 minutes more.

Sauce:
½ cup orange juice
¼ cup white wine
1 tablespoon corn starch

Simmer until thickened.

SKILLET CHICKEN
Serves 4

2 whole chicken breasts, skinned, boned and halved
salt and pepper to taste
2 tablespoons margarine
1 small green pepper, cut into strips
½ cup onion, diced
½ cup celery, sliced
2 tomatoes, chopped
4 teaspoons fresh dill, chopped
½ teaspoon thyme

Sprinkle chicken with salt and pepper. Melt margarine in medium skillet. Brown chicken on both sides and remove from skillet. Add to skillet green pepper, onion and celery. Saute until tender. Add tomatoes, dill and thyme. Place chicken in flat casserole. Pour vegetable mixture over chicken. Bake covered 30-40 minutes in 350° oven until chicken is tender.

POULTRY

WALNUT CHICKEN
Serves 4

2 large whole chicken breasts, skinned, boned and
  cut into 1-inch pieces
1 teaspoon cornstarch
1 tablespoon water
1 egg white
3 tablespoons soy sauce
1 tablespoon bourbon
½ teaspoon sugar
4 tablespoons oil
3 green onions, cut into 2-inch slivers (including stems)
2 slices fresh ginger root, minced
1 garlic clove, minced
¾ cup chopped walnuts

Mix cornstarch, water and egg white. Add chicken and toss until thoroughly coated. In small bowl combine soy sauce, bourbon and sugar. Heat skillet or wok and add 2 tablespoons oil and stir fry chicken 3 to 5 minutes or until completely cooked. Remove from pan. Add remaining oil to pan and saute onions, ginger and garlic 1 minute. Return chicken to pan and continue cooking 1 minute. Add soy-bourbon mixture and cook quickly until sauce has thickened. Stir in walnuts. Serve with rice.

WHITE CHILI
Serves 8-10

1 pound large white beans, soaked overnight in water,
  drained
6 cups chicken broth
2 cloves garlic, minced

2 medium onions, chopped
1 tablespoon oil
2 4-ounce cans chopped green chilies
1 or more teaspoons chili powder (to taste)
2 teaspoons ground cumin
1½ teaspoons dried oregano
¼ teaspoon ground cloves
¼ teaspoon pepper
4 cups diced cooked chicken breasts

Combine beans, chicken broth, garlic and ½ of onions in large soup pot and boil. Reduce heat and simmer until beans are soft, 3 hours or more. Add more chicken broth if necessary. In skillet, saute remaining onions in oil until tender. Add chilies and seasonings and mix thoroughly. Add to bean mixture. Add chicken and continue to simmer for 1 hour.

ORIENTAL CHICKEN SALAD
Serves 4

1 whole boned and skinned chicken breast
2 cups chicken broth
butter lettuce
oriental sauce

Poach chicken in broth for 20 minutes and allow to cool in liquid. Chill for 4 or more hours. Slice chicken into 1 inch or 2 inch strips. Place chicken on a bed of lettuce and pour sauce over.

Oriental Sauce:
2 tablespoons soy sauce
1 tablespoon sesame oil
1 tablespoon honey

1 tablespoon dry sherry
1 teaspoon grated fresh ginger or ¼ teaspoon dried
2 green onions, finely minced
1 tablespoon toasted sesame seeds

Mix above ingredients and pour over chicken.

CHICKEN B'STILLA
Serves 6

1 3-pound chicken, cut up
2 cups onions, chopped
1 cup parsley, chopped
½ cup unsalted margarine
1 teaspoon saffron
2 cups water
salt, pepper
5 eggs, beaten
1½ cups toasted ground almonds or other nuts
¾ cup sugar
1½ teaspoons ground cinnamon
melted margarine
4 sheets filo dough
¼ cup powdered sugar

Combine chicken pieces, onions, parsley, unsalted margarine, saffron, water and salt and pepper to taste in large saucepan. Bring to boil. Reduce heat, cover and simmer 45 minutes or until chicken is tender. Remove chicken from pan and cool. Reserve broth. Remove meat from bones and dice. Set aside.

Place reserved chicken broth in skillet. Bring to simmer. Add eggs. Cook, stirring constantly 7 to 10 minutes until eggs are cooked and scrambled. Set aside. Combine almonds, sugar and

½ teaspoon cinnamon. Set aside. Above mixtures may be prepared ahead and refrigerated.

When ready to assemble dish about 1 hour before serving, brush 12-inch oven proof frying pan with rounded sides with melted margarine. Layer 3 filo sheets in skillet, brushing each sheet with margarine. About 5 inches of dough should hang over edge of pan.

Sprinkle ⅓ of almond mixture and ⅓ of chicken mixture over dough. Top with another ⅓ of almond mixture and ⅓ of egg mixture. Repeat layers until ingredients are used. Fold bottom sheets of filo over filling. Brush with margarine. Top with remaining filo sheet, tucking ends underneath. Brush with margarine.

Bake at 400° 15 to 20 minutes or until golden brown. Cool slightly, then invert onto serving platter. Sprinkle with powdered sugar while still warm. Decorate with remaining cinnamon.

POULTRY

THAI CHICKEN PASTA
Serves 4-6

1 medium cucumber, thinly sliced
1 medium onion, diced
2 cups roughly chopped cabbage
salt
½ cup crunchy peanut butter
2 tablespoons lime juice and pulp, or more to taste
1 tablespoon brown sugar
1 tablespoon tamari or other soy sauce
1 tablespoon Worcestershire sauce
1 teaspoon crushed hot red pepper
1 teaspoon curry powder
1 chicken breast, boned, skinned, poached
1 can chicken broth
¼ teaspoon cloves
2 cloves garlic, minced
6 ounces pasta of choice
¼ cup roughly chopped cilantro, or to taste
8 to10 large basil leaves, roughly chopped

In a large bowl, combine cucumber, onion, cabbage and 1 tablespoon salt. Let stand 30 minutes to 1 hour, then rinse with cold water and drain thoroughly. Set aside.

In heavy saucepan, combine peanut butter, lime juice, brown sugar, tamari, Worcestershire, crushed hot pepper, curry powder, cloves and garlic. Mix well. Don't boil. Stir frequently to avoid sticking.

Cook pasta in boiling salted water. Drain. Add sauce, reserved vegetables, sliced chicken, cilantro and basil and stir well. Season to taste with salt. Add additional lime juice and crushed pepper, if desired.

258

BARBECUED CHICKEN - CHINESE STYLE
Serves 4

1 frying chicken, cut up
⅓ cup soy sauce
3 tablespoons salad oil
1 teaspoon dry mustard
½ teaspoon ground ginger
¼ teaspoon pepper
1 clove garlic, minced

Mix last 6 ingredients together. Brush all sides of chicken with mixture. Let stand 30 minutes or longer, brushing several times with sauce. Put chicken on rack in shallow pan and bake in 350° oven 50 minutes or until tender. Brush with sauce and pan drippings every 15 minutes, until brown and crisp.

RAISIN TERIYAKI CHICKEN
Serves 4

1 chicken (2½ to 3 pounds), cut into serving pieces
½ cup white raisins
½ cup soy sauce
½ cup dry sherry
1 clove garlic, crushed
1 teaspoon brown sugar
½ teaspoon ginger

Arrange chicken in a shallow baking dish, large enough to hold chicken in one layer. Mix remaining ingredients and pour over chicken. Marinate 2 to 3 hours at room temperature. Cover and bake in the sauce in a preheated 350° oven 1 hour.

POULTRY

CHICKEN ESPAÑA
Serves 12

3 frying chickens, cut in pieces
margarine
1 onion, chopped
1 clove garlic, minced
1 green pepper, chopped
¼ pound fresh mushrooms, sliced
salt and pepper
2 to 3 pimientos, cut in strips
3 cups chicken stock
5 ounce package of saffron rice
1 tomato, sliced
1 10-ounce package frozen mixed vegetables
toasted slivered almonds

Using an electric skillet or heavy frying pan, brown chicken in margarine. Remove chicken and set aside. In the same skillet sauté onion, garlic, pepper and mushrooms. Season with salt and pepper to taste. Return chicken to skillet and mix with sautéed ingredients. Add pimiento and 1 cup of the chicken stock. Cover and simmer for 15 minutes. Add rest of stock and simmer another 10 minutes. Add uncooked saffron rice and tomato and cover with mixed vegetables. Cook at high temperature for a few minutes and then simmer for 45 minutes, stirring occasionally. Sprinkle almonds over all.

PICNIC CHICKEN IN BASKET
Serves 4

1 pound chicken breasts,
  boned, cut into wide
  strips
1 pound round sourdough
  bread
½ cup flour
2 tablespoons sesame seeds,
  toasted
½ tablespoon thyme
salt and pepper, to taste
¾ teaspoon tarragon

1 tablespoon ginger, grated
1 medium red onion,
  cut in strips
1 red pepper, cut in
  thin strips
1 yellow pepper, cut in
  thin strips
2 egg whites, slightly beaten
4 tablespoons margarine,
  melted
½ tablespoon poppy seeds

Cut top off of sourdough bread. Scoop out inside of bread, leaving ¾ inch of bread all around. (The inside of the bread can later be used for bread cubes, french toast, or other future use.) Baste inside of bread with some of the margarine seasoned with sesame seeds, thyme and tarragon. Saute onion and peppers lightly in Pam spray. Spread vegetables inside of bread. Set aside.

Dip chicken in egg whites, seasoned with sesame seeds, poppy seeds and grated ginger. Dip in flour, lightly. Sprinkle remaining melted margarine over chicken and bake covered in 350° oven for 40 minutes. This can be prepared early and refrigerated. When ready to use, fill the bread basket with chicken, cover with top of bread, and wrap in silver foil. Heat in 350° oven for 25 minutes. To transport, wrap in newspaper to keep warm. When serving, bread can be torn apart as a wrap for chicken.

Note: Whole chicken, cut into eight pieces, can be used instead of boneless breast.

POULTRY

MIDDLE EASTERN STEAMED CHICKEN
Serves 4

1 roasting chicken (about 3 pounds)
4 cups steamed brown rice or kasha
½ cup chopped walnuts or pine nuts
4 tablespoons seedless raisins
4 tablespoons melted unsalted margarine
3 tablespoons honey
2 pinches each of cinnamon, ginger, cloves, turmeric,
  cumin and pepper
¼ cup peanut oil
fresh mint or watercress

Rinse and pat chicken dry and sprinkle inside and out with salt. Mix together rice (or kasha) with nuts, raisins, 2 tablespoons melted margarine, honey and spices. Stuff chicken with half the mixture, and close cavity. Tie legs together and place chicken in steamer or on a rack an inch above boiling water in a roasting pan. Put remaining rice mixture in aluminum foil, seal, and place next to chicken on rack. Cover roasting pan tightly and steam chicken for about 40 to 60 minutes or until tender (when fork-tested, juices will run clear if done.) Remove chicken. Pat dry with paper towels. Heat oil and remaining margarine in a large skillet over high heat. Lower heat to medium and brown chicken on all sides. Garnish with fresh mint sprigs or watercress; surround with steamed rice.

CHICKEN MOROCCO
Serves 4

1 2½-3 pound broiler or fryer, cut up
salt and paprika to taste
¼ teaspoon pepper

2 tablespoons margarine
½ cup chicken consomme
1 clove garlic
1 medium eggplant, peeled and cut up
4 green onions, chopped
2 tomatoes, peeled, seeded and diced
¼ teaspoon thyme
1 tablespoon parsley, chopped

Sprinkle chicken pieces with paprika, salt and pepper. Melt margarine in skillet and add chicken pieces until browned. Remove from skillet, scrape brown pieces from skillet and add chicken consomme. Add garlic, eggplant, green onions and tomatoes and return chicken to skillet. Sprinkle with salt, thyme and parsley. Cover and simmer 40 minutes. Remove garlic. Serve with rice.

KOREAN CHICKEN
Serves 4-6

1 3-pound fryer, cut into serving pieces

Marinade:
½ cup peanut oil
¼ cup honey
¼ teaspoon powdered ginger
¼ cup chives, minced
1 cup soy sauce
1 clove garlic, minced
¼ teaspoon dry mustard

Combine ingredients to make marinade. Marinate chicken for 3 hours, turning chicken several times. Broil under moderate heat about 15 minutes each side. Baste while broiling.

CHICKEN ARTICHOKE CACCIATORE
Serves 4

1 3-pound fryer cut up or 4 medium breasts, halved
2 6-ounce jars marinated artichoke hearts
2 tablespoons olive oil
flour for dredging
1 can (1 pound) Italian solid pack tomatoes
2 garlic cloves, minced
½ pound mushrooms, sliced
½ teaspoon salt
½ teaspoon oregano
½ teaspoon basil
½ teaspoon ground pepper
¼ cup sherry
fresh chopped parsley

Drain marinade from artichoke hearts into large skillet and add olive oil. Dredge chicken in flour and brown in oil until golden. Transfer chicken pieces from skillet into a 3 quart casserole. In skillet combine tomatoes, artichoke hearts, garlic, mushrooms and spices. Stir over low heat 1 minute. Pour over chicken. Cover and bake at 350° for 1 hour or until tender. During last few minutes add sherry. Garnish with fresh chopped parsley.

POTATO BAKED CHICKEN
Serves 4-6

1 chicken (3 pounds), cut into serving pieces, or 3 pounds split chicken breast
1 egg, or 1 egg white, slightly beaten
2 tablespoons non-dairy creamer
1 cup instant mashed potato flakes

¼ *cup margarine*
½ *teaspoon salt*
⅛ *teaspoon pepper*

Dry chicken well. Blend egg and creamer. Dip chicken first in creamer mixture, then roll in potato flakes, coating thoroughly. (Reserve remaining potato flakes, if any.)

Melt margarine in a baking dish. Arrange chicken, skin side down, in the dish. Sprinkle with some of the salt and pepper. Bake, uncovered, in a preheated 400° oven 30 minutes. Turn chicken; sprinkle with salt, pepper and any remaining potato flake mixture. Bake 30 minutes longer or until fork-tender.

This dish can be frozen.

CHICKEN STEW
Serves 8

2 3-pound chickens, cut up
3 cups endive or cabbage, chopped
1 cup parsnips cut into ½ inch pieces
1 cup carrots cut into ½ inch pieces
1 cup rutabaga cut into ½ inch pieces
1 cup onion, coarsely chopped
1 tablespoon garlic, chopped
1 bay leaf
½ *teaspoon dried thyme*
¼ *cup fresh parsley leaves or cilantro, chopped*
  or 1 tablespoon fresh tarragon, chopped
1½ cups chicken consomme
½ *cup dry white wine*
½ *teaspoon salt*
black pepper to taste, freshly ground

Put the chicken pieces in a large, heavy saucepan. Add the endive, parsnips, carrots, rutabaga, onion, garlic, bay leaf, thyme, parsley or cilantro, chicken stock, wine, salt and pepper. Bring the mixture to a boil, cover, and simmer for 25 minutes. Remove fat from the surface occasionally. Remove the chicken from the pan and pour the vegetable mixture into a food mill or food processor. Puree the vegetables coarsely so the mixture retains its variation in color. Return the sauce to the pan, along with the chicken. Bring it back to a boil and simmer the chicken for 15 minutes. Add the herbs and serve, pouring sauce over the chicken.

Optional: Remove skin from chicken after cooking.

GARDEN CHICKEN WITH RICE
Serves 6

1 teaspoon saffron threads
¼ cup olive oil
3½-pound chicken, skinned and cut into serving pieces
2 onions, chopped
2 small green bell peppers, chopped
¾ pound plum tomatoes (about 6), peeled, seeded and
*   chopped*
2 garlic cloves, minced
4 teaspoons paprika
3 cups Arborio or brown rice
6 cups chicken broth
1 large red bell pepper, roasted and cut into strips
1 cup frozen peas
1 cup minced fresh parsley leaves

Set a rack over a saucepan of boiling water, put the saffron in a saucer on the rack, and let it steam for 3 to 4 minutes, or until it is brittle. Remove the saucer and the rack and crumble the saffron in the saucer. In a large heavy skillet, heat the oil over moderately high heat until it is hot but not smoking and reduce the heat to moderately low. Cook the chicken, patted dry, for 15 to 18 minutes, turning until cooked through. Transfer to a bowl.

Pour off all but 3 tablespoons of the fat from the skillet; cook the onions and the green bell peppers over moderately low heat, stirring occasionally, until the vegetables are softened. Add tomatoes, garlic, paprika, and saffron and cook mixture, stirring, for 1 minute. Add the rice and cook, stirring, for 3 minutes. Add the broth and simmer the mixture, stirring occasionally, for 7 minutes. Transfer the rice mixture to a shallow 5-quart baking dish and arrange the chicken over it. Bake the chicken and rice in middle of a preheated 325° oven for 15 minutes. Sprinkle the red bell pepper and the peas over it, and bake for 5 to 10 minutes more, until the liquid is absorbed and the rice is al dente. Sprinkle with the parsley.

FRUITED CHICKEN
Serves 6-8

2 cut-up chicken fryers
1 medium onion, sliced
1-6 ounce jar sweet and sour sauce
¼ cup chile sauce
1 1-pound can sliced peaches, drained
1 1-pound can sweet pitted dark cherries, drained

Season chicken with salt and pepper. Layer onion on bottom of pan. Mix remaining ingredients and pour over chicken. Dot top layer with margarine. Bake in shallow baking dish for 1½ hours uncovered at 350°. Baste often.

POULTRY

FRUITED CHICKEN CURRY
Serves 4

1 broiler or fryer-3 pounds, cut-up
¾ cup dried apricots
¾ cup dried prunes
¼ cup raisins
2 tablespoons margarine
1 medium onion, chopped
1 tablespoon curry powder
1 teaspoon salt
1 teaspoon sugar
3 cups cooked rice
¼ cup salted peanuts

Combine apricots, dried prunes and raisins with 1 cup of water and set aside for 1 hour. Heat margarine in skillet. Add chicken pieces and brown well on both sides. Remove chicken from pan. Add onion and curry powder, stirring carefully 2-3 minutes so that curry powder does not burn. Return chicken to skillet, skin side down and sprinkle with salt and sugar. Add soaked fruits with liquid, cover and cook until chicken is tender, about 45 minutes. Serve over hot rice and sprinkle with peanuts.

PLUM CHICKEN
Serves 8-10

5 whole chicken breasts, boned
1 10-ounce jar plum preserves
2 tablespoons white vinegar
1 tablespoon grated orange rind
½ teaspoon Kitchen Bouquet
¼ teaspoon allspice
½ teaspoon dry mustard
1 sliced onion

Combine and heat ingredients (except onions and chicken) until blended. Place chicken pieces on top of onion slices. Pour sauce over chicken. Bake approximately 1¾ hours at 350°, basting every half hour.

CHICKEN AND PINEAPPLE BROCHETTE
Serves 4

2 whole chicken breasts, boned and cut to bite-sized pieces
1 cup pineapple chunks and syrup
orange glaze (see below)
2 cups cooked basmati or brown rice

Drain pineapple chunks. (Reserve syrup for orange glaze.) Marinate chicken in glaze several hours. Skewer chicken, alternating with pineapple. Place 5 inches from heat and broil 8 minutes. Turn once and baste several times. Serve with rice.

Glaze:
¼ cup melted margarine
⅔ cup orange juice
1 teaspoon dry mustard
1½ teaspoons grated orange peel
⅓ cup pineapple syrup
1 tablespoon dry white wine

Combine melted margarine, orange juice, dry mustard, grated orange peel, syrup and wine. Bring to a simmer (Do Not Boil). Stir until well blended.

POULTRY

CHICKEN A L'ORANGE
Serves 4

1 chicken, cut up
¼ cup Dijon mustard
1 cup or more bread crumbs
½ cup orange juice
¼ cup white wine

Season chicken to taste. Coat chicken lightly with Dijon mustard. Roll in bread crumbs. Place in shallow casserole. Pour orange juice and wine over all and bake at 350° 45 minutes to 1 hour, basting every 15 minutes. Discard liquid and broil a few minutes until crisp and brown. Garnish with orange slices.

HONEY GLAZED CHICKEN WITH APPLES
Serves 8

2 frying chickens, cut in eighths
salt, pepper, garlic powder
6 tablespoons margarine, melted
½ cup apple juice
½ cup honey
8 apples, cored, peeled, quartered
2 tablespoons brown sugar
2 teaspoons lemon rind, grated
2 teaspoons orange rind, grated
½ cup orange marmalade

Sprinkle chicken pieces with salt, pepper and garlic powder. Melt the margarine. Place the peeled apples around edges of 9 x 13 inch casserole. Place chicken in center. Drizzle all with melted margarine. Heat together apple juice, honey, brown sugar, lemon and orange rind. Baste chicken and apples with mixture. Bake

50 minutes at 350°, basting every 10 minutes, until rich golden brown. Brush orange marmalade over chicken and apples and bake 5-10 minutes to glaze. Serve apples as accompaniment to chicken. Extra apples can be glazed in separate pan if desired to serve with chicken or meat.

CHICKEN APPLE ROLL-UPS
Serves 6

5 tablespoons margarine
1 Golden Delicious apple, peeled and coarsely shredded
1 teaspoon sugar
1 teaspoon lemon juice
1 teaspoon cinnamon
⅛ teaspoon each ground coriander and nutmeg
2 cups cooked chicken, chopped
¼ cup all-purpose flour
¼ teaspoon salt
dash white pepper
¾ cup each chicken broth and light non-dairy creamer
1 egg yolk
12 crepes, 7 inches in diameter
  (see index under Fish Blintzes)
2 tablespoons dry Vermouth
nutmeg

Melt 1 tablespoon of margarine in a medium-sized frying pan. Stir in apple and cook just until tender, stirring frequently. Stir in sugar, lemon juice, cinnamon, coriander and nutmeg. Fold in chicken; set mixture aside. Melt the remaining 4 tablespoons margarine in a medium-sized saucepan over medium heat. Stir in flour, salt and white pepper; cook until bubbly. Gradually add chicken broth and light non-dairy cream, stirring constantly until thickened. Remove from heat. Beat egg yolk in a small bowl; stir in a little of the hot sauce, then return this to the first sauce. Replace over the heat and cook, stirring for a minute or two more. Reserving about half of this sauce, fold remaining sauce into apple-chicken mixture. Fill crepes with apple-chicken-sauce mixture; fold filled crepes into cylinders and place, side-by-side, in a greased shallow rectangular baking dish about 12 inches long. Reheat remaining sauce and stir in Vermouth; pour it over the crepes. Dust with nutmeg. Bake in a 425° oven for 12-15 minutes, until crepes are heated and sauce is lightly browned.

SESAME CRUSTED CHICKEN
WITH PERSIMMON SAUCE
Serves 4

1 pound chicken breasts
1 cup sesame seeds, toasted
1 egg white, beaten
seasoned salt to taste
2 teaspoons ginger
non-stick spray
2 cups persimmon pulp
2 teaspoons ginger
¼ cup white wine

Marinade:
½ cup soy sauce
2 tablespoons lemon juice
½ cup orange juice

Pour marinade over chicken breasts. Refrigerate for several hours. Toast sesame seeds in dry pan on stove. Combine persimmon pulp, ginger and white wine. Set aside. Whip egg white until foamy. Dip chicken pieces in egg white, then in toasted sesame seeds. Place on platter for 20 minutes. Brown in pan that has been sprayed. When browned on both sides, place in shallow pan and pour over persimmon pulp mixture. Cover with silver foil and place in 350° oven for 30 minutes, basting twice. Uncover and bake another 10 minutes. Serve with extra sauce.

Salmon filets may be substituted for chicken breasts.

ROCK CORNISH HENS WITH
DIJON PECAN SAUCE
Serves 4

4 small Rock Cornish hens
½ cup margarine, melted
1 tablespoon flour
1 cup chicken stock
¼ cup Dijon mustard
2 tablespoons dry white wine
1 tablespoon honey
⅓ cup chopped pecans

Preheat oven to 325°. Set hens on a rack in a shallow roasting pan. Brush well with melted margarine. Roast in oven for 15 minutes. Turn hens on side, brush with margarine, and roast another 15 minutes. Continue rotating and brushing hens at 15 minute intervals until hens are upright again. Continue roasting until hens are browned and tender.

Stir flour into pan drippings and cook about 3 minutes. Combine stock, mustard, wine, and honey. Gradually stir the mixture into roux (flour mixture), cooking until bubbly and thick. Add the nuts and spoon over the hens.

Variation: For Curried Pineapple Sauce, bring to a simmer an 8 ounce can of crushed pineapple, 2 tablespoons margarine, and 1 teaspoon curry powder. Lower heat, cover, and simmer 5 minutes.

APRICOT CORNISH HENS
Serves 6

3 Cornish hens
2 cups cold cooked rice
2 tablespoons margarine
3 tablespoons parsley, chopped
3 tablespoons onions, chopped
3 tablespoons chives, chopped
additional melted margarine
1 6-ounce jar of apricot preserves, thinned with
  2 tablespoons orange juice or white wine

Heat oven to 350°. If desired, lightly salt cavities of hens. Combine rice, 2 tablespoons margarine, parsley, onions and chives. Lightly stuff mixture into hens' cavities. Brush hens with melted margarine. Roast for 1½ hours. Baste with juice from pan. When almost done, brush hens with apricot preserves and continue baking until glazed hens are browned.

DUCK 'N MARMALADE
Serves 4

1 duck, cut into quarters
1 8-ounce jar orange or other flavored marmalade
½ cup rose wine

Prick duck with fork. Completely enfold all ingredients in 2 layers of heavy foil. Place in baking pan. Bake 2 hours at 375°.

Remove carefully and pour juices into shallow pan. Refrigerate or freeze until fat has solidified. Discard fat. Can be prepared the day before to this point. Bring duck to room temperature. Spoon half of juices over duck, broil 20-30 minutes. Serve with remainder of juices.

CRISP DUCKLING IN ORANGE SAUCE
Serves 3

1 duck, 4-5 pounds
coarse salt, to season
2 tart apples, cored and quartered

Sauce:
¼ cup unsalted margarine
½ cup light brown sugar
1 tablespoon flour
½ cup freshly squeezed orange juice
½ teaspoon lemon rind, grated
½ cup apple jelly
¼ teaspoon cinnamon
¼ teaspoon nutmeg
ground cloves, to taste

Preheat oven to 350°. Rub cavity of duck with salt and place apples inside. Sprinkle salt on outside skin. Place duck on top rack of oven. Fill a large, deep pan with 1 inch of water and place on the bottom rack to catch drippings. Bake 2 hours or until tender.

Prepare orange sauce as duck cooks. Melt margarine in a saucepan over medium heat. Stir in sugar and flour, blending well. Increase heat, add orange juice, lemon rind, jelly, and spices. Bring to a boil, stirring constantly, until sauce is thick.

Slice duck into serving portions, dress with sauce and serve.

POULTRY

ROAST DUCK
Serves 4

1 duck, about 5 pounds
salt and freshly ground pepper
½ orange, cut into 2 pieces
1 stalk celery with leaves on it
½ onion
1 sprig parsley

1 onion, cut in half
1 stalk celery with leaves on it
2 carrots, chopped
2 sprigs parsley
1 bay leaf
5 peppercorns
1 teaspoon salt
2 cups water
1 cup red wine
neck and giblets of duck
1 tablespoon flour
1 tablespoon margarine

Rub duck inside and out with salt and pepper. Stuff with orange, celery, onion, and parsley. Close the opening with a metal skewer. Preheat oven to 450°. Put the duck on its back in a roasting pan. Roast for ¾ of an hour, then turn duck, remove all drippings, and roast for another ¾ of an hour. Remove duck from oven and discard drippings.

While the duck is roasting, put the remaining ingredients in a large pot. Bring slowly to a boil and simmer for 1 hour. Strain and reserve the broth.

Reduce the oven temperature to 400°. Return duck to oven and continue to cook for another 40 minutes, basting every 10 minutes with the reserved broth. Place duck on serving plate and thicken the gravy with a mixture of 1 tablespoon of flour, 1 tablespoon of margarine, and 1 tablespoon red wine. Serve the gravy on the side.

ROAST BREAST OF TURKEY
Serves 6-8

1 4-pound turkey breast, bone intact, without wings
½ teaspoon salt
freshly ground black pepper (8 turns of the mill)
1 tablespoon vegetable oil
½ teaspoon dried thyme or 2 sprigs fresh thyme
2 small whole onions
1 bay leaf
2 garlic cloves
¼ cup dry white wine
½ cup orange, pineapple or apricot juice
¼ cup chicken stock

Preheat oven to 400°. Sprinkle breast with salt and pepper. Brush with oil inside and out. Rub inside of the breast with thyme. Place turkey in a roasting pan skin side up along with the onions, bay leaf and garlic. Roast 1-1½ hours, basting often, at 350°. Pour off the fat in the pan. Add white wine, juice and chicken stock and roast 10 minutes more. Allow the turkey to rest for 10 minutes before slicing.

POULTRY

FRUITED TURKEY BREAST

1 can of frozen orange juice
¼ cup duck sauce
1 tablespoon Worcestershire sauce
⅓ cup white wine
garlic powder
1 turkey breast
2 cups dried fruit

Mix first 5 ingredients together. Pour over turkey breast and marinate at least 1 hour. Sprinkle cut up fruit over turkey and wrap loosely in tent of silver foil. Seal tightly. Bake 1¾ hours at 400°.

FRUIT-STUFFED TURKEY BREAST ROLL
Serves 6-8

2 apples, peeled and cubed
1 cup cranberries
12 pitted prunes, cut into halves
½ cup walnuts, chopped
2 tablespoons raisins
2 tablespoons sugar
¼ cup brandy
¾ teaspoon ground cinnamon
½ teaspoon salt
½ teaspoon garlic powder
½ teaspoon ground allspice
½ teaspoon black pepper
¼ teaspoon ground cloves
¼ teaspoon ground mace
¼ teaspoon whole dried thyme leaves
1 (4 to 6-pound) turkey breast, boned, butterflied, skin intact
1-2 tablespoons margarine

278

Combine apples, cranberries, prunes, walnuts, raisins, sugar, brandy and ¼ teaspoon cinnamon in container with tight-fitting lid. Toss well to mix and marinate 2 hours or overnight.

Combine salt, garlic powder, allspice, pepper, cloves, mace, remaining cinnamon and thyme. Rub mixture over turkey breast, then refrigerate turkey, covered, 2 hours or overnight. Place filling across widest section of turkey breast, forming long round, about 2-3 inches in diameter. Bring both sides of turkey together abound stuffing and sew up or wrap tightly with kitchen string. Roll will be about 12-14 incles long. Place turkey roll in center of greased sheet of foil. Roll up foil. Bake at 400° for 40 minutes. Reduce heat to 350°, uncover roll, and cook 20 minutes longer. Baste with margarine, if necessary, then return to oven and bake 10 minutes longer.

Remove from oven and let stand 5-10 minutes. Remove strings, then slice in ½ inch slices, fanning them out on a serving platter. Drizzle with pan juices and serve.

POULTRY

MARINATED TURKEY BREAST
Serves 8

1 turkey breast, 4-6 pounds
2 teaspoons salt
1 teaspoon pepper

Marinade:
1 sliced onion
½ cup oil
½ cup vinegar
2 chopped tomatoes
2 medium green peppers, chopped
1 small can sliced olives
chopped parsley

Rub salt and pepper into turkey breast. Combine marinade ingredients, pour over turkey and marinate overnight, basting a few times. Place breast on rack, pour over marinade. Bake at 325° for 2 hours for a 4 pound turkey breast and 2½ hours for a 6 pound breast. Baste often.

MALAYSIAN TURKEY
Serves 8

1 fresh boneless turkey breast half (2½ to 3 pounds)
⅓ cup chunky peanut butter
⅓ cup teriyaki sauce
¼ cup lemon juice
¼ cup vegetable oil
2 teaspoons ground ginger
2 teaspoons sweet basil
2 teaspoons onion powder
2 teaspoons garlic powder
¼ to ½ teaspoon crushed red pepper

Place turkey in plastic bag. Combine remaining ingredients in blender or food processor. Process until smooth; reserve ½ cup sauce. Pour remaining sauce over turkey, turning to coat evenly.

Marinate in refrigerator 30 minutes. Place turkey on grill, set over drip pan (filled with 2 inches of water). Arrange coals around drip pan. Grill, covered, over medium-high coals, or bake in broiler pan, uncovered, at 400° for 1 to 1½ hours or until 170° internal temperature, basting with marinade occasionally. Let stand 10 minutes before carving. Serve with reserved sauce.

POULTRY

STRAIGHT FROM THE GALLEY TURKEY CHILI
Serves 16

3 teaspoons oil
2 pounds ground turkey or 1 pound each
  of ground veal and ground turkey
2 large onions, chopped
1 green pepper, chopped
3 stalks celery, chopped
3 carrots, sliced
½ cup parsley
½ cup fresh cilantro, minced (optional)
2 cups tomato juice
1 28-ounce can of Italian tomatoes, crushed
1 8-ounce can tomato paste
6 fresh tomatoes, chopped
2 cloves garlic, minced
1-2 tablespoons chili powder
1 teaspoon cumin
1 teaspoon coriander (optional)
1 teaspoon thyme
1 teaspoon oregano
ground pepper
½ teaspoon nutmeg
1 15½-ounce can of red kidney beans

Brown ground meat in oil. Add remaining ingredients, except kidney beans. Cook covered, stirring occasionally, for 1 hour. Add kidney beans and cook for 15 minutes more. Adjust seasoning.

"When the grass is tender, it is easily cut."

TSENAH TSADIG

C ould be that grass was the prototype of the salad of today. We still emphasize green, fresh and tender, but we've come a long way baby! Now we are offered a plethora of ingredients: tomato, radish, avocado, jicama, cantaloupe, kiwi, grapefruit and peppers- red, green and yellow. To these we add pasta, chicken, cheese, fish and much, much more. The permutations and combinations are endless.

Classic is the snap of the cold salad on the palate— cleansing greens, prelude or coda to the entree, as you wish. High in popularity today are the salads that serve as meals unto themselves.

CHINESE CHICKEN SALAD
Serves 6-8

Marinade:
2 teaspoons sesame oil
¼ teaspoon salt
2 tablespoons white vinegar
2 tablespoons sugar
4 tablespoons salad oil

Salad:
2 cups cooked, shredded chicken breast
2 cups bean threads (mai fun)
oil for frying
2 tablespoons sesame seeds, roasted
2 green onions, green part only, chopped
½ cup unsalted cashew nuts
2 cups finely shredded lettuce - mix varieties for color

Marinate cooked chicken for 2 minutes. Toss lightly.

Break bean threads or cut with scissors into very small bunches and drop into 2 inches of very hot oil in small batches for a few seconds until the threads fully expand. Do not brown. Remove from oil and drain on absorbent paper. (This can be done several days ahead and kept in covered bowl.) Place in 250° oven uncovered to recrisp. When crisp, add to chicken mixture with roasted sesame seeds, chopped green onions and nuts. Before serving, add shredded lettuce and toss again.

To roast sesame seeds: Put in a dry skillet over medium heat. When they pop or brown they are ready. Be careful, they burn quickly. Or, spread seeds in shallow pan, bake 350° about 10 minutes, being careful not to burn.

SALADS

CHICKEN SALAD PIQUANTE
Serves 8

Salad:
4 chicken breasts, skinned and poached
2 cups purple cabbage, shredded
3 hearts of palm, sliced in ½ inch pieces
1 cup Chinese peas with strings removed
2 green onions, chopped

Dressing:
¾ cup sesame oil
3 tablespoons hot chili oil
3 tablespoons Hoisin sauce
3 tablespoons lemon juice
3 tablespoons lemon peel
3 tablespoons ginger
white pepper

Cube chicken into 1 inch chunks. Combine vegetables. Pour over ½ cup of dressing (or to taste).

GREEN APPLE-CURRIED CHICKEN SALAD
Serves 6 - 8

2 large Granny Smith apples
2 tablespoons lime or lemon juice
3½ cups cubed, cooked chicken or turkey
⅓ cup cooked rice
½ cup mayonnaise
½ cup slivered toasted almonds
1 tablespoon onion, chopped
1 tablespoon curry powder
¼ teaspoon salt

Core and dice apples, combine with lemon or lime juice. Stir in chicken and rice. Blend together mayonnaise, almonds, onion curry powder and salt. Stir into apple mixture. Chill. Mound salad on greens.

CURRIED CHICKEN SALAD #1
Serves 8

1-3½ pound chicken
½ cup green pepper, chopped
½ cup onion, chopped
½ cup celery, chopped
½ cup prunes, coarsely cut
½ cup golden raisins

½ cup seedless grapes
½ cup cantaloupe, diced
4 papayas
lettuce leaves
tomato slices

Cook chicken in boiling salted water until tender, about 35 to 40 minutes, then drain, reserving broth for other use. Remove bones and skin and cut meat into chunks. Combine chicken with green pepper, onion, celery, prunes, raisins, grapes, melon and curry dressing and toss to mix well. Chill. Cut papayas into halves and remove seeds. Spoon chicken salad into papaya cavities and serve garnished with lettuce and tomato slices.

Curry Dressing:
1 cup non-dairy whipping cream
⅓ cup mayonnaise

curry powder
salt, pepper

Whip non-dairy cream, mayonnaise and curry to taste in blender until smooth. Season to taste with salt and pepper.

SALADS

CURRIED CHICKEN SALAD, #2
Serves 6

3 cups diced, cooked chicken or turkey
2 stalks celery, diced
½ cup almonds, chopped
½ cup raisins, grapes or diced apples or combination
¼ cup green onions, chopped
½ cup mayonnaise
¼ cup apple juice
2 teaspoons curry powder
2 teaspoons chutney

Combine all ingredients. Cover and refrigerate. Serve on lettuce or in half cantaloupe.

GRILLED SALMON STEAK SALAD
Serves 4

2 tablespoons olive oil
1 tablespoon Dijon mustard
1 teaspoon minced fresh thyme
salt
freshly ground black pepper
1 tablespoon lemon juice
4 salmon steaks
mixed salad greens

Combine olive oil, mustard and thyme. Season to taste with salt and pepper. Brush salmon steaks with mixture. Prepare hot fire. Add lemon juice to salmon. Place salmon on oiled grill, set 4 to 6 inches from coals. Cook steaks, brushing several times with olive oil mixture about 5 to 6 minutes, or until lightly browned on bottom.

Using wide spatula, turn steaks over and brush cooked side with more marinade. Cook until second side is nicely browned, about 5 to 6 minutes, brushing with more marinade. Flake fish into chunks and serve hot or cold over chilled mixed greens. Top with dressing.

Dressing:
¾ cup yogurt
⅓ cup vinegar
2 tablespoons olive oil
1 tablespoon Dijon mustard
1 tablespoon lemon juice
1 clove garlic, crushed
1 tablespoon chopped fresh dill or fennel
salt
freshly ground black pepper

Combine yogurt, vinegar, olive oil, mustard, lemon juice, garlic and dill. Season to taste with salt and pepper. Stir or shake well. Chill until ready to serve. Makes about 1½ cups.

SALADS

TUNA AND PASTA SHELL SALAD
Serves 6

1 8-ounce package small shell macaroni, cooked, drained
   and rinsed in cold water
1 7-ounce can water packed tuna, drained
½ cup shredded Cheddar cheese
¼ cup toasted almonds
1 cup frozen peas
¼ cup chopped onion
½ cup chopped celery
1 teaspoon fresh chopped dill
½ cup calorie-reduced mayonnaise
½ cup low-fat plain yogurt
1 teaspoon lemon juice
¼ cup calorie-reduced Italian salad dressing
salt and pepper to taste
toasted sesame seeds

Combine all ingredients except sesame seeds. Cover and chill
4 hours or overnight. At serving time adjust seasoning and
garnish with toasted sesame seeds.

CHOPPED NICOISE SALAD
Serves 6

1 large head romaine lettuce, finely chopped
4 large plum tomatoes, seeded, finely chopped
1 green bell pepper, finely chopped
1 cup canned garbanzo beans
4½ ounces Mozzarella cheese, diced
½ cup pitted black olives, finely chopped
½ cup pimiento-stuffed green olives, finely chopped
6 ounces tuna, drained

2 ounces Feta cheese, crumbled
¾ cup olive oil
2 tablespoons red wine vinegar
1½ tablespoons minced fresh basil or 1 teaspoon dried
1 tablespoon Dijon mustard
2 teaspoons fresh lemon juice
pinch of sugar
salt and pepper

Combine first 9 ingredients in large bowl. Blend oil with next 5 ingredients in small bowl. Season with salt and pepper. Pour over salad and toss thoroughly.

MARINATED ARTICHOKE SALAD SUPREME
Serves 20

6 peppers, sliced in thin strips, red, green and yellow
1 large red onion, sliced thin
1 5½-ounce can black olives, sliced
½ cup parsley, chopped
1 5½-ounce can hearts of palm, sliced
6 Italian or small tomatoes, sliced
32 ounces marinated artichokes and ½ of marinade
2 cucumbers, sliced thin
4 tablespoons rice vinegar
2 tablespoons Balsamic vinegar
¼ cup chopped cilantro (optional)
1 tablespoon coarse ground pepper

Mix all ingredients together and refrigerate for approximately 6 hours. Do not marinate overnight.

SALADS

AVOCADO AND MUSHROOM PIQUANT
Serves 8

2 avocados, peeled and sliced
½ pound small button mushrooms
¼ cup oil
3 tablespoons tarragon vinegar
2 tablespoons lemon juice
2 tablespoons water
1 tablespoon chopped parsley
1 clove garlic, minced
¾ teaspoon salt
freshly ground pepper to taste
lettuce, watercress or parsley

Place avocado slices and mushrooms in a deep plastic container with a tight fitting lid. Blend remaining ingredients and pour over vegetables. Cover and chill several hours or overnight. Shake covered container several times during marinating. Serve on lettuce leaves garnished with watercress or parsley.

BELGIAN ENDIVE SALAD
Serves 2-4

2 Belgian endives
½ cup shredded Gruyere cheese
½ cup coarsely chopped walnuts
¼ cup walnut oil, or other oil
2 tablespoons lemon juice
salt
white pepper

Run cold water over endives and pat dry with paper towels. Cut each in 3 sections and loosen leaves. Place in salad bowl. Sprinkle cheese and walnuts over endives. In small bowl beat oil and lemon juice. Season to taste with salt and white pepper. Pour over endives. Toss well.

THAI ASPARAGUS SALAD
Serves 6

3-4 anchovy fillets, pounded to a paste
1 small garlic clove
¼ teaspoon red pepper flakes
½ teaspoon black pepper
3 tablespoons peanut oil
juice of 1 lime
1½ pounds asparagus, sliced diagonally into 1-inch
  lengths, steamed
½ cup loosely packed, chopped cilantro
1 tablespoon dried basil
1 small red onion, thinly sliced into rings

Combine first 6 ingredients, toss with cooked asparagus; add remaining ingredients.

BROCCOLI SALAD
Serves 8

3 cups broccoli
1 /2 cups cherry tomatoes, halved
1¹green onion, diced
2 tablespoons minced parsley
red wine vinaigrette or Italian salad dressing

Steam broccoli 4-5 minutes and chill before combining with remaining ingredients.

SALADS

MARINATED SWEET AND SOUR CARROT SALAD
Serves 12

1½ *pounds carrots, pared and thinly sliced, cooked*
  crisp-tender
1 *medium sweet red onion, thinly sliced*
½ *cup chopped green pepper*
10¾ *ounce can tomato soup*
¾ *cup sugar*
½ *cup red wine vinegar*
1 *teaspoon Worcestershire sauce*
½ *teaspoon salt*

Combine vegetables in serving bowl. Combine remaining ingredients for marinade in a small bowl. Combine vegetables and marinade. Cover and refrigerate overnight.

MARINATED CHINESE SALAD
Serves 4

1 *cucumber, peeled and cut in long thin fingers*
1 *pound fresh bean sprouts*
4 *stalks celery, thinly sliced diagonally*
2 *green onions, chopped*
2 *tablespoons sliced pimientos*
¼ *cup sugar*
¾ *cup apple cider vinegar*
¾ *cup water*

Combine vegetables in a plastic container that can be tightly sealed. Stir together sugar, vinegar and water until the sugar is dissolved. Pour dressing over vegetables. Cover and refrigerate overnight. Stir vegetables or shake covered container occasionally during marinating.

CUCUMBER PACHADI
Serves 8

3 medium pickling cucumbers
1 teaspoon kosher salt
1 onion, peeled and quartered
1 large tomato, peeled, seeded and quartered
3 small green chilis, mild or hot
1 small bunch cilantro, leaves only
¾ cup unflavored yogurt

Peel cucumbers. Cut in half and then in 1 inch pieces. Process 3 pulses and sprinkle with salt. Process the onion, tomato, chilis and cilantro to small pieces. Squeeze water from cucumbers and place in serving bowl. Add chopped mixture and yogurt. Mix well.

FARMER'S CHOP SUEY
Serves 6

2 cups farmer or hoop cheese
2 cups small curd cottage cheese
1 cup sour cream
2 tomatoes, peeled and coarsely cut
2 pickling cucumbers, peeled and chopped
1 small red pepper, seeded and chopped
1 rib celery, chopped
1 small carrot, grated
4 radishes, sliced very thin
1 bunch scallions, cut in 1 inch segments
1 bunch dill, feathery leaves only
1 teaspoon seasoning salt
fresh ground pepper to taste

In large bowl, combine cheeses and sour cream. In another bowl toss vegetables, add to cheese mixture and blend well. Carefully fold in tomatoes and season to taste with seasoning salt and pepper.

CURRIED SPINACH SALAD
Serves 4-6

2 large bunches spinach
2-3 tart apples, depending on size
lemon juice
⅔ cup roasted Spanish peanuts
½ cup golden raisins
⅓ cup thinly sliced green onions
2 tablespoons toasted sesame seeds

Curry Dressing:
½ cup white wine vinegar
⅔ cup salad oil
3 tablespoons finely chopped chutney
1 teaspoon curry powder
½ teaspoon salt
1 teaspoon dry mustard
¼ teaspoon Tabasco sauce

Wash and trim spinach. Tear into bite-size pieces and place in large mixing bowl. Core and dice apples. Toss with lemon juice. Add to spinach in bowl. Add peanuts, raisins, onions and sesame seeds. Combine dressing in blender or glass jar. Toss salad with desired amount of dressing. Unused dressing may be stored in refrigerator indefinitely.

DAY-AHEAD SPINACH SALAD
Serves 6

½ - ¾ *pound spinach*
½ *medium thinly sliced cucumber*
½ *cup thinly sliced radishes*
¼ *cup thinly sliced green onions*
2 *hard cooked eggs, sliced*
¾ *cup thick blue cheese dressing*
½ *cup Spanish peanuts*

Wash spinach and pat dry leaves. Tear into bite size pieces Arrange evenly in a shallow bowl. Evenly layer cucumber slices, radishes, green onions and eggs. Spread dressing over the top. Cover and chill overnight. Just before serving sprinkle with peanuts.

CRUNCHY VEGETABLE SALAD
Serves 6-8

1 *medium size head iceberg lettuce*
½ *cup thinly sliced green onions*
1 *cup thinly sliced celery*
1 *8-ounce can water chestnuts, drained and sliced*
1 *9-ounce package frozen peas*
1 *cup mayonnaise or to taste*
2 *teaspoons sugar*
½ *cup grated Parmesan cheese*
¼ *teaspoon seasoned salt*
3 *hard cooked eggs, chopped*
½ *pound fresh mushrooms, sliced*
2 *medium tomatoes, cut into wedges*

Slice lettuce and place in shallow 4 quart serving dish. Layer onions, celery, water, chestnuts and peas over lettuce. Spread mayonnaise evenly over top. Sprinkle with sugar, cheese and salt. Cover and chill overnight. Just before serving, sprinkle salad with chopped eggs; top with sliced mushrooms and attractively arranged tomato wedges.

TOMATOES WITH DILL AND FETA CHEESE
Serve 6

1 cup Feta cheese, diced
½ cup plain yogurt
½ cup milk
1 tablespoon fresh dill, minced
3 large ripe tomatoes, cut in small wedges
1 head butter lettuce
dill sprigs

Combine cheese, yogurt, milk, and dill and blend well until smooth. Refrigerate.

Arrange tomatoes on leaves of rinsed and crisped lettuce. Pour dressing over tomatoes and top with dill sprigs. Refrigerate reserved dressing and use within 2 to 3 days.

TOMATO BREAD SALAD
Serves 6

3 pounds very ripe plum tomatoes, cut into large cubes
2 cups red onions, thinly sliced
1 cup basil leaves, julienned
⅔ cup extra virgin olive oil
2 tablespoons red wine vinegar
salt and pepper
2½ cups sourdough bread croutons

Combine tomatoes, red onions, basil, olive oil, vinegar, salt and pepper to taste, in a large ceramic or porcelain bowl. Refrigerate until ready to serve, add the following to croutons, toss and serve.

Croutons:
3 tablespoons unsalted butter
3 tablespoons extra virgin olive oil
3 large cloves garlic, minced
1 tablespoon each parsley and chives, chopped
3 tablespoons Parmesan cheese

Saute croutons in butter and oil over medium heat for about 3 minutes. Add garlic and herbs, mix well, place on cookie sheet and bake in a 350° oven until golden. Toss with Parmesan, add to tomatoes and serve.

SALADS

LENTIL AND WALNUT SALAD
Serves 6 - 8

2½ cups dried lentils
3 carrots, peeled and quartered
1 medium size yellow onion, peeled
3 cloves
1½ quarts chicken stock
1 bay leaf
2 teaspoons dried thyme
⅓ cup white wine vinegar
3 garlic cloves, minced
½ cup walnut oil
salt and freshly ground pepper to taste
2 green onions chopped
1 cup walnut halves
Italian parsley, chopped

Rinse the lentils and sort through them carefully discarding any pebbles you may find. Transfer lentils to a large pot and add carrots, onion stuck with the cloves, stock, bay leaf and thyme. Set over moderate heat and bring to a boil. Reduce to a simmer, skim foam, cover, and cook for about 25 minutes (lentil cooking time varies widely), or until lentils are tender but still hold their shape. Do not overcook.

While lentils are cooking, combine vinegar, garlic and walnut oil in a blender or in a bowl of a food processor fitted with a steel blade, and process until smooth and creamy. When lentils are done, drain them, discard the carrots, onion, cloves and bay leaf, and pour lentils into a mixing bowl. Rewhisk dressing and pour it over the still-hot lentils. Toss gently, season generously with salt and pepper and let salad cool to room temperature. Toss again, cover, and refrigerate overnight. Before serving, add green onions and walnuts. Add an additional tablespoon or two

of vinegar or walnut oil to taste, and toss gently. Sprinkle generously with chopped parsley. Serve with freshly ground pepper.

BULGUR SALAD PRIMAVERA
6-8 Servings

Salad:
1 cup bulgur
2 cups boiling water
2 cups chopped tomatoes, very ripe
1 cup shredded carrot
½ cup dried currants
½ cup toasted sunflower seeds
½ cup finely chopped scallions
fresh mint

Dressing:
¼ cup red wine vinegar
3 tablespoons soy sauce
2 tablespoons olive oil
2 cloves garlic, minced
1 tablespoon chopped fresh basil
¼ teaspoon oregano

Place bulgur in a large bowl. Add boiling water, and let stand for
one hour until the bulgur is just tender. Strain and press out
excess moisture. Return bulgur to bowl and add remaining salad
ingredients. Combine dressing ingredients in jar, shake well and
pour over bulgur mixture. Toss well, cover bowl and refrigerate
until 1 hour before serving time. Garnish with mint.

SALADS

PEARL BARLEY SALAD
Serves 6

3 cups water
1½ teaspoons salt, divided
1¼ cups pearl barley
⅓ cup lemon juice
½ cup olive oil
⅛ teaspoon pepper
3 green onions including green tops, chopped
1¼ cups parsley, finely chopped
¼ cup fresh mint leaves, chopped
1 head romaine lettuce
1 cucumber, sliced
1 cup cherry tomatoes

Bring water and 1 teaspoon salt to a boil. Add barley, cover and simmer 35 minutes. Barley will be puffed and almost tender-chewy at this point. Remove from heat and cool. Combine lemon juice, oil, remaining ½ teaspoon salt and pepper. Pour over barley. Toss with a fork. Chill. Add onion, parsley and mint. Cover and refrigerate overnight to blend flavors. Line serving bowl with romaine leaves. Spoon in salad. Garnish with cucumber slices and tomatoes.

RICE SALAD
Serves 8

2 cups cooked rice
¼ cup Italian salad dressing
¼ cup mayonnaise
1 cup sliced radishes
1 cucumber, chopped
1 green pepper

½ *cup celery diced*
½ *cup green onions, diced*

Mix cooked rice and salad dressing. Chill several hours or overnight. Add mayonnaise and fold in vegetables before serving.

INDONESIAN RICE SALAD
Serves 8

2 cups cooked, cooled brown rice
½ *cup raisins*
2 green onions, chopped
¼ *cup water chestnuts, thinly sliced*
1 large green pepper, chopped
½ *cup cashews, toasted*
1 stalk celery, chopped
fresh parsley
½-*1 cup sesame seeds, toasted*

Dressing:
¾ *cup orange juice*
¼ *cup safflower oil*
1 tablespoon sesame oil
¾ *tablespoon tamari sauce or light soy sauce*
2 tablespoons dry sherry
juice of 1 lemon
1-2 cloves garlic, minced
½-*1 teaspoon ginger root, freshly grated*

Combine salad ingredients in a large bowl. Combine dressing ingredients and toss with salad.

SALADS

PISTACHIO RICE SALAD
Serves 6-8

2 cups long grain quick cooking brown rice
3-4 green onions, chopped
1 red bell pepper, chopped
1 green bell pepper, chopped
½ cup snow peas, chopped
¾ cup pistachios
½ cup dried apricots
1 cucumber, sliced
1 cup bean sprouts, blanched but still crisp
rice vinegar to taste
tamari sauce to taste

Cook rice and mix with remaining ingredients. Serve hot or cold.

SOUTHWEST BEAN SALAD
Serves 12-16

1 16-ounce package pinto beans
¼ cup ketchup
¼ cup cider vinegar
¼ cup olive oil
1 tablespoon Worcestershire sauce
3 tablespoons brown sugar, packed
1 tablespoon chili powder
1 teaspoon ground cumin
1 teaspoon salt
¼ teaspoon pepper
¼ teaspoon Tabasco sauce
1½ tablespoons Dijon-style mustard
1 medium red bell pepper, diced

1 medium green bell pepper, diced
1 medium white onion, minced
1 11-ounce can whole-kernel corn, drained
6 ounces corn tortilla chips, crumbled, divided

Rinse beans, pick over to remove any grit. Put in large pot with lid, add water to cover by at least 2 inches and let soak overnight. Or bring beans to boil, cover, remove from heat and let stand 1 hour. Drain and rinse beans, return to pot, fill with fresh water to cover by at least 2 inches and bring to boil. Reduce heat slightly and simmer 1-1½ hours or until tender but not falling apart. Drain, rinse under cold running water to stop cooking, and drain well again.

Dressing:
In 1-quart non-aluminum saucepan combine ket-chup, vinegar, olive oil, Worcestershire sauce, brown sugar, chili powder, cumin, salt, pepper and Tabasco sauce. Bring to boil, reduce heat to low and simmer 10 minutes. Remove from heat, whisk in mustard and set aside.

To assemble salad: In large bowl combine cooked beans, bell peppers, onion and corn. Just before serving fold half of the crumbled chips into salad, add dressing and toss. Sprinkle remaining chips over top. Serve at room temperature.

SALADS

SUMMER PASTA SALAD
Serves 4-6

4 quarts water
1 pound pasta, ziti or penne
Juice of 2 lemons
⅓ cup extra virgin olive oil
3 small green zucchini
3 small yellow crookneck squash
4 cloves garlic, minced
2 pounds very ripe plum tomatoes, peeled and seeded
¼ cup basil leaves, julienned
salt, sugar and pepper to taste

Bring water to boil, add pasta, cook al dente. Drain and rinse in cold water. Place in large bowl and add lemon juice, tossing well. Add half the olive oil, toss again. Set aside.

Slice all zucchini in half lengthwise, then into ½ inch slices on the bias. Heat remaining oil in large skillet over medium high heat. Add zucchini and saute quickly until tender, about 2 minutes. Add garlic and cook 1 minute. Add tomatoes, basil, salt, sugar, and pepper. Pour vegetables over pasta and toss. Taste and correct seasoning. May be served chilled or at room temperature.

FRESH FRUIT SALAD WITH HONEY DRESSING
Serves 8

1 red apple, cut in cubes
1 avocado, sliced
1 orange, peeled and sliced
1 pineapple, peeled, cored and sliced
½ cup chopped dates

Arrange apple, avocado, orange and pineapple pieces on lettuce-lined platter. Garnish with dates. Serve with dressing.

Dressing:
2 8-ounce cartons peach yogurt or peach kefir
2 tablespoons oil
3 tablespoons honey
¼ teaspoon poppy seeds

Stir together yogurt, oil and honey until well blended. Chill until serving time. Garnish with poppy seeds. Makes about 2 cups.

SAUERKRAUT SALAD
Serves 8-10

3 cups sauerkraut, drained
1 1-pound can garbanzo beans, drained
1 cup chopped celery
1 green pepper, chopped
2 tablespoons diced pimiento
2 green onions, chopped
½ cup oil
¼ cup vinegar
¼ cup sugar
1 teaspoon pepper

Combine all ingredients. Cover and refrigerate 12 hours or overnight.

SALADS

ROASTED PEPPERS

6 peppers, red, yellow or green

Preheat oven to 375°. Place peppers on rack in middle of oven. Bake for 20 to 30 minutes or until skin has darkened. Turn each pepper over and continue to bake until all are blistered. Enclose in brown bag until cool. Remove seeds. Peppers are now ready for recipe.

ROASTED PEPPER SALAD
Serves 6

6 roasted peppers, cut into oblong pieces
⅓ cup virgin olive oil
3 garlic cloves, minced
salt and pepper to taste
2 tablespoons balsamic vinegar
1 2-ounce can of anchovies
parsley

Layer peppers in bowl. Cover with olive oil, garlic, salt and pepper. Cover with plastic and refrigerate. When ready to serve, arrange peppers on platter, sprinkle balsamic vinegar and garnish with anchovies and parsley.

LITTLE ITALY BREAD SALAD
Serves 6

½ loaf day-old French or Italian bread
2 tomatoes, peeled, seeded, and cut into ½-inch dice
1½ tablespoons capers
½ cup fruity olive oil
¼ cup red wine vinegar
coarse salt and freshly ground pepper to taste
3 cucumbers, peeled, halved, seeded,
  and cut into ½-inch dice
½ small red onion, peeled and thinly sliced
1 bell pepper, red, yellow, or green, cored, seeded,
  and cut lengthwise into very thin strips

Cut the bread into ½-inch-thick slices and remove the crusts. Set aside. Mix together the tomatoes, capers, oil, vinegar, salt, and pepper. In a wide, shallow bowl or large platter make a layer of bread slices. Scatter the cucumbers, onion, and bell pepper strips over the bread. Pour a ladleful of the tomato mixture over the bread and vegetables. Continue layering until all the ingredients are used up ending with tomato mixture. Set the dish aside at room temperature or in the refrigerator for at least 1 hour. It is important for the bread to absorb the liquid from the vegetables and tomato mixture. If the dish seems too dry, sprinkle on more oil and vinegar.

SOUPS

*"If the pot has ingredients,
the plate will have food."*
YIDDISH PROVERB

Soup is so versatile.
Depending on its contents, it can be a first course
or a whole meal. It can warm with its heat, like
barley and beans in the winter, or it can cool like
gazpacho in the summer.

What's in the pot is up to you—for although
recipes are known to call for exact ingredients,
who among us has not hesitated to add a carrot,
an onion, even a rutabaga together with liquid
left from steamed vegetables and spices and
seasoning that come to hand, and mind?
Nevertheless, we won't go wrong if we start with
the game plans that follow.

BASIC BEEF STOCK
Yields 3 quarts

4 pounds bones with some meat on them
3 quarts water
1 cup onions, thinly sliced
1 cup carrots, sliced
1 cup celery, sliced
2 bay leaves
1 teaspoon dried thyme or 1 sprig fresh thyme
4 whole black peppercorns
2-3 sprigs fresh parsley

Put bones in a large kettle, cover with cold water and bring to a boil. Let boil for 3 minutes and drain. Return bones to kettle and add 3 quarts water, onion, carrots, celery, bay leaf, thyme, peppercorns and parsley. Bring to a boil and simmer for at least 4 hours, skimming the fat and residue from the surface from time to time. Strain and discard the solids If you wish to make this stock as fat free as possible, refrigerate. When cold, the fat will rise to the surface and harden making it easy to scrape off and discard. Use this stock as a base for other soups and other recipes. Can also be used alone with cooked diced vegetables. This stock can be frozen.

CHICKEN STOCK
Yields 2½ quarts

4 pounds chicken bones (backs, necks, wings)
10 cups water
6 whole peppercorn
1 cup onion, cut into quarters
½ cup carrots, coarsely chopped
½ cup celery, coarsely chopped
5 sprigs fresh parsley

SOUPS

1 bay leaf
½ teaspoon dried thyme or 1 sprig fresh thyme
1 whole clove
1 garlic clove
2 sprigs fresh dill weed
salt and pepper to taste

Place bones in a heavy kettle. Add the remaining ingredients and bring to a boil. Simmer uncovered for 1 hour, skimming the surface from time to time to remove the fat and residue which comes to the surface. Strain through cheesecloth or fine strainer. If you wish to remove excess fat, refrigerate, and when fat rises to the surface and hardens, scrape off.

VEGETABLE STOCK
Yields 10 Cups

1 potato
1 whole celery or 1 small celery root
1 onion, peeled, studded with 4 cloves
2 leeks (white part only)
1 carrot
4 ripe tomatoes, quartered
1 turnip, small
1 teaspoon dried whole thyme
2 bay leaves
10 peppercorns, crushed
12 cups water
2 tablespoons soy sauce (low sodium)
1 tablespoon salt

Combine all ingredients in large stockpot. Slowly bring to boil. Simmer about 2 hours, reducing to about 10 cups. Strain liquid. Check seasoning.

JERUSALEM ARTICHOKE SOUP
Serves 4-6

3 tablespoons margarine
1 onion, sliced
1 9-ounce box frozen artichoke hearts, thawed
1 pound Jerusalem artichokes, peeled and diced
1 quart chicken broth
1½ cups watercress leaves
salt and freshly ground pepper

Melt the margarine in a large saucepan, add the onion, and cook gently about 5 minutes. Add the artichoke hearts and Jerusalem artichokes, then cook and stir 5 minutes longer.

Pour in the chicken broth, bring to a boil, then cover and simmer about 20 minutes, until the vegetables are very tender. Puree in a blender or food processor until smooth, then add the watercress leaves and process a few seconds more, until finely chopped and the soup is flecked with green. Season to taste with salt and pepper.

BARLEY MUSHROOM SOUP
Serves 6-8

4 tablespoons medium sized barley
1½ cups beef stock or water
⅓ cup margarine
¾ pound mushrooms, thinly sliced
1 large onion, chopped
4 cups boiling water or stock or half of each or more
  if needed
½ cup carrots, raw and grated
¾ cup small raw potatoes, peeled and cubed

SOUPS

½ cup celery, finely chopped
salt, pepper and cayenne to taste

Soak barley in beef stock or water for at least 1 hour. In a large soup kettle, melt margarine and saute mushrooms and onion over a low flame about 5 minutes. Add 4 cups stock or water or combination of both, bring to a boil and then add carrots, potatoes, celery, drained barley and seasonings. Bring to a boil again. Lower the flame and simmer gently until the barley is tender, about 40 minutes.

Note: Rice can be substituted for barley.

VEGETARIAN BARLEY SOUP
Serves 12

1 medium green pepper, chopped
½ cup onion, chopped
1 clove garlic, minced
2 tablespoons oil
6 cups water
4 medium tomatoes, peeled and chopped
½ teaspoon basil
½ teaspoon oregano
⅛ teaspoon pepper
½ cup barley
2 cups broccoli pieces
3 medium carrots, julienne
1 cup celery slices
2 teaspoons salt to taste

Sauté green pepper, onion and garlic in oil in a 4½ quart Dutch oven. Add water, tomatoes, basil, oregano and pepper. Bring to a boil and stir in barley. Cover and simmer about 40 minutes.

Add remaining vegetables. Return to boil and simmer 20 minutes or until vegetables are tender. Add salt.

CURRIED CARROT SOUP
Serves 6

2 teaspoons oil
1 onion, coarsely chopped
1 teaspoon dried thyme
1 bay leaf
4 or 5 carrots, average size, sliced
1 tablespoon curry powder
5 cups vegetable stock, heated
3 ounces Neufchatel low-fat cream cheese
salt and pepper to taste
3 tablespoons parsley, chopped
parsley sprigs

In saucepan, over moderate fire, heat oil. Gently sauté onions and stir with thyme and bay leaf until glazed. Add carrots. Stir in curry powder. Pour in vegetable stock. Simmer, uncovered, 40-50 minutes. Remove bay leaf.

In blender, blend soup mixture and cheese until smooth. Return mixture to saucepan. Reheat and season. Add parsley sprigs.

SOUPS

CELERY ROOT SOUP
Serves 4-6

1 quart chicken soup
2 medium sized celery root
6 large fresh tomatoes, peeled and seeded
1 medium onion, chopped
2 tablespoons margarine
salt and pepper to taste
1 teaspoon dried basil
2 tablespoons parsley, chopped
fresh basil or dill to garnish

Bring soup to a boil. Pare celery root, coarsely dice and place in boiling stock. Cook until tender, about 30 minutes. Saute tomatoes and onions in butter or margarine until soft. Add salt and pepper, basil, and parsley, to soup and add vegetables. Put into blender or food processor and puree. Correct seasoning. Serve hot with fresh basil or dill for garnish.

CORN AND BEAN SOUP
Serves 8

1 pound (2½ cups) dry small white beans
2 quarts regular-strength chicken broth
2 teaspoons dry savory leaves or dry thyme leaves
1 can (28 ounce) pear-shaped tomatoes
1 can (17 ounce) cream-style corn
pepper
extra-virgin olive oil
salt

Sort the beans to remove any debris; rinse and drain. To a 4-5 quart pan, add beans, broth and savory. Bring to a boil over high

318

heat; reduce heat, cover and simmer until beans are tender to bite, about 1½ hours. With a knife, cut through tomatoes in can to make small pieces; add to soup along with corn and pepper to taste. Cover and simmer about 30 minutes longer to blend flavors. With spoon or potato masher, mash some of the beans to thicken soup slightly. If made ahead, let cool, cover and chill up to 2 days; reheat to serve. Ladle soup into wide bowls. Add a swirl of olive oil to taste to each portion. Add salt to taste.

EGG LEMON SOUP
Serves 6

6 cups rich chicken stock
¼ cup long grain white rice
3 large eggs, separated, at room temperature
¼ cup freshly squeezed lemon juice
salt to taste

In a soup pot, bring chicken stock to a boil. Add rice. Cover the pot, and cook over medium heat until rice is just tender, about 15 minutes. Remove pot from the heat, leave it uncovered, and spoon out about 1 cup of the liquid. Beat egg whites to soft peaks. While continuing to beat, add yolks and beat for about 2 minutes. Slowly add lemon juice and then 1 cup of stock, beating all the while. Whisk this mixture into the soup until well blended. Add salt to taste. Heat (but do not boil) the soup over a low flame stirring constantly, before serving.

SOUPS

FRESH CHINESE PEA POD SOUP
Serves 4

2 teaspoons sesame-seed or safflower oil
2 onions, coarsely chopped
1 teaspoon dried sweet basil
5 cups vegetable stock, heated
3 ounces Neufchatel low-fat cream cheese
¾ pound fresh Chinese pea pods (snow peas), washed
 and strings removed
vegetable seasoning, to taste
parsley sprigs

In a saucepan, heat oil and gently sauté onion until glazed. Add basil and vegetable stock. Simmer very gently, uncovered, 30 minutes. Remove from fire. Cool 10 minutes. In blender or food processor, puree broth with cream cheese and Chinese pea pods. Season with vegetable seasoning and bring to near boil. Garnish with parsley sprigs and serve immediately,

HERBED SQUASH SOUP*
Serves 8

1 large onion, cubed
5 cups squash in any combination (zucchini, butternut,
 summer, etc.)
1 large potato, cubed
3 tablespoons olive oil
4 tablespoons dry vegetable bouillon (or 4 bouillon cubes
 prepared in 3 cups of boiling water)
½ cup fresh basil (or 2 teaspoons dry basil)
1 tablespoon thyme
pepper to taste

½ cup milk or half-and-half
dill (optional)

Saute onion in oil until glazed. Add potato and squash. Simmer in bouillon until just tender. Place in food processor and puree. Return to pot and adjust seasonings. Add milk and heat. When serving, sprinkle with dill.

*The squash and tomato soups may be served together for a two-color effect. Simultaneously pour 1 cup of each soup into a bowl from each side. Sprinkle with dill or basil.

PUMPKIN SOUP
Serves 12

1 onion, chopped
4 ribs celery, chopped
1 leek, chopped
4 ounces margarine
3 pounds pumpkin or 2 16-ounce cans pumpkin
5 cups broth
1 teaspoon nutmeg
salt and pepper to taste
½ cup non-dairy creamer
1 cup parsley, finely chopped

Saute onion, celery and leek in margarine. If using canned pumpkin add contents to vegetables; if using fresh pumpkin, cut inside of pumpkin into pieces. Mix with sauteed vegetables, broth, and cook until tender. Puree in food processor. Add nutmeg, salt and pepper. Simmer for 10 minutes. Add non-dairy creamer and heat again, being careful not to boil. Add dollop of creamer and sprinkle with parsley.

SOUPS

LENTIL PUMPKIN SOUP
Serves 10

1 tablespoon canola oil
2 large onions, coarsely chopped
½ cup lentils, washed and sorted
5¼ cups low-fat chicken broth
1½ cups cooked pumpkin (or other yellow squash)
1 teaspoon salt (or to taste)
¼ teaspoon freshly ground pepper
dash of hot pepper sauce
2 bay leaves

Heat the oil in a pot large enough to hold all the ingredients. Add ¼ cup chicken broth and onions and cook until the onions are lightly browned. Stir in the lentils and the rest of the broth. Add the pumpkin, salt, pepper, hot pepper sauce, and bay leaves. Simmer, covered until the lentils are tender, about 1 hour. Remove bay leaves. Puree in the blender or food processor.

At serving time, bring to a simmer. Adjust the seasonings. Do not boil.

CREAMY LITE SPINACH SOUP
Serves 6

A food processor works, but this is one of the few cases where a blender is a better choice if you have one.

1 large or 3 smaller bunches of spinach
2 cups vegetable broth
1 or 2 cloves garlic
1 cup Ricotta cheese

322

½ cup cream or milk
salt and freshly ground pepper

Wash the spinach well and remove the large, tough stems. Shred or chop the spinach coarsely. You should have 4 cups, lightly packed.

Combine the spinach with the vegetable broth, garlic and Ricotta in the blender. Blend on high speed for about 1 minute, scraping down the inside of the container with a spatula if necessary so all the ingredients are thoroughly blended.

Pour the soup into a saucepan. Add cream or milk, salt and pepper. Heat it just to a simmer. (If it boils, you lose that brilliant green color.) Serve warm or chilled.

SPINACH-PEAR SOUP
Serves 4

3 cups vegetable stock (see index)
2 leeks (white part only), cut in 1 inch slices
1 onion, halved
2 teaspoons arrowroot, dissolved in 2 tablespoons water
1 cup fresh spinach, chopped (or ½ cup frozen spinach thawed
*   and drained)*
white pepper, to taste
vegetable seasoning, to taste
1 or 2 drops Pernod liqueur
1 firm pear (not overly ripe) or apple, cored and thinly sliced

In vegetable stock, simmer leeks and onion 35 minutes, until tender. Remove from fire. Cool 10 minutes.

In food blender, puree leeks and onion with some of the broth until creamy and smooth. Add dissolved arrowroot. Return mixture to pot; bring back to a boil. With wooden spatula, stir in spinach. Season with pepper and vegetable seasoning. Remove from fire and add Pernod.

Place 2 or 3 slices of pear in each bowl, pour soup over, and serve immediately.

FRESH TOMATO SOUP
Serves 4-6

1 tablespoon butter or margarine
3 large carrots, sliced
3 medium potatoes, sliced
4 large tomatoes, peeled and quartered
6 cups boiling water
salt
pepper
dried tarragon
marjoram
croutons
sour cream (optional)

Melt butter or margarine in a soup kettle. Add carrots, potatoes, tomatoes and saute the mixture for about 3 minutes, stirring constantly. Add 6 cups boiling water and season with salt, pepper and a pinch each of the tarragon and marjoram. Cover and simmer for about 1 hour or until the vegetables are tender. Puree the mixture. Heat and serve with croutons and a topping of sour cream.

LENTIL-TOMATO SOUP
Serves 8

1 cup lentils and water to cover
1 teaspoon oil
1½ teaspoons mustard seeds
1 cup chopped onions
8 cups water
10 medium tomatoes, chopped or thinly sliced
½ cup chopped cilantro
1 tablespoon curry powder or to taste
salt

Cook lentils until tender or cook in pressure cooker with 2 cups water, following manufacturer's directions. Drain lentils.

Heat oil in saucepan over medium heat. Add mustard seeds, cover pan and heat until seeds pop. Add and saute onions until tender. Add 8 cups water with tomatoes and cilantro. Simmer 10 minutes.

Add cooked lentils and 2 tablespoons curry powder or to taste. Bring to boil, stirring. Simmer 10 minutes, stirring occasionally. Season to taste with salt.

TOMATO, BASIL, ORANGE SOUP
Serves 6-8

1 onion, diced
4 carrots, diced
3 ribs celery, diced
1 tablespoon garlic, chopped
3 tablespoons olive oil
2 large cans of pear tomatoes, broken up

SOUPS

4 cups of chicken broth
2 cups of orange juice
1 bunch of fresh basil, chopped
salt and pepper

Saute onion, carrots, celery, and garlic in olive oil until tender. Add tomatoes with juice, chciken broth, orange juice and basil. Heat until very hot. Add salt and pepper to taste.

FRESH VEGETABLE SOUP
Serves 12 -14

1 tablespoon oil (olive or your choice)
1 cup onions, chopped
1 tablespoon garlic, chopped
2 cups tomatoes, ripe and diced
2 cups zucchini, cut into small ½ inch cubes
1 cup carrots, cut into ¼ inch cubes
1 cup white turnips, cut into ¼ inch cubes
1 cup celery, chopped
1 pound dried navy beans
freshly ground pepper to taste
10 cups defatted chicken stock
¼ cup fresh basil, chopped
salt to taste

Heat oil in a kettle. Add onions and garlic. Cook them briefly and add cubed and chopped vegetables. Cook 10 minutes. Add beans, pepper and stock. Bring to a boil and simmer for 1 hour and 45 minutes. Add basil and salt.

FRESH VEGETABLE SOUP PUREE
Serves 4

2 cups fresh chopped vegetables
  (include onion, potato, and both green and yellow
  vegetables for a balanced dish)
2 cups water
2 tablespoons thyme
2 tablespoons basil
butter, margarine or oil (optional)
salt and pepper
grated Parmesan cheese (optional)

Combine vegetables, water and seasonings in saucepan and bring to a boil, stirring frequently. Reduce heat, cover and simmer 15 minutes. Transfer to blender and puree until smooth. Return soup to pan and add optional butter, margarine or oil. Season to taste with salt and pepper and sprinkle with Parmesan cheese.

Note: This soup can also be served chilled with a dollop of yogurt.

SOUPS

MUSHROOM VEGETABLE SOUP
Serves 6

1 pound fresh mushrooms
2 tablespoons margarine
1 cup carrots, finely chopped
1 cup celery, finely chopped
1 cup onions, finely chopped
1 clove garlic, minced
14 ounces beef broth
2 cups water
¼ cup tomato paste
2 tablespoons parsley flakes or ¼ cup minced fresh parsley
1 bay leaf
¼ teaspoon salt (optional)
¼ teaspoon pepper
2 tablespoons dry sherry

Dampen mushrooms and wipe them off to clean them. It's best not to soak them as they absorb water. Slice half of them and set aside.

Chop remaining mushrooms and sauté in 1 tablespoon margarine in a large pot. Add carrots, celery, and onion and cook 5 to 7 minutes, stirring often. Stir in garlic, broth, water, tomato paste, parsley, bay leaf, salt, if desired, and pepper. Simmer, covered for 1 hour.

Puree soup in a blender.

Sauté the sliced mushrooms in the remaining 1 tablespoon margarine. Return pureed soup to pot; add sautéed mushrooms and sherry. (Alcohol evaporates during heating, leaving only the flavor). Reheat over moderate heat, stirring.

HERBED VEGETABLE SOUP
Serves 8 -10

2 onions, chopped
2 garlic cloves, minced
2 carrots, chopped
2 stalks of celery, chopped
½ stick unsalted butter or margarine
1 teaspoon dried marjoram
1 bay leaf
½ teaspoon dried basil
salt and pepper
4 cups chicken stock or canned chicken broth
1 cup canned tomato puree
1 10-ounce package frozen spinach
1 10-ounce package frozen peas
1 10-ounce package frozen corn
⅓ cup fresh parsley leaves, chopped

In a kettle, over moderately low heat, cook the onions, garlic, carrots and celery in the butter with marjoram, bay leaf, basil and salt and pepper to taste, stirring occasionally until the vegetables are softened. Add the stock and the tomato puree, and bring the liquid to a boil. Add the spinach, peas, and corn, returning the liquid to a boil, breaking up the vegetables, and simmer the soup for 5 minutes, or until the vegetables are just tender. (Discard the bay leaf.) In a food processor, pulsing the motor several times, puree the soup coarsely in batches. The soup may be prepared in advance and kept covered and chilled. Reheat as needed. Sprinkle with parsley.

SOUPS

FISH SOUP WITH VEGETABLES
4 Servings

1½ pounds firm white fish
1½ pounds fresh fish bones, including heads
1¾ cups fish broth (see below) or use water
1 cup onion, chopped
2 cups green or red peppers, preferably one of each, chopped
2 cloves garlic, finely minced
1½ cups leeks, both white and green parts, chopped
2 cups tomatoes, seeded, skinned, chopped
1 cup potatoes, peeled, cut into ½ inch cubes
¼ cup olive oil
1 teaspoon loosely packed saffron, optional
1 hot dried red pepper, optional
salt and freshly ground pepper to taste
1 bay leaf
2 sprigs fresh thyme or ½ teaspoon dried
1 cup dry white wine
½ cup heavy cream
2 tablespoons anise-flavored liqueur, optional
¼ cup parsley, finely chopped
8 slices French bread croutons (see below)

Cut fish into 1½ inch cubes. There should be about 4 cups. Set aside. Cook fish broth. Prepare the onion, peppers, garlic, leeks, tomatoes and potatoes and set aside in separate batches. Add cold water to the potatoes to prevent discoloration. Set aside. Heat the oil in a pot and add onion. Cook until wilted. Add peppers, garlic, saffron and leeks and cook, stirring, about 1 minute. Add hot red pepper, salt, pepper, bay leaf and thyme. Cook about 3-5 minutes. Add the tomatoes and cook, stirring, about 1 minute. Add the wine and potatoes and cover. Cook 10 minutes. Add fish broth and fish. Cook 5 minutes. Add the cream and bring to boil. If desired, add liqueur. Serve piping hot with chopped parsley and 2 croutons for each serving.

Fish Broth:
In a large saucepan or small kettle, combine about 1½ pounds fresh fish bones (with head but gills and eyes removed) and 3 cups water. Bring to boil and simmer about 25 minutes. Stir once during cooking. Drain solids and reserve broth.

Fresh Bread Croutons:
Rub outside of 1 section of French bread (large enough to make 8 slices) with a peeled clove of garlic. Cut into 8 slices. Brush each slice with half teaspoon olive oil. Place under broiler, turning once, until crisp and golden.

ITALIAN FISH SOUP
Serves 4

2 carrots, finely diced (1½ cups)
1 medium onion, finely diced (⅔ cup)
1 leek, washed well and diced
1½ tablespoons olive oil
2 large cloves garlic, minced (2 teaspoons)
¾ teaspoon thyme
4 large tomatoes, peeled, seeded, and coarsely chopped
⅓ cup dry white wine
1½ pounds assorted firm fish filets (e.g., halibut,
* red snapper), cut into 1-inch pieces*
4 cups fish stock, heated
2 tablespoons fresh parsley, minced
salt to taste
freshly ground black pepper to taste

In a large, heavy saucepan, cook carrots, onion, and leek in oil, stirring until the onion is translucent, about 5 minutes. Stir in garlic and cook vegetables for another minute.

Add thyme, tomatoes, and wine, and simmer mixture for 5 minutes. Add fish, and simmer mixture for another 5 minutes.

Add hot stock, bring soup to a boil, and simmer it for 5 minutes. Stir in parsley, salt, and pepper.

BEEF SHANK SUPPER SOUP
Serves 6

4 pounds meaty beef shanks, cut into pieces, 1½ inches thick
1 large onion, finely chopped
2 stalks celery, finely chopped
1 can (28-ounce) whole tomatoes
1 tablespoon oregano
1 teaspoon thyme
¼ teaspoon ground cloves
1 bay leaf
1½ teaspoon salt
6 cups water
½ cup pearl barley
4 large carrots, cut into 1-inch chunks
1 package (9-ounce) frozen green beans, cut
1 cup parsley, finely chopped

In a large kettle (about 8 quarts), brown shanks in their own fat over medium heat. Transfer meat to a bowl. Add onions and celery to drippings in kettle. Cook and stir over medium heat until onions are limp. Add tomatoes and their liquid. Stir in oregano, thyme, cloves, bay leaf, salt and water. Return meat and any juices to kettle. Cover and bring to a boil. Reduce heat and simmer gently 1½ hours.

Remove kettle from heat and cool until meat can be handled. Pull meat off bones and cut into 1-inch pieces. Discard fat and gristle. Return meat and any bones with marrow to kettle. Chill the soup until surface fat has solidified. Lift off fat and discard. Bring soup to a simmer. Stir in barley and simmer, covered, until tender. Add beans and cook, uncovered, 10 minutes. Correct seasoning. Stir in parsley.

TURKEY BARLEY SOUP
Serves 8

turkey carcass, browned in oven
½ teaspoon salt and pepper, or to taste garlic salt and
  pepper
2 teaspoons dried dill
2 teaspoons parsley
1 tablespoon Worcestershire sauce
4 stalks celery
4-5 whole carrots
water to cover
1 cup barley
2 packages dried mushrooms
3 tablespoons dried vegetable broth

Simmer all ingredients, except barley, mushrooms and vegetable broth, until the vegetables are soft. Lift out turkey carcass, remove meat and set aside. Add barley, dry mushrooms and more liquid if necessary to vegetable broth. Cook 45 minutes. Add turkey meat and heat through.

SOUPS

AFTER HOLIDAY TURKEY BEAN SOUP
Serves 8

turkey carcass and bones
2 onions, halved
3 bay leaves
3 large carrots
6 stalks of celery with leaves
1 cup parsley
2 chicken bouillon cubes
1 8-ounce can tomato paste
salt to taste
½ teaspoon ground black pepper
¾ cup barley
2 cups assorted beans such as black, red, baby limas,
* green and orange split peas*

Brown turkey and bones in roasting pan in 400° oven. Remove to large soup pot breaking it up if necessary. Add remaining ingredients and cover with water. Simmer 2 hours covered. Remove meat from bones. Discard bones and bay leaves, puree onion, celery, parsley and carrots. Return with meat to soup pot. Adjust seasonings.

APPLE-CURRY SOUP
Serves 6-8

2 tart apples, sliced
2 medium onions, diced
2 stalks celery, diced
1 clove garlic, minced
2 tablespoons margarine
2 teaspoons curry powder
2 tablespoons flour

4 cups chicken broth
salt and pepper to taste
2 cups non-dairy cream
unpeeled red apple slices and parsley for garnish

Cook 2 apples, onions, celery and garlic in margarine until tender but not browned. Blend curry powder and flour and add to mixture. Add broth and seasonings. Slowly bring to boil; reduce to simmer. Cook 30 minutes. Puree in blender when cool and stir in cream. Chill. Float thin apple slices and parsley sprigs. Should be served cold.

BEET BORSCHT
Serves 8-10

2 cans beets, sliced or julienne
2 bottles prepared borscht
1 cucumber, seeded and chopped
1 lemon, thinly sliced
1 teaspoon dill weed
3 tablespoons chopped chives
4 cups sour cream
2 cups beer
salt and pepper to taste

Combine all ingredients and chill.

Optional: Beets can be put in blender if thicker consistency is preferred.

SOUPS

A TASTE OF SUMMER SOUP
Serves 8

2 onions, chopped
vegetable spray
1 tablespoon oil
2 pounds zucchini, sliced
chicken or powdered broth to cover
½ cup fresh watercress
¼ cup fresh basil and/or thyme
nutmeg to taste
1 cup non-dairy creamer or milk

Using a large casserole with cover, spray with vegetable oil. Saute chopped onions in oil. Cover and cook for 25 minutes. Add zucchini, broth, basil or thyme. Cook for 25 minutes. Add watercress to mixture. Do not cook. When cool, puree in food processor. Add nutmeg and non-dairy creamer or milk. Chill and serve.

COLD BROCCOLI SOUP
Serves 6

2 pounds broccoli, chopped
4 cups vegetable broth
1 cup celery, chopped
½ cup green onion, diced (white and light green part)
1 teaspoon salt, or to taste
lemon wedges
low-fat yogurt
cucumber, chopped

Put first 5 ingredients in a saucepan. Cover and cook over medium heat until broccoli is tender, 8 to 10 minutes. Transfer to a blender or processor and puree smooth. Transfer to a bowl, cover and chill at least 3 hours. Serve with lemon wedges, yogurt, and cucumber.

GAZPACHO
Serves 6

2 Bermuda onions, chopped
2 pickling cucumbers, chopped
½ cup each celery and green onion, thinly sliced
1 green, 1 red pepper, seeded and chopped
7 large tomatoes, peeled and cut into 8 pieces
5 garlic cloves
¼ cup light olive oil
1 jalapeno, minced
1 tablespoon red wine vinegar
1 teaspoon soy sauce
3 cups tomato juice
parsley or watercress, chopped
garlic croutons

Process first four ingredients on pulse mode 4-5 seconds until mixture is chunky, remove to bowl. Process 6 tomatoes until small, add to first mixture. Process remaining tomato with garlic, tomato juice, olive oil, chili, vinegar, and soy sauce. Chill overnight, garnish with chopped parsley or watercress and serve with garlic croutons.

SOUPS

GAZPACHO
Serves 4-6

1 onion, quartered
4 or more tomatoes, peeled and quartered
1 cucumber, peeled and quartered
2 green peppers, cut into chunks
3 tablespoons olive oil
¼ cup red wine vinegar
1 cup tomato or vegetable-tomato juice
½ cup parsley
3 tablespoons fresh or dried dill
1 teaspoon hot pepper sauce
salt and pepper to taste

Blend above ingredients in blender or food processor. Process only to a coarse grind. Refrigerate several hours or overnight. Serve with assorted garnishes: cut up avocado, jicama, raw green pepper, celery, mushrooms and red or green onion.

ANOTHER GAZPACHO
Serves 8

1 pound, 14 ounce canned tomatoes
1 8-ounce can tomato soup (condensed)
1 can liquid (water, consomme, beef broth, etc.)
½ of a long cucumber (peeled)
1 green pepper (medium size)
3 or 4 scallions
¼ cup apple cider vinegar
pepper to taste

Blend in food processor all the above except vinegar and pepper, which are added after blending, and chill.

338

SOUPS

HERBED TOMATO SOUP*
Serves 8

1 onion, cubed
olive oil
1 potato, peeled and cubed
1 large fennel bulb (anise), white only, cut up, or fresh dill
10 tomatoes, peeled, seeded and chopped
*2 cups chicken broth (or 3 bouillon cubes and 2 cups
   of water)*
½ cup chopped parsley
½ cup fresh basil, chopped
salt and ground pepper, to taste

Sauté onions. When glazed add potato, fennel and chopped tomatoes. Sauté for ten minutes. Add broth and herbs and cook
until vegetables are tender. Pour into processor and puree. Pour
back into pan and heat with seasonings to taste. This soup may
be served chilled or reheated. To serve, sprinkle with green leaf
from fennel bulb, or fresh dill.

* The squash and tomato soups may be served together for a
two-color effect. Simultaneously pour one cup of each soup into
a bowl from each side. Sprinkle with dill or basil.

SOUPS

COLD STRAWBERRY BUTTERMILK SOUP
Serves 4

2 pint boxes fresh strawberries, washed and hulled
* (or 2 boxes of frozen)*
1 cup orange juice
½ teaspoon cinnamon
½ cup superfine sugar
1 cup buttermilk
2 cantaloupes

Set aside 6 strawberries. Puree remaining berries in food processor or blender. Strain into bowl. Add orange juice, cinnamon, sugar and buttermilk and sliced reserved strawberries. Cover and chill 8 hours or overnight. Cut melons in half making a saw-tooth edge. Scoop out seeds. Turn upside down on paper towel to drain. Cover with plastic wrap and refrigerate until ready to serve. To serve, fill melon halves with soup. Garnish with strawberry slices.

2-TONE FRUIT SOUP
Serves 4-6

2 ripe cantaloupes, peeled and cut into chunks
1 small can (6½ ounce) frozen pineapple juice
½ ripe honey-dew, peeled and cut into chunks
½ cup Amaretto (or to taste)
1 teaspoon fresh mint

Puree cantaloupes, add pineapple juice. Place in bowl. Puree honey-dew and mint. Add Amaretto. Place in separate bowls. To serve, use 2 ladles to simultaneously pour soup into individual dishes, so that the colors appear side by side.

Optional: With a teaspoon, put a drop of cantaloupe mixture in center of honey-dew and vice versa.

RASPBERRY SOUP
Serves 6

1 10-ounce package frozen raspberries, thawed
1 11-ounce can mandarin oranges and juice
1 cup orange juice
½ cup dry red wine
1 cup Chablis wine
⅓ cup lemon juice
¼ cup tapioca
mint sprigs for garnish

Combine all ingredients except tapioca and mint. Add 1 cup of mixture to tapioca and cook until clear and thickened. Add remaining ingredients and chill. Garnish. If necessary add more of any ingredient. Sugar may be added to taste.

PEAR PEA SOUP

1 large can pears and juice (or four ripe pears, peeled)
1 cup onion, chopped
1 cup leek,sliced
1 cup celery, sliced
1 potato, peeled and cubed
1/4 cup unsalted butter or margarine
4 cups chicken or vegetable stock
1 bay leaf
1 16-ounce package frozen peas, thawed
salt, pepper, nutmeg to taste
⅓ cup half-and-half or non-dairy creamer

SOUPS

¼ cup fresh mint, minced
paprika

Sauté first 5 ingredients in butter or margarine about 15 minutes. Add stock, bay leaf and simmer 20 minutes. Add peas and mint and cook 10 minutes longer or until vegetables are soft. Season, and discard bay leaf. Puree in processor. Add cream. Serve chilled with additional pear, peas and mint if desired as garnish. Sprinkle lightly with paprika.

WINTER SOUP
Serves 10

1 large celery root, peeled and cubed
2 tablespoons dry dill or ½ cup fresh dill
3 carrots, cut up
3 celery stalks, cut up
1 red or yellow pepper, cut up (not green)
1 onion, diced and sauteed
1-8 ounce can tomato puree
1-8 ounce can stewed tomatoes
¼ cup dry vegetable broth
½ cup parsley
1 teaspoon ground pepper
2 teaspoons basil
1 teaspoon thyme
½ cup or more buttermilk to thin soup

Cover celery root with water and simmer for 20 minutes. Add dill. Add all other ingredients and sauteed onion, except buttermilk. Simmer for 20 minutes until all are tender. Cool. Put cooked soup in processor and pulse until mixture is coarse as desired. Return to stove, heat and correct seasonings. Add more broth if necessary to taste. Add buttermilk, heat and serve.

Optional: One tablespoon sour cream on top of each serving and a sprinkle of dill.

"The master of the house at the commencement of the meal cuts the bread and says the benediction and the guest pronounces the grace after the meal. The master of the house breaks bread so that he may do so with a pleasant eye (cutting larger pieces than the guest would.) The guest pronounces the grace in order that he may bless the master of the house."
TALMUD

How gratifying for the host and hostess, for besides the good company of their guests, they receive a blessing for their efforts! A nice reward when you have worked hard to prepare a traditional company meal.

Memories, memories—mama knew how to take a dish and make it her own. So we're just following her example when we add a little bit of this and that to the old-time recipes. Try them. You'll like them.

CHALLAH
Yields 1 loaf or 35 rolls

2 packages dry yeast
2 cups warm water
6 cups flour
2 eggs
2 tablespoons oil
4 tablespoons sugar
2 tablespoons salt
1 beaten egg
poppy or sesame seeds

Soften yeast in water in a small bowl. Set aside. Sift flour into a large bowl. Make a well in center of flour. Place eggs, oil, sugar, salt and softened yeast in well. Mix together until a ball of dough is formed. Add more flour if necessary. This process may be done in an electric mixer with the dough hook. Place ball of dough in greased bowl. Turn once to grease top of dough. Cover and let rise until double in bulk, about 1 hour. Punch down. Knead on floured board. Divide dough in half and shape each half into a loaf. Place in greased loaf pans. Brush top of loaves with beaten egg or milk. Sprinkle with seeds. Cover and let rise again until double in bulk, about 1 to 2 hours. Bake at 375° for 45 minutes or until golden brown.

Dough can be divided and shaped into individual rolls. If desired, the dough may be braided to form loaves instead of baking in loaf pans.

TRADITIONAL

CABBAGE BORSCHT
Serves 12-15

3 quarts beef broth
3½ pounds stewing beef, cut in pieces
3-4 marrow bones
1 16-ounce can whole tomatoes
2 medium onions, chopped
3 cloves garlic, minced
1 8-ounce can sauerkraut with juice
1 medium head cabbage, cored and thinly sliced
salt and pepper to taste
¼ cup lemon juice
¼ cup sugar
¼ cup dry red wine
1 can julienne beets (optional)

Place broth, beef, bones, tomatoes, onions and garlic in large soup pot and bring to boil. Skim off brown foam that accumulates on top. Lower heat. Add sauerkraut and cabbage. Simmer 1½ hours until meat is tender. Season soup with salt, pepper, lemon juice and sugar. Continue cooking to combine flavors. Cool and store in refrigerator at least 2 days before serving. Remove hardened fat. Reheat to serve and add wine. Adjust seasoning if desired. Add julienne beets if desired.

HASSIDIC BLACK BEAN SOUP
Serves 8

2 cups black beans
3 tablespoons margarine or chicken fat
2 onions, chopped
1 cup celery, chopped
1 bouquet garni of parsley, thyme, bay leaf

1 beef bone, with some meat on it
6 cups beef or chicken soup
4 cups water
salt, pepper to taste
4 tablespoons Slivowitz (plum brandy)
2 tablespoons lemon juice
2 hard boiled eggs, chopped, to garnish
1 tablespoon parsley, chopped, to garnish
½ lemon, sliced thin, to garnish

Cover beans in water for 6 hours; drain. In a kettle, melt 3 table-spoons margarine and add chopped onions, celery and bouquet garni. Cook over low heat 10 minutes. Add beef bone, beans, soup, water, salt, pepper and bring to boil. Reduce heat, simmer for 4 hours (adding more liquid if necessary). Discard the beef bone, bouquet garni and add Sliviowitz. Season with lemon juice. Garnish with chopped hard-boiled eggs, chopped parsley and lemon slices.

HOLIDAY SWEET AND SOUR CABBAGE
Serves 20

2 large onions, chopped
2 tablespoons oil
2 large cabbage heads, shredded
½ pound dried apples
2 mangoes, sliced
2 teaspoons sour salt
1 lemon, sliced
3 tablespoons brown sugar or 1 tablespoon brown sugar
  substitute
1 8-ounce can tomato sauce

Saute onions in oil, add cabbage and continue to saute until wilted. Add other ingredients and simmer for 45 minutes. Best cooked and refrigerated the day before serving. Reheat.

STUFFED CABBAGE ROLLS
Serves 12

1 cabbage
2 tablespoons oil
2 onions
1 clove garlic
1 stalk celery, cut up
½ green pepper, cup up
2 cans (8 ounces) tomato sauce
½ cup red wine
brown sugar
a little honey

juice of 1 lemon
salt and pepper
1 pound ground meat or turkey
1 cup rice, half cooked
1 egg
2 large tart green apples, grated
⅛ cup grated onion
raisins
1 small potato, grated
6-8 ginger snaps (optional)

Cover cabbage with hot water in large pot. Cover and boil 15-20 minutes or until soft. Slowly take leaves apart and cut away hard part of leaf.* Cut 2 onions into pot with oil and garlic, celery, green pepper and saute. Add tomato sauce, red wine, brown sugar, honey, lemon juice, seasonings and enough water to fill about ⅓ of the pot. Simmer. Mix meat, rice, egg, 1 grated apple and a little brown sugar, onion and garlic if you wish. Place a small ball in a cabbage leaf and roll up envelope style. Place in pot with any leftover leaves and sprinkle with second grated apple, raisins, potato and ginger snaps. Cover. Bring to boil and simmer about 1 hour or until meat is done. The dish is better made 1 day ahead.

*Or, freeze cabbage. Thaw and remove core. Slowly take leaves apart.

CABBAGE KUGEL
Serves 6-8

1 head cabbage
4 eggs, slightly beaten
2 onions, chopped and sauteed
¼ cup oil or margarine
½ cup matzoh meal or 2 large potatoes, grated and drained
½ teaspoon salt
¼ teaspoon white pepper

Shred cabbage, soak in hot water for 15 minutes, repeat; squeeze out water. Mix remaining ingredients together, grease pan, bake at 350°, 1 hour. Can be frozen.

TZIMMES FOR ROSH HOSHANA
SERVES 12-15

6 large yams
10 large carrots, sliced and cooked
¼ pound margarine
brown sugar, to taste
orange juice, to taste
cinnamon and nutmeg
salt and pepper
1 cup cooked soup giblets and short rib if possible

Bake yams until very tender. Mash with carrots. Add other ingredients, a little at a time as needed for smooth texture. Use cooked giblets and small piece of soup meat (short rib). Chop and mix into the above mixture. Put mixture into 3 quart casserole and bake at 350° for 45 minutes.

TRADITIONAL

TZIMMES WITH FRUIT AND SHORT RIBS
Serves 10

vegetable oil
6 pounds short ribs
4 cups diced onions
1 pound pitted prunes
1½ pounds dried apricots
2½ pounds carrots, sliced
6 ounces red horseradish
2 pounds sweet potatoes, sliced
2 tablespoons salt
¾ cup sugar or more to taste
½ teaspoon ground cloves
1 pinch nutmeg
4 cups boiling water

Brown ribs in hot oil. Mix in onions and cook until soft. Cover and simmer 1 hour stirring occasionally. Soak dried fruit in hot water. Cool ½ hour. Preheat oven 325°. Combine all ingredients including soaking liquid into a large baking casserole. Cover and cook for 3 hours. Uncover for last 30 minutes to brown top slightly.

POTATO DUMPLING TZIMMES
Serves 8-10

2 onions, sliced
1-1½ pound piece of brisket
5 pounds carrots
½ cup brown sugar
salt and pepper to taste
8-9 white potatoes, grated and drained
½ grated onion

1 egg
¼ cup chicken fat or ½ cube margarine
2-3 sweet potatoes (optional)

Saute 2 sliced onions with brisket until brown. Slice carrots; cook in water to barely cover with brown sugar and salt for 15 minutes. Mix grated drained potatoes with grated onions, egg, fat, salt, pepper and the starch that settles at bottom of potato liquid. Make balls and add to carrot mixture Cook until balls are firm and transfer to 300° oven along with brisket and onions. Bake for at least 2 hours uncovered. Casserole should be glazed. Cubed sweet potatoes may be added around inside of pot the last hour of baking.

APRICOT NOODLE KUGEL
Serves 8

12 ounces fine noodles
4 ounces dried apricots
3 tablespoons orange marmalade
4 eggs
12 ounces sour cream
⅓ cup sugar
2 teaspoons cinnamon
4 tablespoons melted butter
2 ounces sliced almonds, lightly toasted
2 tablespoons melted butter

Cook noodles according to directions. Add apricots to food processor one at a time, and process orange marmalade, eggs, sour cream, sugar, cinnamon and 4 tablespoons melted butter. Fold this mixture over the cooked, drained noodles, add nuts, and blend evenly. Swirl 2 tablespoons melted butter into bundt pan or pyrex dish. Bake at 350° for 1 hour.

TRADITIONAL

BLINTZ SOUFFLE
Serves 8

Filling:
8 ounces cream cheese
2 cups small curd cottage cheese
2 egg yolks
1 tablespoon sugar
1 teaspoon vanilla extract

Batter:
½ cup unsalted butter, softened
⅓ cup sugar
6 eggs, lightly beaten
½ cups sour cream
½ cup freshly squeezed orange Juice
1 cup flour
2 teaspoons baking powder

Preheat oven to 350°. Butter a baking dish (9 x 13 inches) and set aside.

Blend together filling ingredients until smooth. Set aside. To prepare batter, mix butter and sugar until fluffy, blend in eggs, sour cream, and orange juice. In a separate bowl, combine flour and baking powder, "sifting" together with a fork. Add to butter mixture and blend well. Pour half of batter into baking dish. Spread filling over the top with a knife; some will settle into the batter. Pour remaining batter over filling. (At this point, souffle can be refrigerated several hours or overnight, if desired. Cover until ready to use. Before baking, remove from refrigerator and allow to stand until room temperature.)

Bake uncovered 50 to 60 minutes or until puffed and golden. Serve immediately with toppings of sour cream, flavored syrup, or assorted jams.

NO-SHELL BLINTZES
Serves 4

4 quarts water
1 tablespoon salt
2 pounds Hoop cheese
¼ cup sugar
¼ cup flour
4 eggs
½ teaspoon salt
½ pound margarine

Bring 4 quarts salted water to boil. Blend cheese, eggs, sugar, flour and salt well. Make balls about the size of an egg and drop into boiling water. Cover and cook about 6 minutes until blintzes rise. Remove from water with slotted spoon and drain on paper toweling. Melt margarine in casserole and add blintzes, turning them so they are all coated with margarine. Bake at 375° for 1 hour. Serve with sour cream or jelly or can be topped with sauteed onions and mushrooms.

TRADITIONAL

HAMANTASCHEN
Yields 40

⅓ cup sugar
¼ cup vegetable shortening
¼ pound margarine
½ cup orange juice
1 teaspoon orange rind
2⅔ cup flour
pinch salt

Cream sugar, shortening, margarine and orange rind. Gradually add flour and salt alternately with juice. Chill dough, then roll on floured surface. Cut into 3 inch rounds. Fill with filling (see below). Moisten fingers and pinch edges together to form triangle. Bake on greased cookie sheet in 350° oven 20-30 minutes, or until golden brown.

Filling #1:
1 can prune butter (lekvar), apricot butter or poppy seed
½ cup raisins
½ cup walnuts, chopped
grated orange rind to taste

Combine all ingredients; mix well.

Filling #2:
1 pound prunes, pitted
wine or brandy to cover
2 teaspoons lemon juice
rind of one lemon

Soak prunes until soft. Heat with liquid over medium heat for 15 minutes. Drain. Chop or pulverize. Add lemon juice and rind.

MACADAMIA MANDELBROT
Yields 40

⅓ *cup safflower oil*
1 cup sugar
¼ *cup light molasses*
1 egg
2 cups flour
2 teaspoons baking soda
1 teaspoon ground cloves
1 teaspoon ground ginger
2 teaspoons ground cinnamon
½ *teaspoon salt*
1 cup macadamia nuts, coarsely chopped
½ *cup raisins*
sugar

Beat together oil, sugar, molasses and egg; in a separate bowl mix flour, baking soda, cloves, ginger, cinnamon and salt. Combine wet and dry ingredients; add nuts and raisins and mix well. Cut dough in half; roll each half into a log about 2 inches in diameter and about 12-14 inches long. Sprinkle sugar (and any fine bits of macadamia nuts) on a large piece of foil; roll the logs back and forth on the sugar and nuts until they are completely covered. Place logs in jellyroll pan; bake at 350° for about 12 minutes. When done, the logs will have flattened out. Remove from oven and cut the logs in 1½ x 3 inch slices. Place cookies back in oven about 5 minutes or until they have dried and are crisp. Place slices on rack to cool.

MOTHER'S SPICY MANDELBREAD
Yields 36

1 stick margarine
½ cup white sugar
½ cup brown sugar
1 tablespoon oil, generous
2 eggs, beaten
2¼ cups flour
2 tablespoons molasses
2 teaspoons ginger
1 teaspoon cloves
2 teaspoons nutmeg
2 teaspoons cinnamon
2 teaspoons baking powder

¾ teaspoon baking soda
1 cup walnuts or almonds,
   ground
lemon or orange rind (optional)

Topping:
1 teaspoon oil
¼ cup almonds, blanched,
   sliced (optional)
1 teaspoon cinnamon
½ teaspoon ginger
¼ cup sugar

Cream together margarine, sugars and oil. Add eggs, flour, molasses, spices, baking powder, baking soda and ground nuts (lemon or orange rind optional). Flour hands and form the dough into 3 long flat loaves with rounded ends about 3 inches wide and 1 inch high. Brush lightly with oil, put blanched sliced almonds, cinnamon or sugar on top (optional). Place on greased cookie sheets. Bake at 375 for 25 minutes. Remove from oven, reduce temperature of oven to 250°. Slice on bias and sprinkle topping over all. Return to oven and bake 20 minutes longer.

MANDELBROT
Yields 50

3 eggs
1 cup sugar
½ cup oil
3 cups flour, sifted

3 teaspoons baking powder
¼ teaspoon salt
1½ cups slivered almonds or walnuts or poppy seeds
1 teaspoon almond flavoring
½ teaspoon cinnamon
1 teaspoon vanilla
2 tablespoons orange juice and rind of 1 orange

Beat eggs well and add sugar gradually. Mix thoroughly. Add rest of ingredients in given order, blend well. Form into 5 long rolls on a floured board. Place on lightly greased cookie sheets. Bake at 375° for 15 minutes. Remove from oven and cut into slices while still hot. Put slices, cut side down on cookie sheets. Bake at 350° for 10 minutes. May be frozen.

Variation: Add chocolate chip or candied fruits

STRUDEL
Yields 30

2½ cups flour (add a little more as needed)
½ pound sweet butter
½ pint vanilla or strawberry ice cream, melted
preserves
chopped nuts
raisins
cocoanut
cinnamon
sugar

Mix first 3 ingredients together. Blend and refrigerate in bowl or plastic bag overnight. Divide dough into 4 balls and roll into rectangles.

Spread with: preserves, chopped nuts, raisins, cocoanut, cinnamon and sugar. Roll-up like a jelly roll and cut ¾ inches apart and ¾ inches through. Bake on greased cookie sheet at 325° for 30 minutes. Freezes very well.

RUGELACH
Yields 30

2 cups flour
½ cup butter or margarine
½ cup cottage cheese (small curd)

Crumble butter into flour, add cottage cheese and mix with fork. Shape into loaf. Cut loaf into 4 pieces and wrap in wax paper. Refrigerate 24 hours. Roll out each piece of dough into 10 x 5 inch rectangle.

Filling:
cinnamon
nutmeg
sugar
orange marmalade or other flavor
chopped nuts
raisins

Sprinkle dough with cinnamon, nutmeg and sugar. Combine orange marmalade or other jam with nuts and raisins. Spread filling on center of each rectangle and roll up. Cut into 1 inch slices. Bake on greased cookie sheet in 350° oven for 12-15 minutes or until lightly browned.

WOLFGANG PUCK'S GEFILTE FISH
Serves 12

1 head (about 2½ pounds) green cabbage
3 tablespoons matzoh meal
1 quart Fish Stock
1 tablespoon olive oil
½ medium (5 ounces) onion, minced
2 pounds white fish fillets, such as pike, carp or whitefish, cut into chunks
3 eggs, separated
½ cup Italian parsley leaves, chopped
2 tablespoons (6 or 7 sprigs) fresh tarragon leaves, chopped
2 to 3 teaspoons salt
½ teaspoon freshly ground white pepper
Cayenne pepper to taste
1 medium carrot, peeled and cut into julienne
1 medium leek, white part only, cut into julienne

Preheat oven to 375°. Blanch head of cabbage in boiling salted water, about 5 minutes, then place in a basin of cold water. Remove the whole leaves and cut away the tough core. As you peel off the outer leaves, you may have to return the head of cabbage to the boiling water to soften the inner leaves. Dry on a clean towel and reserve.

Dissolve 3 tablespoons matzoh meal in ½ cup fish stock. Reserve until needed. In a small skillet, heat the olive oil. Over medium heat, saute the onion until wilted, 4 to 5 minutes. Do not brown. Cool.

In a wooden bowl or on a chopping board, chop the fish fine with a chopper or a large knife. Add stock, cooled onions, 3 egg yolks, chopped parsley and tarragon, 2 teaspoons salt, white pepper and cayenne and continue to chop until well combined. In a clean medium bowl, whisk egg whites until firm but not stiff. Stir a little into the fish mixture, then, quickly but gently fold in the remaining whites. To test for flavor, bring a little fish stock to a simmer, add a small ball of fish mixture and cook for about 5 minutes. Taste and correct seasoning.

Heat fish stock and spoon a little into an 11 x 17 inch baking dish. Moisten your hands with cold water while dividing the fish mixture into 12 portions, about 4 ounces each, and enclose each portion in 1 or 2 cabbage leaves. You will find that when the leaves get smaller, you will have to use 2 leaves to wrap fish. As each package is formed, place in the prepared baking pan, seam-side down. This size pan holds the 12 packages comfortably. Pour the remaining stock over the fish and top with the julienned carrots and leeks. Cover pan with foil and bake for 30 minutes. Let cool in the stock and refrigerate until needed.

Presentation:
Place 1 package of fish on each of 12 plates, garnishing with some of the julienned carrots and leeks. Serve with homemade horseradish, white or red.

To make white horseradish, finely grate peeled fresh horseradish into a small bowl, cover with plastic wrap and refrigerate until needed. To make red horseradish, boil ½ pound red beets until tender. Peel and then finely grate into medium bowl. Add about ½ cup grated horseradish, or to taste, and combine thoroughly. Refrigerate, covered, until needed.

CHAROSES
Serves 8

2 large apples (McIntosh or Red Delicious)
¼ pound walnuts, about 1 cup
⅓ cup sweet red wine
½ teaspoon freshly grated ginger root
½ teaspoon ground cinnamon

Peel, core and quarter apples. Chop apples and walnuts; add wine to moisten to make a semi-fine mixture. Season with ginger root and cinnamon.

GEFILTE FISH
Serves 9-10

1 whitefish fillet (3 pounds)
¾ pound halibut or pike fillets
2 eggs
2 onions, finely chopped
2 teaspoons salt
½ teaspoon pepper
2 tablespoons matzoh meal
½ cup ground almonds (optional)
horseradish

Fish Stock:
bones, head and skin of the whitefish
3 pounds additional fish bones and heads
2 onions, sliced
3 carrots, sliced
3 sprigs parsley
1 teaspoon salt
6 cups water

363

TRADITIONAL

Put the whitefish fillets on a board, skin side down. Slip the blade of a knife between the flesh and skin the fish. Be sure the skin is free of scales and there are no bones left in the fillets. For the stock, rinse bones and heads (eyes removed) of all fish under cold running water. Combine all ingredients for stock in a large, deep saucepan or pot. Bring to a boil. Skim off foam as it accumulates. Cover and simmer for 30 minutes. Strain and return to the pan. Taste for correct seasoning.

Grind the whitefish and halibut or pike fillets in 2 batches in a food processor until fine. Return half the fish to the food processor and add 1 egg, half the chopped onions, 1 teaspoon salt and ¼ teaspoon pepper. Process to thoroughly mix. Transfer to a large bowl. Repeat with the other half of the fish and the remaining egg, onion, salt and pepper. Transfer to the bowl and mix with the first batch. Stir in the matzoh meal. Add the carrots to the strained stock and bring to a simmer. With moistened hands, shape the fish mixture into ovals or balls using ¼ or ⅓ cup of the mixture for each one. Carefully drop the fish balls into the simmering stock. Add enough hot water to barely cover them, pouring it carefully near the edge of the pan. Bring back to a simmer, cover and simmer over low heat about 1 hour. Let cool in the stock.

Chill the fish with a little of the stock for a least 4 hours before serving. Chill the carrots and the remaining stock in separate containers. To serve, garnish each fish ball with a carrot slice and add a spoonful of the jellied stock to the plate. Serve with horseradish.

TRADITIONAL

MATZOH BALLS
Yields 8

3 eggs at room temperature, separated
½ cup plus 1 tablespoon matzoh meal
½ teaspoon kosher salt
½ teaspoon white pepper, freshly ground
½ cup to 1 cup chicken stock

Bring a large pot of salted water (or 2 smaller ones) to a boil and let simmer. (Matzoh balls need room to expand while cooking.) Beat egg whites until very stiff. Add egg yolks and continue beating until well blended. Gradually sprinkle small amounts of matzoh meal over top of eggs and gently combine with a rubber spatula, always reaching to bottom of bowl. Season with salt and pepper. Refrigerate for at least 1 hour. Have a small bowl of water ready. Moisten hands with water and shape full teaspoons of mixture into balls. Drop carefully into simmering water. Cover and cook 15 minutes. Remove with perforated spoon. Serve in hot chicken soup.

To make in advance: keep drained matzoh balls in small saucepan with some chicken soup or stock. Reheat gently and discard liquid, which will be cloudy.

TRADITIONAL

MATZOH FARFEL PUDDING
Serves 8

2 cups matzoh farfel
3 eggs
½ teaspoon salt
⅓ cup sugar
¼ cup melted butter or margarine
1 teaspoon cinnamon
½ cup raisins
2 large apples, grated

Soak farfel for 2-3 minutes. Drain. Beat eggs and salt. Add sugar, butter or margarine, matzoh farfel, cinnamon, raisins and apples. Bake in 8-inch square pan in 350° oven for 45 minutes.

MATZOH PUDDING
Serves 10

1 box egg matzoh
1 quart bottle concord grape wine
12 ounce jar of apricot or plum jam
8 eggs
cinnamon
½ cup lemon juice
3 small apples, grated
salt to taste

Break up matzoh and pour wine over it. Grate apples and mix with jam, cinnamon and lemon juice. Beat eggs, add salt and mix with matzoh. Grease large pyrex pan, layer matzoh and fruit ending with matzoh on top. Bake in 350° oven for 1 hour.

EASY POTATO PUDDING
Serves 10

6 medium potatoes
1 onion
1 carrot
¼ cup matzoh meal
1 teaspoon salt
¼ teaspoon pepper
3 eggs, beaten well
4 ounces butter or margarine, melted

Put the first 6 ingredients into meat grinder or food processor. Add beaten eggs and put into a well greased pan approximately 8 x 10 inches. Brush top of mixture with melted margarine and bake in 375° preheated oven for 45 minutes to 1 hour.

Variation: Add 3 grated zucchini to above ingredients.

PASSOVER CARROT KUGEL
Serves 6

4 eggs, separated
½ cup sugar
1 cup raw carrots, grated (tightly packed)
1 apple, shredded
¼ cup red wine
2 tablespoons lemon juice
½ teaspoon lemon peel, grated
⅓ cup potato flour

Preheat oven to 375°. Beat egg yolks with sugar until light. Add grated carrot, shredded apple, wine, lemon juice, lemon peel, and potato flour. Blend well.

TRADITIONAL

Beat egg whites until stiff peaks form and fold them into the carrot mixture.

Spoon into a well-greased 1½ quart casserole. Bake 35 minutes, or until golden brown. If you serve immediately, the carrot kugel will be very puffy. Served cold, it will fall a bit.

SWEET CARROT PUDDING FOR PASSOVER
Serves 8-10

2 cups grated carrots, raw, lightly packed
½ cup shredded unpared apple
1 lemon, grated rind and juice
½ cup potato flour
2 tablespoons matzoh meal
1 cup sugar
½ cup red sweet wine
8 eggs, separated

Mix thoroughly carrots, apple, lemon rind, juice, potato flour, matzoh meal, sugar, wine and egg yolks. Beat egg whites until stiff and fold into carrot mixture. Pour into well greased 8 x 8 inch pan and bake at 375° for 45 minutes. Serve hot.

Wine Sauce:
½ cup cold water   *2 eggs, separated*
½ cup honey   *1 cup red wine*
1 teaspoon potato flour   *1 teaspoon orange rind*

Combine water, honey and potato flour in saucepan. Cover and cook over low heat, stirring constantly, until thickened and smooth. Beat egg yolks well and without washing beaters add a small amount of hot mixture slowly. Slowly add to saucepan, stirring constantly. When thoroughly mixed, remove from heat. Stir in wine; beat egg whites and fold into mixture. Add rind. Pour over pudding.

PASSOVER CARROT TORTE
Serves 10

5 eggs, separated
1 cup sugar
1 cup raw carrots, grated
1½ cups ground almonds
½ cup potato starch
½ lemon, juice and grated rind
¼ teaspoon cinnamon
1 tablespoon liqueur (optional)

Beat egg yolks with sugar until light and lemon colored. Add grated carrots, almonds, potato starch, lemon juice, rind and cinnamon. If desired, add 1 tablespoon liqueur. Beat egg whites until stiff, fold into carrot mixture. Grease 9 inch springform pan generously, pour mixture into pan and bake in 375° oven for 1 hour.

TRADITIONAL

MATZOH FARFEL PILAF
Serves 10

4 tablespoons margarine
2 diced onions
2 ribs diced celery
1 pound chopped mushrooms
1 box matzoh farfel
4-5 cups hot chicken broth
2 large diced, unpeeled apples (optional)
6 eggs, beaten
salt and pepper to taste

Heat greased casserole in 350 oven for a few minutes to heat thoroughly while you saute onions, celery and mushrooms in margarine. Add farfel and saute for 2 minutes longer. Combine with remaining ingredients and place in warmed 2 or 3 inch high casserole and bake at 350° for 45 minutes stirring mixture frequently to brown evenly.

PASSOVER FILBERT MACAROONS
Yields 20

3 egg whites
1 cup sugar
8 ounces ground filberts or almonds
a few drops of lemon juice or other flavor extract

Beat egg whites with sugar until stiff. Add filberts and juice or extract. Place small mounds of mixture on greased cookie sheet. Bake in 325° oven for 20 minutes.

Note: For chocolate macaroons, include 2 ounces grated bittersweet chocolate in recipe. Add to egg whites with nuts.

CHOCOLATE CHIP COOKIES FOR PASSOVER
Yields 2 dozen

2 eggs
¼ cup sugar
½ cup oil
1 cup chocolate chips or broken semi-sweet chocolate bar
1 cup cake meal
2 tablespoons potato starch
1 cup nuts

Cream eggs, adding sugar and oil gradually. Add nuts, chocolate chips, and sifted meal and starch. Refrigerate 4-5 hours. Drop by teaspoon onto a lightly greased cookie sheet. Bake in preheated 350° oven. Bake 20 minutes or until brown.

CINNAMON-NUT PASSOVER COOKIES
Yields 20

1 cup matzoh meal
1 cup matzoh farfel
¾ cup sugar
rind of 1 lemon and 1½ teaspoons lemon juice
¼ teaspoon salt
2 eggs, beaten
1½ teaspoons cinnamon
½ cup nuts
½ cup melted margarine

Mix dry ingredients. Add nuts. Then add eggs, margarine, rind and lemon juice, mixing well. Roll into balls and flatten with small glass. Bake at 350° for 15-20 minutes in preheated oven.

TRADITIONAL

HONEY CAKE COOKIES

1 egg
2 tablespoons oil
orange juice
honey cake mix
½ cup ground nuts

Mix beaten egg with 2 tablespoons oil and orange juice to make ½ cup. Add to cake mix with ½ cup nuts. Spoon mixture on to greased baking sheet. Bake in 350° oven for 12 minutes. Remove from pan and place cookies on rack to cool.

CHOCOLATE BROWNIES FOR PASSOVER
Yields 30

6 eggs, separate 5, 1 whole
1⅓ cups sugar
⅔ cup oil
⅔ cup potato starch
1 cup chopped nuts
⅓ cup cocoa
1 teaspoon instant coffee crystals
pinch salt

Lightly grease 9 x 13 inch baking pan. Beat 5 egg yolks and 1 whole egg until smooth. Add remaining ingredients (except egg whites) gradually, and blend well. Beat egg whites until stiff; fold into chocolate batter. Pour into baking pan. Bake at 350° for 45 minutes until tester comes out clean.

PASSOVER BROWNIES
Yields 20

4 ounces unsweetened chocolate
1 cup margarine
3 tablespoons instant coffee
4 eggs
1½ cups sugar
1 cup cake meal
½ cup walnuts
2-2½ cups miniature marshmallows
1 12-ounce package chocolate chips

Melt chocolate, margarine and instant coffee. Cool. Beat eggs and add sugar, chocolate mixture and cake meal. Pour mixture in a 9 x 13 inch pyrex dish, generously sprinkle with nuts and bake at 325° for 20 minutes or until toothpick comes out dry. Remove from oven. Cover brownies with marshmallows and return to oven, which has been turned off, until the marshmallows get soft.

Melt 12 ounce package of chocolate chips with 1 tablespoon margarine and spread this mixture over marshmallows. You may have to use your fingers to spread or swirl the marshmallows. Cool slightly. Place in freezer. Remove from freezer 2 hours before serving.

TRADITIONAL

PASSOVER BANANA CAKE
Serves 6-8

7 egg yolks
1 cup sugar
¼ teaspoon salt
1 cup mashed bananas
¾ cup sifted potato starch
1 cup coarsely chopped walnuts
7 egg whites, stiffly beaten
sliced bananas
whipped cream

Beat the egg yolks until thick. Add the sugar and salt and beat until fluffy and lemon colored. Stir in the bananas and potato starch, then the walnuts. Fold in the egg whites. Pour into 2 greased 9-inch layer cake pans.

Bake at 350° oven 30 minutes or until a toothpick comes out clean. Cool on a cake rack. Spread whipped cream and sliced bananas on one layer and cover with other layer. Cover with additional cream and bananas.

PASSOVER APPLE CAKE
Serves 10-12

6 eggs
1 cup sugar
1½ cups cake meal
⅔ cup oil
1 tablespoon cinnamon
1 cup raisins
1 cup chopped nuts
8 Granny Smith apples, peeled and sliced

Preheat oven to 350°. Use a large greased 9 x 13 inch pan. In a large mixing bowl mix the eggs, sugar and cake meal together. Add oil and mix very well. Batter will be very thick. Combine the cinnamon, raisins, nuts and sliced apples. Spread ⅓ of the batter in the baking pan. Layer half of apples. Spread remaining batter over apples (mixture may not cover completely.) Cover with rest of apples. Sprinkle on topping and bake for 1½ hours. Let cool. Slice in squares to serve.

Topping:
⅔ cup chopped walnuts or pecans
1 cup sugar
4 teaspoons cinnamon

Mix all ingredients together. Sprinkle over top of cake.

PASSOVER NUT TORTE
Serves 10

8 eggs, separated
1⅓ cup sugar
juice and rind of 1 lemon or orange
⅓ cup matzoh meal
3 cups (¾ pound) ground filberts or almonds

Combine egg yolks and sugar. Beat until lemon colored. Add rind, juice, matzoh meal and almonds. Beat egg whites until stiff, but not dry, and add to mixture. Pour into large, greased springform pan. Bake in 350° oven for 1 hour.

TRADITIONAL

PASSOVER CARROT CAKE

1 package honey cake mix
⅓ cup sour cream
1 cup grated raw carrots
⅓ cup golden seedless raisins
¾ cup pecans or walnuts
1 teaspoon grated fresh lemon or orange peel

Prepare cake mix according to directions substituting sour cream for ¼ cup of liquid called for on the box. Add carrots, I raisins, nuts, peel and spread mixture evenly on greased and floured sheet cake pan (13 x 9 x 2 inch). Bake 40 minutes to 1 hour. Cool in pan. Sprinkle with powdered sugar or desired frosting.

Note: This cake can be made with yellow cake mix by adding the following ingredients to the dry mix before proceeding:

1 teaspoon nutmeg
1 teaspoon cinnamon
½ teaspoon allspice

CHOCOLATE CREAM PASSOVER CAKE
Serves 10

⅓ cup unsalted butter
2 ounces semi-sweet chocolate
1⅓ cups matzoh meal
½ cup extra fine sugar
9 ounces semi-sweet chocolate
11 ounces cream cheese, at room temperature
⅔ cup granulated sugar
6 eggs

3-4 teaspoons vanilla, to taste
⅓ cup heavy cream

Melt butter and 2 ounces of chocolate, stir until smooth. Add matzoh meal and sugar and press into bottom and sides of lightly greased 9 inch springform pan. Bake in 350° oven 8-10 minutes. Refrigerate at least 1 hour. Melt 9 ounces of chocolate, stir and set aside. Beat cream cheese, add sugar gradually and add eggs, 1 at a time. Add vanilla, chocolate and cream. Mix well. Pour into prepared crust and bake 30-35 minutes in preheated 375° oven. The center of the cake will be soft. Refrigerate at least 4 hours.

PASSOVER CHEESE LATKES
Serves 4

3 eggs
1 cup milk
1 cup cottage cheese
1 cup matzoh meal
¾ teaspoon salt
½ teaspoon ground cinnamon
1 tablespoon sugar

Beat eggs. Add milk and cheese. Mix matzoh meal with other ingredients. Add to egg mixture and beat. Carefully drop from tablespoon onto hot, greased frying pan. Brown on one side, turn, brown on the other.

TRADITIONAL

PASSOVER BLINTZES
Serves 8

Crepes:
4 eggs, whipped
10 tablespoons potato starch
1 cup of milk (low fat)
salt-dash
1 tablespoon melted margarine or butter

Filling:
1 pound Hoop cheese, or Ricotta, or combination
1 egg
2 tablespoons lemon or orange rind
1 tablespoon sugar
½ cup raisins or currants
vanilla (optional)

Crepes:
Using beater, add potato starch gradually to whipped eggs alternately with milk until combined. Add salt and melted margarine. Let stand at room temperature for at least an hour or overnight in refrigerator.

Lightly grease a 7 or 8 inch hot skillet with oil. Mix batter well and often. Add 2 tablespoons of batter and tip skillet so that batter covers bottom of pan evenly. When set on one side, loosen with spatula and turn over. Brown and turn out crepe on plate covered with wax paper. Repeat with rest of batter, separating each crepe with wax paper.

Spoon about 3 tablespoons of filling onto center of each crepe. Roll and fold in sides. Bake or fry in margarine or butter until golden brown on both sides. May be frozen before cooking. Optional: Serve with sour cream, jam and cinnamon.

CRUNCHY STICKY MATZOH
Yields 2 dozen

6 matzohs
shortening for frying

Syrup:
1½ cups sugar
1 cup water
juice of 1 medium lemon
½ teaspoon ground cinnamon (and some ginger optional)

Wet matzoh completely. Do not soak. Wrap in damp towel for ½ hour. Cut each matzoh into quarters and deep fry until golden on both sides. Drain on paper towels. Cook sugar, water and lemon juice for 30 minutes. Add pieces of matzoh and cook for 2 minutes. Remove with slotted spoons to tray. Sprinkle with cinnamon and cool.

VEGETABLES

If vegetables are good for the intelligentsia, and we have it on good authority that they are, then it follows that they're good for the rest of us as well.

We Californians are lucky. We can go into almost any supermarket and choose from a stunning array of vegetables. Not only do we find the usual, but the new varieties genetically engineered to add color and taste to our table.

We are thankful for the new and the old; the carrot that was brought to America by the colonists, the potato that came to us from South and Central America by way of Ireland and the native squashes and corn.

Vegetables are on everybody's "good for you" list and prepared in interesting new ways and combinations they can stand by themselves and meet nutritional standards. Ask any vegetarian.

VEGETABLES

CAULIFLOWER PEAS AND POTATOES
IN SPICY SAUCE
Serves 6-8

1 small head cauliflower, cut into florets
2 large potatoes
½ cup vegetable oil
2 teaspoons cumin seeds plus 1 teaspoon ground cumin
2 tablespoons ground coriander
1 teaspoon turmeric
½ teaspoon cayenne
1 10-ounce package tiny frozen peas
1½ cups fresh ripe tomatoes, chopped (may substitute
 ¾ cup tomato puree)
3 cups water, boiling
3 teaspoons kosher salt
3 tablespoons fresh cilantro leaves, finely chopped

Slice cauliflower florets. Peel potatoes and cut each into eight pieces. Heat oil in large, deep, heavy pan. When hot, add cumin seeds and cook about 15 seconds. Add cumin, coriander, turmeric and cayenne, stir and immediately add cauliflower and potatoes. Cook until vegetables begin to sear, about 5 minutes. Add tomatoes and cook until puree thickens, about 3 minutes. Add boiling water and salt . Reduce heat and simmer vegetables, covered, about 15 minutes. Add frozen peas and cook 5 minutes more. Sprinkle with cilantro.

VEGETABLES

CUCUMBER AND SNAP BEANS
Serves 8

2 cucumbers, peeled, seeded and cubed
2 cups snap beans, stems trimmed
2 tablespoons oil or ½ cup chicken broth
¼ cup scallions
½ cup parsley

Saute cucumber for 2 minutes. Add snap beans, scallions and parsley and saute for 2 minutes. If broth is used, use liquid to "saute" instead of oil.

BROCCOLI SOUFFLE
Serves 8

1½ tablespoons margarine, melted
½ cup cornflake crumbs
3 eggs, beaten
½ cup mayonnaise
½ cup half and half or liquid non-dairy creamer
2 tablespoons flour
2 tablespoons chopped onion
2 10-ounce packages frozen chopped broccoli, thawed and
   drained
salt and pepper to taste

Grease 9 x 9 inch square baking pan with margarine. Sprinkle a layer of crumbs on bottom of greased pan. Combine all remaining ingredients in a large bowl. Spoon mixture over crumbs. Bake at 350° for 35 to 45 minutes. Cut into 16 small squares. May be frozen.

STIR FRY BROCCOLI AND ASPARAGUS
Serves 4

2 tablespoons olive oil
1 medium onion, thinly sliced
1 tablespoon shredded fresh ginger
3 cloves garlic, minced
3 cups fresh broccoli, florets and trimmed stems
1 pound asparagus, trimmed and cut in 2 inch pieces
2 tablespoons fresh lemon juice
1½ teaspoons sugar

In wok or large skillet, heat oil; stir-fry onion, ginger, garlic and salt. Add broccoli and asparagus. Stir over high heat until well coated. Add lemon juice and sugar. Stir-fry 2 minutes longer, or until vegetables are crisp-tender.

DIJON GLAZED CARROTS
Serves 8

2 pounds carrots, peeled and thickly sliced
1 teaspoon salt
2 cups water
3 tablespoons butter or margarine
3 tablespoons Dijon mustard
¼ cup brown sugar
¼ cup fresh parsley, chopped, for garnish

Cook carrots in salted water until crisp-tender. Drain well and return to saucepan. In a small sauce pan combine butter, mustard and sugar. Heat until butter melts and mixture is bubbly. Pour glaze over carrots and simmer uncovered slowly until carrots are heated and glazed. Transfer to serving bowl and garnish. with parsley.

VEGETABLES

GINGER-LIME CARROTS
Serves 8

3 pounds carrots, peeled and cut into ¼ inch slices
3 cups water
3 tablespoons margarine or butter
3 tablespoons honey
2 tablespoons fresh lime juice
1 tablespoon grated lime rind
1 tablespoon grated fresh ginger
lime slices for garnish

Steam carrots until crisp-tender, about 10 minutes. Drain. In a small saucepan, heat remaining ingredients, except lime slices, until margarine melts and mixture becomes bubbly. Stir margarine mixture into drained carrots. Heat over low heat, stirring constantly, until carrots are glazed, about 2 minutes. Transfer to serving bowl and garnish with lime slices.

CARROT RING
Serves 8

¾ cup shortening
¾ cup brown sugar
2 eggs, beaten
1 teaspoon baking powder
1½ teaspoons baking soda
¾ teaspoon salt

2 cups carrots, grated
¾ teaspoon nutmeg
2 teaspoons water
1 teaspoon cinnamon
2 cups flour

Cream shortening and sugar until light and fluffy. Add eggs, carrots and water. Sift flour with remaining ingredients. Add to mixture. Pour into a greased tube pan. Bake at 350° for 45 minutes. Remove from oven and cool 5 minutes. Turn out onto serving platter. Fill center with green vegetables.

Optional: subsitute ¾ teaspoon powdered ginger for the nutmeg and cinnamon.

CARROT SOUFFLE
Serves 6

2 cups cooked carrots, pureed
2 teaspoons lemon juice
2 tablespoons onion, minced
1/2 cup butter, softened
1/4 cup sugar
1 tablespoon flour
1 teaspoon salt
1/4 teaspoon cinnamon
1 cup milk
3 eggs

Preheat oven to 350°. Beat all ingredients together until smooth. Pour into a 2 quart, lightly buttered souffle dish or casserole. Bake at 350°, uncovered, for 45 minutes to 1 hour or until center is firm to touch.

Carrots may be cooked and pureed hours ahead of time; add lemon juice and cover tightly until ready to mix.

VEGETABLES

GLAZED CARROTS AND BRUSSEL SPROUTS
Serves 10

1 pound carrots, peeled and cut in 1½ inch pieces
2 10-ounce packages brussel sprouts
2 tablespoons chopped onion
2 tablespoons margarine
2 tablespoons cornstarch
1 10½-ounce can condensed consomme or stock
⅓ cup apple juice
2 teaspoons lemon juice
1 tablespoon brown sugar
⅛ teaspoon ground cloves

Steam carrots and brussel sprouts, drain. Set aside. In a saucepan saute onions in margarine. Soften and dissolve cornstarch in a small amount of consomme. Add all remaining ingredients to onions in saucepan. Cook, stirring constantly, until thickened. Stir in vegetables until thoroughly combined.

ORIENTAL ASPARAGUS
Serves 6

1 small garlic clove
3 anchovy fillets
¼ teaspoon red pepper flakes
½ teaspoon black pepper
3 tablespoons peanut or sesame oil
1 lime
1½ pounds young asparagus
½ cup chopped cilantro
1 tablespoon dried basil
1 small onion

388

Mash anchovy fillets and garlic. Blend with oil and juice of lime. Steam the asparagus, cut into 1 inch lengths, until just tender.

Combine asparagus with anchovy dressing. Then toss well with the cilantro, basil and thinly sliced onion.

CHINESE ASPARAGUS
Serves 4

1 pound fresh young asparagus
1 teaspoon sugar
½ teaspoon cornstarch
2 tablespoons soy sauce
2 tablespoons water
2 tablespoons peanut oil
2 cloves garlic, minced

Wash asparagus carefully and cut diagonally into ½ inch lengths. Stop cutting when you reach the white of woody part. Mix together the sugar, cornstarch, soy sauce and water. Heat oil slowly in large frying pan or a Chinese cooking wok. Add garlic and cook until golden. Add asparagus and soy sauce mixture. Stir well and cover, cooking over medium high heat. Remove cover every minute or so to stir. Cook only until tender crisp, about 5 minutes or less.

VEGETABLES

CORN PUDDING
Serves 6

2 cups water
½ cup hominy grits
1 tablespoon butter
1 16 ounce can cream-style corn
½ cup yellow corn meal
2 eggs and 2 egg whites, beaten
¼ cup low fat milk
1 cup Monterey Jack cheese, grated
1 4-ounce can green chilis, drained and minced
Cayenne to taste

Boil water in saucepan and gradually add grits, stirring constantly. Reduce heat, cover and simmer until water has been absorbed. Stir in butter. Transfer grits to a large bowl, and stir in remaining ingredients. Place mixture in a greased 1½ quart casserole. Place casserole in oven and bake for 1 hour, or until a skewer comes out clean.

CURRIED CORN
Serves 8

16-ounce bag frozen corn kernels, defrosted
8-ounce can tomato sauce
1 teaspoon powdered ginger
½ teaspoon cumin
1 medium onion, minced finely
¼ teaspoon pepper
¼ teaspoon salt
½ teaspoon curry powder
3 tablespoons oil

Saute onions and cumin in hot oil until light brown. Add ginger, curry powder, pepper and saute again on lower heat for 3 minutes or more until brown. Add tomato sauce, salt, and let simmer until thick. Add the corn and simmer again for 5-6 minutes, until corn is cooked. Taste-add more salt if required.

(The curried corn should not be runny; however, if too thick, you may add ¼ cup of water.)

EGGPLANT CREPES
Serves 8

2 medium eggplants, peeled and thinly sliced lengthwise
1 small onion, finely chopped
1 clove garlic, minced
3 tablespoons butter or margarine
1 9-ounce package frozen, chopped spinach, thawed and
thoroughly drained
2 eggs, beaten
2 cups Ricotta cheese
¼ cup Parmesan cheese
1 tablespoon parsley, chopped
½ teaspoon oregano
spaghetti sauce

Place eggplant slices on foil lined baking sheet. Bake at 350° until almost tender. Saute onion and garlic in butter. Add remaining ingredients except spaghetti sauce. Place about 1 to 2 tablespoons filling in center of each eggplant slice. Roll up and arrange in baking dish. Spoon spaghetti sauce over rolls. Bake at 375° for 15 to 20 minutes or until hot and bubbly.

VEGETABLES

EGGPLANT NOUVELLE
Serves 12

1 large eggplant, sliced thin
2 or 3 tablespoons olive oil
3 ounces Gorgonzola cheese
1 teaspoon basil
¼ cup pine nuts
1 red pepper, roasted

Salt sliced eggplant for ½ hour and drain. Place on greased cookie sheet, spread with olive oil and bake in 350° oven until tender. This may be prepared ahead. Spread with cheese and basil and broil until lightly browned. Add pine nuts and roasted pepper which has been cut into strips for garnish.

EGGPLANT AND SWEET PEPPER FRITTATA
Serves 8-10

10 eggs or 2½ cups low-cholesterol egg product
½ cup whole or lowfat milk
¼ teaspoon cayenne pepper
1 teaspoon salt
3 tablespoons olive oil
½ large red bell pepper, cut into small pieces
½ large green bell pepper, cut into small pieces
1 baby eggplant, or ¾ cup regular eggplant, skinned and cut into pieces
2 tablespoons freshly grated Parmesan cheese

Beat eggs, milk, cayenne pepper, and 1 teaspoon salt in a medium bowl. Set aside. Heat the broiler. In 2 large (10 inch) ovenproof skillets, saute peppers and eggplant in olive oil until softened, about 3 minutes. Divide the egg mixture between both pans, stirring over low heat until eggs just begin to set, about 2 minutes. Cover and cook over low heat until the eggs are completely set and the bottom of the egg mixture is golden, about 5 minutes. Sprinkle the tops of the egg mixture with Parmesan cheese. Remove the lids and transfer the pans to the broiler. Broil until the tops are golden, about 2 minutes. To serve, run a rubber spatula around the edges to loosen the frittatas, slide onto warm platters.

STUFFED EGGPLANT
Serves 8

8 small eggplants, halved lengthwise
2 medium onions, finely chopped
¼ cup butter
2 cups crumbled Feta cheese
½ cup grated Parmesan cheese
½ cup milk
1 egg, beaten
2 tablespoons parsley, chopped
salt and pepper
16 slices tomato
olive oil

Scoop out eggplant pulp, reserve shells. Chop pulp. Saute onions in butter until golden. Add eggplant pulp. Cook and stir for 5 minutes. Transfer mixture to mixing bowl. Add cheeses, milk, egg and parsley. Season to taste with salt and pepper. Spoon mixture into reserved eggplant shells. Top each with tomato slices and brush with oil. Place in greased baking pan. Bake at 350° for 40 minutes.

VEGETABLES

FIESTA RATATOUILLE
Serves 6

1 medium eggplant (unpeeled), cut into ¾ inch pieces
1 teaspoon coarse salt
½ cup golden raisins
10 tablespoons (or more) olive oil
2 large red onions, thinly sliced
2 garlic cloves, minced
1 red bell pepper, cut into ¾ inch pieces
1 yellow bell pepper, cut into ¾ inch pieces
2 small zucchini, cut into ¾ inch thick rounds
2 small yellow squash, sliced
salt and pepper
3 tablespoons balsamic vinegar or red wine vinegar
1½ tablespoons sugar
3 tablespoons toasted pine nuts
2 tablespoons fresh parsley, minced

Place eggplant in large bowl. Sprinkle with salt. Add enough cold water to cover. Place raisins in small bowl. Add enough hot water to cover. Let eggplant and raisins stand 30 minutes.

Drain eggplant and raisins. Set raisins aside. Pat eggplant dry with paper towels. Heat 3 tablespoons oil in heavy large skillet over high heat. Add onions and garlic and saute 3 minutes. Reduce heat to medium-low. Cover partially and cook until onions soften and carmelize, stirring occasionally, about 35 minutes. Add bell peppers and cook until tender, stirring frequently, about 12 minutes. Transfer pepper mixture to bowl. Do not rinse skillet.

Heat 5 tablespoons oil in same skillet over medium heat. Add eggplant and saute until soft and brown, stirring frequently and adding more oil to skillet if sticking, about 20 minutes. Add to pepper mixture. Heat 2 tablespoons oil in same skillet over medium heat. Add zucchini and yellow squash and saute until golden about 7 minutes. Return all vegetables to skillet and cook 4 minutes, stirring occasionally. Season with salt and pepper.

Mix vinegar and sugar in small bowl until sugar dissolves. Add vinegar mixture and raisins to vegetables and cook 3 minutes, stirring occasionally. Transfer vegetables to large bowl. Mix in pine nuts and parsley. Cool completely. (Vegetables can be prepared 1 day ahead. Cover and refrigerate. Bring to room temperature before serving.)

LIMA BEAN SPECIAL
Serves 8

3 cups large dried lima beans
water
salt
3 tablespoons brown sugar
¼ cup butter or margarine
1 large can pear halves, drained, reserve juice
butter, as needed
cinnamon

Cover beans with water and soak overnight. Add salt to water and cook until beans are tender but not mushy. Drain. Place beans in greased casserole. Stir in sugar and butter. Place pears on top of beans, close together, with centers up. Fill hollows of pears with butter, brown sugar and sprinkle well with cinnamon. Add juice from pears, reserving some for basting. Bake at 300° for 2 hours or longer. Baste often. Do not cover. If juice dries out, add more pear juice.

VEGETABLES

ORIENTAL EGGPLANT
Serves 10

2 tablespoons olive oil
1 pound slender Oriental eggplants, stems trimmed
4 fresh oregano sprigs about 4 inches long, or 1 teaspoon
  dry oregano leaves
1 clove garlic, thinly sliced
½ teaspoon red preserved ginger in syrup, thinly sliced,
  or ½ teaspoon fresh ginger, thinly shredded
¾ cup white wine vinegar
⅓ cup sugar
½ teaspoon Oriental sesame oil

Line a 10 x 15 inch pan with foil; brush with oil. Cut eggplants in quarters length-wise; lay skin down in a single layer in pan. Brush cut sides with olive oil. Bake, uncovered, in a 475° oven until eggplant is browned and soft when pressed, 15-25 minutes. Sprinkle eggplant with oregano, garlic and ginger. Cool. Lay a wide-mouthed 1-pint jar on its side. Fill jar with eggplant (so strips are vertical when jar is upright) trimming pieces to make them ¾ inch short of rim. Set jar upright. In a 1-1½ quart pan, combine vinegar, sugar and sesame oil. Bring to a boil, stirring until sugar dissolves; pour over vegetables to cover. Reserve extra liquid. Put lid on jar and shake to release bubbles. Chill overnight; if needed, add reserved liquid to cover vegetables. Serve, or chill up to 2 weeks; turn jar over occasionally to keep tops moist.

VEGETARIAN PAELLA
Serves 4-6

olive oil
2 onions, chopped
4 tomatoes, peeled, seeded and finely chopped
3 leeks, white part only, chopped
6 medium artichoke hearts, halved and sprinkled with lemon
3 red peppers, roasted, peeled, and cut into thin strips
½ head of cauliflower, broken into florets
½ cup peas
5 cups vegetable broth
4 cloves garlic, minced
¼ cup parsley, minced
1 pound short grain rice

Cover heavy, wide, flat-bottomed pan with ½ inch olive oil. Heat pan. Add onions and cook until onions are tender, stirring occasionally. Continue cooking until onions are golden and beginning to carmelize. Add tomatoes and leeks and continue cooking until all liquid has evaporated. Stir in artichoke hearts and pepper strips, cauliflower and peas and add 1 cup stock. Bring to boil. Simmer 10 minuites. Stir in garlic and parsley. Add remaining stock and stir in rice. Cook over medium heat until rice is done, about 20 minutes. Do not stir once rice has been added. Cool 10 minutes before serving.

VEGETABLES

VEGETARIAN CHILI
Serves 8

¾ *cup olive oil*
3 *zucchini, cut into ½ inch dice*
2 *onions, cut into ½ inch dice*
4 *cloves garlic, finely chopped*
2 *large red bell peppers, cored and cut into ¼ inch dice*
1 *can (35 ounces) Italian plum tomatoes, with juice*
1 ½ *pounds ripe plum tomatoes, cut into 1 inch dice*
2 *tablespoons good-quality chili powder*
1 *tablespoon ground cumin*
1 *tablespoon dried basil*
1 *tablespoon dried oregano*
2 *teaspoons freshly ground black pepper*
1 *teaspoon salt*
1 *teaspoon fennel seeds*
½ *cup fresh Italian (flat-leaf) parsley, chopped*
1 *cup canned dark red kidney beans, drained*
1 *cup canned chick-peas (garbanzos), drained*
½ *cup fresh dill, chopped*
2 *tablespoons fresh lemon juice*
1 *cup sour cream*
2 *cups Monterey Jack cheese, grated*
4 *scallions, white bulbs and 3 inches green, sliced diagonally*

Heat ½ cup of oil in a large skilled over medium heat. Add zucchini, and saute until just tender, 5 to 7 minutes. Transfer zucchini to a large flameproof casserole or dutch oven. Heat the remaining ¼ cup oil in skillet over low heat. Add onions, garlic, and bell peppers. Saute until wilted, about 10 minutes. Transfer mixture to casserole, along with oil remaining in skillet. Place casserole over low heat. Add canned tomatoes and their juice, the fresh tomatoes, chili powder, cumin, basil, oregano, pepper, salt, fennel seeds, and parsley. Cook, uncovered, stirring often, for 30 minutes. Stir in kidney beans, chick-peas, dill, and lemon juice, cook for another 15 minutes. Stir well, adjust seasonings to taste. Serve with bowls of sour cream, cheese, and scallions.

DOLMAS (STUFFED GRAPE LEAVES)
Serves 40

Filling:
1 tablespoon margarine or butter
1 large onion, chopped
1 cup rice, uncooked
1 teaspoon salt
¼ teaspoon pepper
1 cup water
juice of 1 lemon
1 cup pine nuts
½ cup chopped parsley

1 pound grape leaves
(can be purchased at Greek or Armenian deli)
2 tablespoons oil
1 cup water

Filling: saute onion in margarine until lightly golden. Add uncooked rice, salt, pepper, 1 cup water and juice of ½ lemon. Cover and simmer 10 minutes, or until liquid is absorbed. Add pine nuts and parsley. Rinse grape leaves, spread leaf out, removing stem. Place leaf bottom side up. Put filling in center of each leaf. Roll leaf, tucking in sides. Arrange open side down in shallow pan so that sides touch. Add juice of ½ lemon and oil to cup of water and pour over grape leaves. Simmer 30 minutes, partially covered.

VEGETABLES

FRESH TOMATO CASSEROLE
Serves 8-10

½ cup butter or margarine
1 cup hot water
1 8-ounce package herb seasoned stuffing
3 medium tomatoes, peeled and diced
½ cup chopped green pepper
1 tablespoon minced parsley

Melt butter or margarine in hot water. Stir in all remaining ingredients. Spoon into greased 1½ quart casserole. Bake covered at 350° for 20 to 25 minutes. Remove cover during last 5 minutes of baking. Garnish with lemon twist if desired.

TAMALE PIE
Serves 6-8

1 onion, chopped
1 green pepper, chopped
½ cup vegetable oil
1 28-ounce can tomatoes
1 cup yellow cornmeal
2 cups milk
3 eggs
1 1-pound can whole kernel corn, drained
½ teaspoon each salt, black pepper and cayenne pepper
1 tablespoon chili powder
2 cups sliced black olives
1 cup shredded Cheddar cheese

Saute onion and pepper in oil until tender. Stir in tomatoes and simmer 20 minutes. Stir cornmeal into milk and cook until mushy. Beat eggs in large bowl, and stir in cornmeal mush, corn, seasonings and olives. Layer cornmeal and tomato mixture in 2 quart greased casserole and top with cheese. Bake in 350° oven for 1 hour.

COLD BELL PEPPERS STUFFED
WITH RICOTTA CHEESE AND HERBS
Serves 6

Peppers:
3 medium-size yellow peppers
3 medium-size red bell peppers
3 cups whole milk Ricotta cheese
2 eggs, beaten
⅓ cup freshly grated Parmesan cheese
3 garlic cloves, finely chopped
1 teaspoon chopped fresh rosemary or ¼ teaspoon, dried, crumbled
salt and pepper

Lightly oil 9 x 13 inch baking dish. Char peppers over gas flame or in broiler until blackened in several spots on all sides. Wrap in plastic bag and let stand 20 minutes to steam. Peel charred skin off peppers. Rinse peppers under running water. Cut 1 inch off peppers at stem end. Remove seeds. Pat peppers dry with paper towels. Arrange peppers cut side up in prepared baking dish. Preheat oven to 325°. Mix Ricotta, eggs, Parmesan, garlic and rosemary in medium bowl. Season with salt and pepper. Spoon stuffing into peppers. Bake until filling begins to set and tops are just crusty, about 35 minutes. Cool, then cover and refrigerate at least 4 hours. (Can be prepared 1 day ahead.)

VEGETABLES

SOUTHWEST STUFFED PEPPERS
Serves 6

1 large onion, chopped
4 cloves garlic, minced
3 tablespoons vegetable oil
1 package taco salad seasoning mix
1 14-ounce can Mexican seasoned stewed tomatoes
1 14-ounce can Mexican style chunky tomato sauce
1 16-ounce can vegetarian refried beans
1 jalapeno pepper, minced
6 large poblano peppers
2 cups jack cheese, grated
4 cups cooked rice

Saute onion and garlic in large heavy skillet about 10 minutes. Add taco salad seasoning, tomatoes, tomato sauce, refried beans and jalapeno and cook about 20 minutes. Broil peppers until blistered all around, put in plastic bag for 15 minutes to facilitate peeling. Remove skins and seeds. Cut in half or leave whole. Arrange peppers in oiled casserole. Fill peppers with vegetable mixture, bake for 25 minutes at 350°, add grated cheese and continue to bake until casserole is bubbling and cheese is melted. Serve over a bed of rice with the following salsa and blue corn chips.

Salsa:
2 avocados, pitted and peeled
½ cup red onion, chopped
½ cup cilantro, chopped
1 tomato, chopped
2 tablespoons lime juice
1 jalapeno chili, minced
½ teaspoon Mexican oregano
1 clove garlic, minced

VEGETABLES

Mash avocados coarsely, add remaining ingredients. Mix well, check seasoning and serve with peppers.

VEGETARIAN GREEN PEPPER MEXICANA
Serves 8

1½ cups pinto beans, cooked
3 medium onions, chopped
2 stalks celery, chopped
3 cloves garlic, diced
¾ teaspoon basil
¾ teaspoon oregano
¼ teaspoon black pepper
2 teaspoons chili powder
12 ounce can diced tomatoes in juice

½ cup cashews
½ cup raisins
2 tablespoons red wine vinegar
¾ cup brown rice, cooked
2 tablespoons vegetable oil
4 large green bell peppers
1 quart spicy tomato or spaghetti sauce

Pour oil into pot; saute onions, celery and garlic until soft. Add spices, diced tomatoes and vinegar to pot. Combine raisins, cashews, brown rice and pinto beans. Add to pot and heat to a simmer; continue cooking for 10 minutes. Cut peppers in half, remove seeds and blanch. Fill peppers with about ½ cup of filling each. Cover with sauce and bake in 350° oven 40 minutes.

VEGETABLES

BAKED SAUERKRAUT AND MUSHROOMS
Serves 8

1 quart sauerkraut, rinsed and drained
1 ounce dried mushrooms soaked for ½ hour in ½ cup
 water (save liquid)
1 large onion, diced
1 large tart apple, diced
1 teaspoon caraway seed (optional)
2 tablespoons butter
½ cup brown sugar
salt and pepper to taste

Brown onion and dried (sliced) mushrooms in butter. Add all ingredients, including water from mushrooms. Bake in a buttered casserole dish at 325° for 1 hour. Add more brown sugar for a sweeter taste or more water for more moist flavor.

WONDERFUL SAUERKRAUT
Serves 6-8

28 ounce jar of sauerkraut
1 pound soup bones
1 cup chili sauce or ketchup
1 whole onion, halved
½ cup tightly packed fresh dill, chopped
pepper to taste
sweetener to taste

Cook all ingredients covered on low flame for 1½ hours. Discard onion.

RED CABBAGE CONFIT
Serves 8

8 cups thinly sliced red cabbage (about 2 pounds)
3 cups onion, sliced thin
1 bay leaf
¼ teaspoon dried thyme, crumbled
4 dried allspice berries
2 garlic cloves, crushed
salt and pepper
2 tablespoons olive oil
1 Granny Smith apple, peeled and grated coarse
1 cup dry red wine vinegar or more to taste
2 tablespoons sugar
¾ cup water
⅓ cup dried currants

In a kettle of boiling salted water, blanch cabbage for 2 minutes and drain it. Put the oil in the cleaned kettle and cook the onion, bay leaf, thyme, allspice berries, garlic, salt and pepper to taste over moderately low heat, stirring until the onion is softened. Add cabbage, apple, wine vinegar, sugar, and water, and bring the liquid to a boil. Simmer the mixture, covered, stirring occasionally, for 30 to 35 minutes, or until cabbage is tender. Discard the allspice berries, and add currants. Simmer the mixture, uncovered, stirring occasionally for 10 to 15 minutes more, or until most of the liquid has evaporated. Discard bay leaf and garlic and season the confit with salt, pepper and the additional vinegar.

VEGETABLES

CRANBERRY CABBAGE
Serves 8

1 tablespoon oil
1 small onion, chopped
1 large cabbage, coarsely cut
1 large green apple, peeled, cut in 1-inch pieces
1 16-ounce can of jellied cranberry sauce
2 tablespoons broth

In a 3-quart casserole heat oil and saute chopped onion until soft. Add cabbage and stir until tender. Add broth, seasoning, and cut up apples. Cover and simmer for 30 minutes. Add jellied cranberry sauce. Another head of cabbage can be added to this recipe if desired.

This can be served in scooped out orange, ramekin or cabbage leaf.

UNSTUFFED CABBAGE
Serves 6-8

Sauce:
28 ounce can Italian plum tomatoes, cut up
15 ounce can tomato sauce
1 cup water
¼ cup catsup
¼ cup onion soup mix
¼ cup brown sugar
¼ cup lemon juice
½ teaspoon powdered ginger

2 pounds ground beef
1 teaspoon minced garlic

2 onions, chopped
1 teaspoon salt
½ teaspoon pepper
1¼ cups brown rice (cooked)
1 green pepper, diced
1 head cabbage, cut in wedges

Combine sauce ingredients, set aside. Saute beef, garlic and onion until meat is browned. Add salt, pepper and rice. Add 1 cup of the sauce. Top with green pepper. Lay cabbage on top. Pour rest of sauce overall. Let rest in oven with heat off for 20 minutes before serving. This dish tastes better when prepared ahead and reheated (350° for about 1 hour).

SPINACH FRITTATA
Serves 6-8

vegetable spray
2 tablespoons oil
2 packages frozen chopped spinach, drained, squeezed dry
6 eggs, beaten
1 pint cottage cheese
½ cup grated Kasseri cheese
¾ cup matzoh meal
½ teaspoon salt

Spray 3-quart glass baking dish with vegetable spray. Add oil and heat in 350° oven. Mix all ingredients, spinach last, and pour into hot dish. Bake at 350° for 45 minutes or until center is firm. Cut into squares when cool.

GARDEN TORTA
Serves 6

3 pounds spinach
4 zucchini, sliced thin
4 eggs, beaten
¼ cup light cream or milk
¼ cup chopped parsley
3 tablespoons Parmesan cheese
¼ cup oil
2 slices white bread
¼ teaspoon pepper, pinch thyme
4 green onions, sliced in 2 inch julienne

Steam cleaned spinach. Drain well and chop. Saute zucchini in oil until tender crisp. Add cheese to spinach. Add eggs in 4 steps, mixing well after each addition. Soak bread in cream or milk and add to spinach mixture. Add seasonings and parsley. Fold in zucchini and green onions. Turn into greased flat casserole and bake at 350° for 35 minutes. Can be served hot or at room temperature.

SPINACH-PECAN PIE
Serves 8

1 9-inch pie shell, baked and cooled
2 eggs, beaten
1 cup milk
½ teaspoon brown mustard
1 cup grated Swiss cheese
¼ cup onion, chopped
1 tablespoon flour
1 cup vegetables such as spinach, broccoli or mushrooms
½ cup pecans

Mix eggs, milk and mustard. Combine cheese, onion, flour and vegetables; put into crust. Pour egg mixture on top. Top with pecans. Bake at 325° for 50 minutes or until knife comes out clean.

SPINACH STRUDEL BAKE
Serves 8

1 bunch green onions, chopped
1 bunch fresh dill, chopped
1 bunch parsley, chopped
¼ cup margarine
1 tablespoon cornstarch
2 packages frozen chopped spinach, drained
6 eggs, beaten
1 pound Feta cheese
1 pound cottage cheese
6 strudel leaves (filo)
melted margarine or butter

Saute onions, dill and parsley in margarine. Stir in cornstarch. Add spinach and saute until combined. In a bowl combine eggs and cheeses. Stir in vegetable mixture. Take 2 strudel leaves and brush each with margarine and place on 9 x 13 inch greased baking pan. Spread half cheese and vegetable mixture over leaves. Place 2 more strudel leaves, each brushed with margarine, over filling. Spread remaining filling over leaves. Top remaining 2 strudel leaves, each brushed with margarine. Bake at 350° until browned.

VEGETABLES

SPINACH SOUFFLE
Serves 6 - 8

3 eggs
1 package frozen chopped spinach, well drained
2 cups cottage cheese
2 tablespoons melted butter
6 ounces sharp Cheddar cheese, grated
3 tablespoons flour
1 teaspoon instant minced onion
3 tablespoons Parmesan cheese, grated
½ teaspoon garlic powder
⅛ teaspoon pepper
salt to taste

Topping:
½ cup cornflake crumbs
½ cup Cheddar cheese, grated
¼ cup butter, melted

Beat eggs very well. Add and thoroughly combine all remaining ingredients, except topping. Pour into 9 x 9 inch greased baking pan or 1½ quart casserole Combine crumbs and cheese and sprinkle over souffle. Drizzle butter over topping. Bake at 350° for 1 hour 15 minutes or until firm. May be cut in small pieces and served cold or hot as an appetizer.

SPINACH SOUFFLE OVER RICE
Serves 8

8-ounce package herb rice mix or 1 cup brown rice
10-ounce package chopped spinach, drained
½ cup cottage cheese
¼ teaspoon nutmeg
6-ounces Gruyere cheese
½ cup green onion, chopped
5 eggs, beaten
1¼ cups yogurt
½ teaspoon salt
¼ teaspoon white pepper
3 tablespoons Parmesan cheese

Cook rice mix or brown rice as directed. Cool. Press cooked rice into well buttered 10 inch pan. Combine all ingredients except Parmesan cheese and spoon over rice. Sprinkle on Parmesan cheese.

Bake at 375° for 35-40 minutes until set.

VEGETABLES

SPINACH AND RICE GALA
Serves 8

1 tablespoon oil
1 large onion, chopped
2 cups mushrooms, sliced
1 clove garlic
1 egg or 2 egg whites
1 tablespoon whole wheat flour
1 ½ cups low-fat cottage cheese, blended until smooth
10 ounces frozen chopped spinach, drained
3 cups cooked brown rice
pepper
½ teaspoon thyme
2 tablespoons Parmesan cheese
2 tablespoons sunflower seeds

Heat oil and saute onion, mushrooms and garlic until tender. Mix egg, flour and cottage cheese. Add to sauted vegetables with spinach. Stir in rice, pepper, thyme and 1 tablespoon Parmesan cheese. Bake in 8 x 12 inch dish and top with Parmesan cheese and sunflower seeds at 375° for 30 to 40 minutes.

ZUCCHINI BAKE
Serves 4

1 onion, chopped
2 teaspoons vegetable oil
15 ounces part-skim Ricotta cheese
3 eggs, beaten or equivalent egg substitute
½ cup grated Cheddar or Gruyere cheese
½ cup milk, lowfat
2 cloves garlic, minced

salt and pepper to taste
2 cups grated zucchini, water squeezed out

Saute onion and garlic in oil; cool. Mix in remaining ingredients adding zucchini last. Turn into 9 inch pan sprayed with cooking spray. Bake in preheated 350° oven 1 hour.

BAKED ZUCCHINI
Serves 10

1 pound zucchini, sliced into rounds
1 large onion, peeled and chopped
½ cup butter or margarine
salt and pepper
6 eggs
¼ cup plus 2 tablespoons whole wheat flour
2 cups milk
8 ounces Cheddar or Jack cheese, grated
1 tablespoon oregano
1 tablespoon basil
1 teaspoon garlic powder

Saute zucchini and onion in butter in a large skillet. Season to taste with salt and pepper. In a bowl beat eggs and combine with remaining ingredients. Pour ½ liquid mixture into greased 9 x 13 inch casserole dish. Arrange zucchini/onion mixture evenly in dish. Top with remaining ½ of liquid cheese mixture. Bake at 350° for 50 to 60 minutes or until casserole is firm and lightly browned.

For flavor variation replace 1 cup milk with 8 ounce can tomato sauce.

VEGETABLES

YELLOW AND GREEN
SERVES 4

2 cups yellow summer squash, cut in narrow
   lengthwise strips
2 cups spinach noodles, cooked
1 large tomato, diced
1 tablespoon oil
pepper
1 teaspoon basil
½ cup low-fat cottage cheese

Steam squash until tender. Combine with remaining ingredients. Toss gently. Serve hot or cold.

ZUCCHINI SQUARES
Serves 12

4 eggs
1 cup flour
4 cloves garlic, minced
1 teaspoon fresh ginger, minced
1 teaspoon seasoned salt
paprika to taste
½ cup onion, chopped
3 cups Cheddar cheese, shredded
3 cups zucchini, sliced
½ cup oil
½ cup cilantro, chopped

Beat eggs. Add flour, spices, cheese, zucchini and oil. Mix well. Pour into 11 x 18 inch baking dish. Top sparingly with cilantro. Bake at 375° for 45-55 minutes. Cut into squares. Serve warm.

ACORN SQUASH
Serves 4

2 acorn squash
1 apple, chopped fine
1 tablespoon orange rind
¼ cup orange juice
¼ teaspoon cinnamon
2-3 tablespoons margarine or butter
¼ teaspoon nutmeg

Cut squash in half and place on baking dish. Bake until soft and tender at 350°. Remove from oven, remove seeds and mash pulp. Mix apple, orange rind, orange juice, butter, cinnamon and nutmeg. Add to squash pulp and fill shell. Heat in 350° oven for 10 minutes.

Variation, spaghetti squash: Pierce all over with fork. Bake in 350° oven 45 minutes (until tender). Remove from oven, cut in half. Remove seeds. Fork pulp until it becomes spaghetti-like and add ingredients as above or use a spaghetti sauce with ½ cup sliced sauteed mushrooms.

VEGETABLES
SQUASH STUFFED WITH MUSHROOM KASHA
Serves 8

2 cups cooked kasha
¼ pound mushrooms
butter or margarine
1 tablespoon oil
1 medium onion, finely chopped
1 green pepper, finely chopped
1 tomato, peeled, seeded and chopped
½ cup firmly packed chopped parsley
salt, pepper
2 yellow crookneck squash and 2 zucchini, each about
* 7 inches long, or 2 acorn squash or 2 butternut squash*

Topping:
2 tablespoons butter
3 tablespoons flour
2 cups milk
2 eggs
1 cup grated Parmesan or Romano cheese

Prepare kasha according to package directions. Chop mushrooms. Heat 2 tablespoons butter and the oil in skillet, add mushrooms, onion, green pepper and tomato and saute, stirring often over moderately high heat until vegetables are tender, but not dry. Fold in cooked kasha and parsley and season to taste with salt and pepper.

Cut squash in half lengthwise and hollow out centers, leaving shells ½-inch thick. Bring plenty of water to boil in 4-quart saucepan and parboil squash in 2 batches for 1 minute each or more, depending on type of squash. Drain and arrange in lightly greased baking pan just large enough to hold them. Fill with stuffing.

416

Prepare topping by melting 2 tablespoons butter and stirring in the flour. Cook, stirring for 1 minute. Add milk all at once and whisk until mixture comes to boil and thickens. Cook about 2 minutes.

Beat eggs in small bowl, and add a little of the white sauce to warm them. Return eggs to white sauce, stirring constantly, and remove from stove. Season to taste with salt and pepper. Add half the cheese, and pour topping over squash, covering each one completely. Sprinkle with remaining cheese.

Bake at 350° 15 to 20 minutes.

ONION CHEESE BAKE
Serves 4

3 large Bermuda onions, thickly sliced
¼ teaspoon salt
¼ teaspoon black pepper
⅛ teaspoon cayenne pepper
¾ cup grated Cheddar cheese
¼ cup seasoned bread crumbs
3 teaspoons butter or margarine

Grease 1 ½-quart baking dish. Place onion slices in dish in a single layer. Season with salt, black pepper, and cayenne pepper. Sprinkle grated cheese over onion slices. Top with bread crumbs and dot with butter or margarine. Bake uncovered at 375° for about 30 minutes.

VEGETABLES

STUFFED ZUCCHINI WITH SPINACH
Serves 6-8

2 large zucchini
1 onion, diced
1 package frozen chopped spinach, thawed
1 cup spaghetti sauce
salt, pepper
Italian seasoning
½ pound mushrooms, chopped
margarine

Cut zucchini lengthwise in half and remove pulp and seeds. Chop the pulp. Saute onion and mushrooms in margarine. Add chopped zucchini pulp amd simmer for 1-2 minutes. Add spinach, seasonings and ½ cup of spaghetti sauce.

Fill zucchini halves with the above mixture. Cover with remaining sauce. Place in pan with some liquid. Bake at 350° oven for 45 minutes or until the zucchini is soft.

Variations: 1 pound meat and ¼ cup cooked rice may be added to mixture. Broccoli may be used instead of spinach.

VEGETABLE SOUFFLE
Serves 8

2 tablespoons margarine
2 tablespoons flour
½ cup beef or chicken broth
2 eggs, separated
2 10-ounce packages frozen, mixed vegetables, drained

Melt margarine in saucepan. Stir in flour until smooth and

bubbling. Add broth, stirring constantly until sauce is thickened. Beat egg yolks, stirring constantly. Continue adding sauce to yolks, keeping mixture smooth. Combine entire mixture in saucepan along with vegetables. Beat egg whites until stiff. Fold into vegetable mixture. Spoon into greased souffle dish or casserole. Bake at 375° for 30 minutes.

POTATO BALLS
Serves 4 - 6

3 medium raw potatoes, peeled
1 potato, cooked, peeled and mashed
1 egg, beaten
salt and pepper to taste
flour as needed
boiling water
1 onion, finely chopped
margarine or butter

Grate potatoes. Squeeze out excess liquid. Stir in mashed potato, egg and season to taste with salt and pepper. Add flour as needed to roll into medium size balls. Drop potato balls in boiling water and cook for about 5 minutes Remove from water and drain. In a large skillet saute onion in butter or margarine. Add potato balls and saute slowly, constantly turning so onions stick to balls, until potato balls are browned.

VEGETABLES

WARM LEMON POTATOES
Serves 6

3 pounds Yukon Gold potatoes cut in 1 inch cubes,
cooked tender

Dressing:
¼ cup fresh lemon juice
2 tablespoons mustard, whole-grain preferred
1 egg yolk
1 tablespoon lemon zest
⅓ cup extra virgin olive oil
½ cup snipped chives
salt and fresh ground pepper to taste

In a large bowl, whisk the lemon juice, mustard, egg, lemon zest, salt and pepper. Slowly whisk in oil until dressing is thick. Stir in chives. Toss the potatoes and dressing and serve warm.

POTATOES ERIN
Serves 6 - 8

1½ pounds frozen shredded potatoes, defrosted
2-3 green onions, chopped
¼ cup mayonnaise
½ pound cheese, shredded
½ cup buttermilk
3 ounce can french fried onions

In buttered 11 inch round or square casserole, lay half the potatoes, half the mayonnaise spread on potatoes, half the green onions, half the buttermilk and half the cheese. Repeat.

Bake 350 for 20 minutes. Top with french fried onions. Bake 25 minutes longer.

Bake 350° for 20 minutes. Top with french fried onion. Bake 25 minutes longer.

PECAN TOPPED YAMS
Serves 8-10

2½-3 pounds yams, baked and scooped out
(canned may be used)
2 eggs, beaten
¾ cup brown sugar, divided
½ cup melted butter or margarine, divided
1 teaspoon salt
1 teaspoon cinnamon
½ cup orange juice (more if potatoes are dry)
1 cup chopped pecans or walnuts

Mash potatoes. Add eggs, ¼ cup brown sugar, ¼ cup melted butter or margarine, salt, cinnamon and juice. Spoon into greased 1½ to 2 quart casserole or souffle dish. Top with nuts and remaining brown sugar. Drizzle with ¼ cup melted butter or margarine. Bake uncovered at 375° for 50 minutes or until thoroughly heated.

VEGETABLES

FRUIT OF PARADISE
Serves 10

8-10 yams
8-10 large Pippin or Granny Smith apples
2 under-ripe bananas, cut into slices
1 small can cling peaches
1 small can chunk or crushed pineapple, light syrup
½ cup brown sugar
½ cup butter or margarine
juice and grated rind of 1 orange and 1 lemon

Bake yams. Cool. Peel and slice apples ¼ inch thick. Melt butter and brown sugar, add apples, cook until soft. Beat skinned yams, add remaining ingredients. Bake in large casserole at 350° for 1 hour. Garnish with almonds and coconut if desired.

SKEWERED VEGETABLES
Serves 10

½ cup vegetable oil
⅓ cup lemon juice
3 tablespoons red wine
1 tablespoon lemon pepper seasoning
2 teaspoons red pepper flakes
1 teaspoon seasoned salt
1 yellow crookneck squash, cut into chunks
1 medium zucchini, cut into chunks
1 small onion, cut into wedges
16 medium mushroom caps
cherry tomatoes
3 tablespoons Parmesan cheese, grated

VEGETABLES

In large bowl, combine oil, lemon juice, wine, lemon pepper seasoning, red pepper flakes and seasoned salt; blend well. Add vegetables; cover and refrigerate 30 minutes or overnight. Remove vegetables; reserve marinade. Thread vegetables onto metal or wooden skewers. (If using wooden skewers, soak them in water 15 - 20 minutes before adding vegetables.) Broil kabobs 6 inches from heat 12 -15 minutes, brushing often with reserved marinade. Sprinkle with Parmesan cheese and broil until lightly browned.

SHEPHERD'S PIE
Serves 4

3 medium brown onions, quartered
4 large carrots, cut in 2 inch pieces
1 celery root, cleaned and cut into large cubes
4 parsnips, peeled and quartered
½ pound mushrooms, wiped clean
1 small cauliflower, in florets
1 small head broccoli, in florets
4 tablespoons vegetable oil
4 cloves garlic, minced
fresh herbs as available including parsley, thyme and
*   tarragon*
salt and pepper to taste

Sauce:
2 tablespoons butter, one tablespoon olive oil
1 medium onion, cut in 1 inch pieces
3 cloves garlic, finely chopped
½ cup red wine
4 tablespoons flour
3 cups vegetable stock, heated
2 tablespoons parsley, chopped
½ teaspoon each thyme and tarragon

VEGETABLES

Heat oil in wide pot with heavy bottom. Add onion and cook about 10 minutes. Stir in garlic and wine, reduce by half. Add flour and cook 3 minutes, add stock and whisk until smooth. Bring to boil and turn to simmer for 25 minutes. Add parsley and check seasoning.

Potato Blanket:
4 large baking potatoes
⅓ cup light cream (or milk)
3 tablespoons butter

Cut up potatoes and cook until soft. Mash and mix in cream, butter and salt and pepper to taste.

Blanch cauliflower and broccoli for about one minute in pot of boiling water. Melt half the butter and a tablespoon of oil in a large skillet. Add onions and carrots and cook about four minutes. Add salt and ½ cup water and lower heat, cover and cook about four minutes.

In second pan, heat remaining butter and add fresh mushrooms. Cook until brown, add salt, garlic and a little water. Add to casserole with celery root and parsnips. Cook over low heat, covered, for another 3 minutes, then add the sauce, cauliflower, broccoli and herbs.

Transfer vegetables and sauce to a heatproof casserole, cover with mashed potatoes and bake at 375° for about 40 minutes.

SAVORY VEGETABLE CHEESE BAKE
Serves 8

1 large potato, diced
1 small zucchini, diced
1 small eggplant, diced
2 green bell peppers, cored, seeded and diced
2 medium carrots, diced
1 small onion, diced
2 tablespoons fresh parsley, chopped
1½ teaspoons salt
¼ teaspoon black pepper, freshly ground
¼ cup Kasseri cheese, crumbled
½ cup Feta cheese, crumbled
4 medium ripe tomatoes, sliced
1 cup rice, cooked (white or brown)
2 tablespoons red wine vinegar
1 cup Jack cheese, grated
½ cup Romano cheese, grated
½ cup shelled green peas or green beans

Preheat oven to 350°. Lightly butter a 9 x 13 inch (or larger) shallow baking dish.

Mix together the first 12 ingredients. Layer half the tomato slices in the bottom of the pan. Spread half the vegetable mixture. Layer cooked rice, remaining vegetables and cover with the remaining tomato slices. Sprinkle with vinegar.

Cover pan with aluminum foil and bake 1 hour and 30 minutes. Remove foil, sprinkle with Jack and Romano cheeses, and return to the oven, uncovered, until cheeses have melted. Serve hot.

VEGETABLES

BLACK BEAN CHILI
Serves 4

2 cups black beans, soaked 8 hours or overnight
1 bay leaf
4 teaspoons cumin seeds
4 teaspoons Mexican oregano
4 teaspoons Hungarian paprika
½ teaspoon cayenne pepper
3 tablespoons chili powder
3 tablespoons corn oil
4 medium onions, cut into1 inch dice
1 28-ounce can peeled tomatoes
4 cloves garlic, minced
1 or 2 teaspoons chipotle chili, seeded and pureed
4 tablespoons cilantro, chopped

Cover soaked and rinsed beans with fresh water and bring to boil with a bay leaf. Lower heat and simmer while you prepare the remaining ingredients.

Heat a heavy skillet over medium heat. Add cumin seeds and after about a minute, add oregano, stirring the pan so herbs don't burn. After about 5 minutes, remove from heat and add paprika and cayenne. Process to a coarse powder.

Heat oil in large skillet, saute onions til soft. Add garlic, ground herbs and chili powder, cook 5 minutes. Add tomatoes and chipotle chili to taste. Simmer for 25 minutes and add mixture to the beans. Add water to keep beans covered and continue to cook until beans are soft. Season to taste and serve with garnishes that can include fresh green chilis, chopped, grated cheese and cilantro.
Note: chipotle chilis can be found in your market's specialty foods.

VEGETABLE TORTE
Serves 8

½ pound leeks
½ pound green cabbage, cut in wedges
½ pound zucchini, trimmed
1 bunch green onions, cut up
½ pound Swiss chard, cut up
1 pound potatoes, peeled
3 eggs, beaten
6 tablespoons bread crumbs
½ teaspoon nutmeg
8 tablespoons Parmesan cheese, grated
¼ cup olive oil
salt, pepper

Place leeks, cabbage, zucchini, green onions, Swiss chard and potatoes in large saucepan. Cover halfway with water and boil 30 minutes until potatoes are tender. Drain well. Cool slightly, then chop vegetables into ½ inch pieces. Place in large bowl. Add eggs, crumbs, nutmeg, cheese, oil and season to taste with salt and pepper. Pour into greased 10-inch pie plate or spring form pan. Bake at 350°, 45 minutes. Cool, then cut into wedges to serve.

Note: Instead of cooking whole, vegetables may be cut into ½ inch pieces and steamed in small amount of water 10 minutes or until tender.

VEGETABLES

VEGETABLE PATE, TRI-COLOR

1 pound carrots, peeled, cut into 1-inch chunks
1 package (9-ounces) frozen artichoke hearts
2 tablespoons butter or margarine
1 medium onion, chopped
3 tablespoons chopped fresh dill or 1½ teaspoons dried
dill weed
1 package (10-ounces) frozen chopped spinach, thawed and
squeezed dry
5 large eggs
1 cup heavy or whipping cream
4 ounces cream cheese
½ cup Parmesan cheese
½ cup milk
salt
⅛ teaspoon pepper
⅛ teaspoon nutmeg

Grease and line sides and bottom of a 3½ x 4½ inch loaf pan with waxed paper. Grease again and set aside. Cook or steam carrots in 1-inch of boiling water until fork-tender, 15-20 minutes. Drain and set aside. In another saucepan cook artichokes according to package instructions, but omit salt. Drain. In medium skillet melt butter or margarine. Add onion and 1 tablespoon fresh or ½ teaspoon dried dill; saute over medium heat until onion is tender. Add spinach. Remove from heat; set aside.

In medium bowl, combine eggs, cream, cheeses, milk, salt, pepper, nutmeg and set aside. In medium bowl of food processor or blender, combine spinach mixture and ⅓ of the cream mixture. Blend or process until smooth-about 30 seconds. Pour into bottom of loaf pan, spreading evenly with spatula.

Rinse and dry work bowl or blender container, then add cooked carrots, ⅓ of the cream mixture and dill. Blend or process until smooth-about 30 seconds. Carefully spread carrot mixture on top of spinach layer. Again rinse and dry bowl or processor. Add artichoke hearts, remaining cream mixture and remaining dill. Process or blend until smooth. Carefully spread artichoke mixture over carrot layer, smoothing out top.

Preheat oven to 375°. Place loaf pan in a roasting pan in oven. Fill roasting pan with hot water. Bake 1 hour, 15 minutes or until center of pate is firm to touch. Remove from oven. Let stand 10 minutes. Unmold onto serving plate, remove waxed paper and cool at room temperature. Chill.

THIS FOR THAT

2 tablespoons = 1 fluid ounce
4 tablespoons = ¼ cup
1 cup = 8 ounces

2 cups = 1 pint
2 pints = 1 quart
16 ounces = 1 pound

2¼ cups granulated sugar = 1 pound
1 cup granulated sugar = 1 cup packed brown sugar or
  2 cups sifted powdered sugar
3½ cups confectioners' sugar = 1 pound
2¼ cups brown sugar firmly packed = 1 pound

---

1 tablespoon lemon juice = ½ teaspoon vinegar
1 lemon = 3 to 4 tablespoons of juice

---

1 ounce chocolate = ¼ cup cocoa
1 ounce chocolate = 3 tablespoons cocoa + 1 tablespoon oil

---

1 cup all purpose flour less 2 tablespoons = 1 cup cake flour
1 cup cake flour = ⅞ cup all purpose flour
5 pound bag flour = 20 cups
1 teaspoon baking powder = ⅓ teaspoon baking soda
  + ½ teaspoon cream of tartar
1 teaspoon baking powder = ¼ teaspoon baking soda
  + ½ cup buttermilk or yogurt
1 tablespoon cornstarch for thickening = 2 tablespoons all
  purpose flour or 4 teaspoons quick cooking tapioca
2 teaspoons dry yeast = ⅔ ounce cake compressed yeast

---

1 cup buttermilk = ⅞ cup whole milk + 1 tablespoon vinegar
1 cup buttermilk = 1 cup milk + 1¾ teaspoons cream of tartar
1 cup milk = ½ cup evaporated milk + ½ cup water
1 cup fruit juice = 1 cup milk (when baking) or
  1 cup fruit pureed
1 quart whole milk = 1 quart skim milk + 3 tablespoons cream
To sour milk add 1 tablespoon lemon juice or vinegar to 1 cup milk

---

1 cup heavy cream = ¾ cup regular milk + ⅓ cup butter, melted
1 cup light cream = ⅞ cup regular milk + 3 tablespoons
  butter, melted

THIS FOR THAT

½ pint heavy cream = 2 cups whipped cream
8 ounces sour cream = 8 ounces yogurt or 6 ounces cream
   cheese + 3 tablespoons milk
Whipped cream - add 3 or 4 drops lemon juice to each cup
   of cream before whipping for firmness
1 pound grated cheese = 4 to 5 cups

---

1 medium onion = 1 teaspoon onion powder
1 large onion, chopped = 1 cup
1 tablespoon dry parsley flakes = 3 tablespoons chopped
   fresh parsley
1 tablespoon chopped fresh herbs = 1 teaspoon dried
1 medium garlic clove = ⅛ teaspoon garlic powder
1 medium garlic clove = ¾ teaspoon garlic salt
1 medium onion = 1 teaspoon onion powder

---

1 cup rice = 3-4 cups cooked rice
1 slice bread = ⅓ cup bread crumbs

---

8 egg whites = 1 cup
6 medium eggs = 4 large eggs
2 yolks or 2 whites = 1 whole egg in baking
2 ounces egg substitute = 1 whole egg
1 egg = 2 tablespoons real mayonnaise in baking
Meringues - add ¼ teaspoon white vinegar during beating
   for each 3 egg whites

---

1 cup tomato juice = ½ cup tomato sauce + ½ cup water
1 pound carrots = 4 cups shredded or 3½ cups diced
1 pound apples = 3 cups peeled, diced or sliced
2 very ripe bananas = 1 cup mashed
1 pound fresh cranberries = 3½ cups sauce

PASSOVER USE

½ cup regular flour = 2 tablespoons cake meal + 6
   tablespoons potato starch
1 cup regular flour = ¼ cup matzo cake meal + ¼ cup potato starch

INDEX

A

Acorn Squash, 415
Almonds
Almond Chicken Stir Fry, 245
Armenian Rice Pilaf with Apricots
    and Almonds, 206
Mushroom Almond Pate, 27-28
Antipasto
Chicken Antipasto, 36-37
Herring Antipasto, 32-33
APPETIZERS, 11-37
Artichoke Cheese Dip, 18
Artichoke Spinach Dip, 18-19
Artichoke Squares, 19
Baba Ghanoush, 29-30
Brie En Croute, 22
Cheese Puffs, 21
Cheese-Chili Appetizer, 20-21
Chicken Antipasto, 36-37
Confetti Pate, 26-27
Crispy Tortilla Strips, 13
Drunken Chicken Drumettes, 37
Egg Salad and Caviar Supreme, 24-25
Garlic-Sesame Spread, 14
Glazed Onions Spumante, 26
Guacamole with Homemade Salsa, 16
Herring Antipasto, 32-33
Herring Apple Delight, 31
Hot Cheese Chili On Chips, 20
Hot Salami, 37
Lox and Cream Cheese Mold, 33
Marinated Vegetables II, 35-36
Melted Brie with Fruits, 22-23
Mexican Dip, 17-18
Mother's Festive Chopped Herring, 32
Mushroom Almond Pate, 27-28
Olive, Cheese and Curry
    on Toasted Muffin, 23
Pita Crisps, 13
Quick Mix Guacamole, 15
Refried Beans Ole, 17
Rikki's Eggplant Melange, 29
Salmon Tartar, 34
Salsa Dip, 15
Sardine Rollups, 35
Savory Tuna, 34

Spicy Spanish Eggplant, 28
Spinach Ball Appetizers, 25-26
Stuffed Cheese Rolls, 24
Vegetable and Eggplant Caponata, 30
Won Ton Crisps, 13-14
Zucchini Delight, 31
Apples
Apple Nut Bundt Cake, 71-72
Apple Slices Au Chocolat, 120
Apple Sour Cream Cake, 72
Apple-Curry Soup, 334-335
Apple-Ricotta Pie, Low Cal, 119
Chicken Apple Roll-Ups, 271
Cinnamon Baked Apples with Pecans, 121
Deep Dish Apple Pie, 122
Fresh Apple Cake 71
Fruity Apple Pudding, 123
German Apple Cake, 73
Green Apple-Curried
    Chicken Salad, 286-287
Herring Apple Delight, 31
Honey Glazed Chicken
    with Apples, 270-271
Passover Apple Cake, 374-375
Spirited Baked Apples, 119-120
Applesauce
Applesauce Orange Nut Bread, 51-52
Chocolate Applesauce Cake, 74
Pumpkin-Applesauce Cake, 83
Apricots
Apricot Cornish Hens, 274
Apricot Mousse, 124
Apricot Noodle Kugel, 353
Armenian Rice Pilaf with Apricots
    and Almonds, 206
Curried Apricot Rice, 209
Pineapple-Apricot Cheesecake Cookies, 114
Artichokes
Artichoke Cheese Dip, 18
Artichoke Spinach Dip, 18-19
Artichoke Squares, 19
Chicken Artichoke Cacciatore, 264
Jerusalem Artichoke Soup, 315
Marinated Artichoke Salad Supreme, 291
Asparagus
Chinese Asparagus, 389
Oriental Asparagus, 388-389
Stir Fry Broccoli and Asparagus, 385

INDEX

INDEX

INDEX

INDEX

INDEX

INDEX

INDEX

INDEX

Z

W

Jewish Family Service of Los Angeles
AROUND OUR TABLE • CALIFORNIA COOKS KOSHER
6505 Wilshire Boulevard
Los Angeles, California 90048

Please send me _____ copies $25.00@ $ _____
    of Around Our Table
    Postage and Handling (First Copy) 2.50@ $ _____
    Additional copies to same address 1.50@ $ _____
    California Residents,
      please add appropriate sales tax $ _____
                   Total $ _____

Please make checks payable to Jewish Family Service of Los Angeles
    Check Enclosed

    Please charge my: ❑ VISA
               ❑ Mastercard Expiration Date: _____

Card Account Number: _____

Card Holder's Signature _____
(Complete reverse side of order form)

- -

Jewish Family Service of Los Angeles
AROUND OUR TABLE • CALIFORNIA COOKS KOSHER
6505 Wilshire Boulevard
Los Angeles, California 90048

Please send me _____ copies $25.00@ $ _____
    of Around Our Table
    Postage and Handling (First Copy) 2.50@ $ _____
    Additional copies to same address 1.50@ $ _____
    California Residents,
      please add appropriate sales tax $ _____
                   Total $ _____

Please make checks payable to Jewish Family Service of Los Angeles
    Check Enclosed

    Please charge my: ❑ VISA
               ❑ Mastercard Expiration Date: _____

Card Account Number: _____

Card Holder's Signature _____
(Complete reverse side of order form)

**Sending a copy of Around Our Table • California Cooks Kosher
to a friend is a long lasting reminder of your thoughtfulness.
Proceeds will benefit Jewish Family Service Senior Services.**

Mail book to: Name _____

                  Address _____

                  City _____

                  State _____ Zip _____

All copies will be sent to your address unless otherwise specified. If you
wish books sent as gifts, please note below and enclose your gift cards with
this order.

Send gift(s) to: Address(es):

_____   _____

_____   _____

_____   _____

_____   _____

_____   _____

- -

**Sending a copy of Around Our Table • California Cooks Kosher
to a friend is a long lasting reminder of your thoughtfulness.
Proceeds will benefit Jewish Family Service Senior Services.**

Mail book to: Name _____

                  Address _____

                  City _____

                  State _____ Zip _____

All copies will be sent to your address unless otherwise specified. If you
wish books sent as gifts, please note below and enclose your gift cards with
this order.

Send gift(s) to: Address(es):

_____   _____

_____   _____

_____   _____

_____   _____

_____   _____